Building a
Virtual Private
Network

Building a Virtual Private Network

Meeta Gupta

WITH

NIIT

Premier
Press

Premier

The Premier Press logo and related trade dress are trademarks of Premier Press, Inc. and may not be used without written permission.

Press

ISBN: 1-931841-81-0

Library of Congress Catalog Card Number: 2002106508

Printed in the United States of America

03 04 05 06 07 BH 10 9 8 7 6 5 4 3 2 1

Premier Press, a division of Course Technology
2645 Erie Avenue, Suite 41
Cincinnati, Ohio 45208

Publisher:
Stacy L. Hiquet

Marketing Manager:
Heather Hurley

Acquisitions Editor:
Stacy Hiquet

Project Editor/Copy Editor:
Elizabeth A. Barrett

Interior Layout:
Bill Hartman

Cover Design:
Phil Velikan

Indexer:
Sherry Massey

For Prashant—Gone too soon.

Acknowledgements

So many people have helped me pull this book together that it is truly the result of a team effort. As usual, thanks Anita for giving me the opportunity to write on something that I enjoy and allowing me sufficient time to work on it. Angshuman, the TOC was wonderful to work on, but I made a few changes to it. Many thanks are also due to Priyanka and Sunil, who not only helped me convert my words into figures but also did their own bit of value-add. Sunil, I have all the gratitude in the world for you. You spared the time to correct the graphics even when you were overloaded with other work. I owe you a huge one there.

I have leaned heavily on three people in the course of writing this book. My heartiest thanks to Elizabeth Barrett for all the hard work she put in the book to make it look like English. Does anything ever escape her vigilant eyes? TG, you are unbelievable! Thank you for meticulously going through the scripts, suggesting corrections, and guiding me where I stumbled. You are also one of the most wonderful people I've ever come across. Thank you for all the support, technical as well as moral. A huge thank you also to Sandip Bhattacharya, who lent his technical expertise to and helped me with the two most important chapters of the book.

In the past, I have been negligent in mentioning some unsung heroes who work quietly yet efficiently behind the scenes. Now I would like to rectify that mistake. Although "thanks" does not suffice, a huge thanks to Vineet Whig and Shantanu Phadnis. Also, a big thanks to Stacy Hiquet for making this book happen in the first place.

And finally to the people who are my lifeline. These are the people who I lean on when the times are hard and laugh with when times are good—my family. Thank you for just being there. How can you guys put up with the crazy schedule I keep?

About the Author

Meeta Gupta holds a Masters degree in Computer Engineering. For the past two years, she has been working with the KSB division of NIIT, where she has authored and co-authored several books for various publishers. These books include *SAN Fundamentals*, *PHP Professional Projects*, *TCP/IP Bible*, and *A+ Certification Guide*. Meeta has been a Subject Matter Expert (SME) for various Instructor-Led Trainings (ILTs), articles, Computer-Based Trainings (CBTs), and Web-Based Trainings (WBTs) developed for various networking technologies. Besides writing, Meeta also has experience training a wide range of clients, from students to corporate clients, about various technologies.

About NIIT

NIIT is a global IT solutions corporation with a presence in 38 countries. With its unique business model and technology creation capabilities, NIIT delivers software and learning solutions to more than 1000 clients across the world.

The success of NIIT's training solutions lies in its unique approach to education. NIIT's Knowledge Solutions business conceives, researches, and develops all the course material. A rigorous instructional design methodology is followed to create engaging and compelling course content. And, NIIT has one of the largest learning material development facilities in the world with more than 5000 years of combined employee experience.

NIIT trains over 200,000 executives and learners each year in IT areas using stand-up training, video aided instruction, computer-based training and Internet-based training. NIIT has developed over 10,000 hours of instructor-led training and over 3000 hours of Internet- and computer-based training. NIIT has been featured in the Guinness Book of World Records for the largest number of learners trained in one year!

Quality is the prime focus at NIIT. Most NIIT processes are ISO-9001 certified. Further, NIIT was the 12th company in the world to be assessed at Level 5 of SEI-CMM. NIIT's Content (Learning Material) Development facility is the first in the world to be assessed at this highest maturity level.

IDC ranked NIIT among the Top 15 IT Training Providers globally for the year 2000. Through the innovative use of training methods and its commitment to research and development, NIIT has been in the forefront of computer education and training for the past 20 years.

NIIT has strategic partnerships with Computer Associates, IBM, Microsoft, Oracle, and Sun Microsystems.

Contents at a Glance

Contents

Introduction

Goal of the Book

VPNs are a must for all organizations planning to compete in the global competitive marketplace. To put this remarkable solution to effective use, network administrators and other IS professionals must have an in-depth knowledge of all technologies related to VPNs and their implementation.

This book aims to provide the kind of knowledge an administrator requires to give his or her company a competitive edge by implementing secure and efficient VPNs. This book will cover all aspects of VPN implementation, starting with basic VPN concepts and then moving on to the practical and real-life aspects of VPN implementation. This book outlines the way an organization should plan for VPNs, what design considerations to keep in mind, which architecture to use for best results, and much, much more.

The first part of the book provides you with an overview of VPN technology. This part introduces you to VPN concepts and covers the various elements included in the VPN technology.

The second part covers tunneling concepts. This part also introduces you to the most important tunneling protocols based on the layers at which they function. PPTP, L2F, and L2TP, which operate at Layer 2, are covered in one chapter, while a separate chapter is dedicated to IPSec, which functions at Layer 3 of the OSI model and has emerged as the most important protocol in VPN technology.

The third part of this book is aimed at building and implementing VPNs. This part introduces you to the design considerations you must keep in mind when you plan your VPN setup and provides generic step-by-step instructions for VPN implementation. This part also covers the implementation of VPNs on two of the most popular networking platforms—Windows 2000 and Linux.

The fourth part of this book is dedicated to VPN security issues. Here, you'll learn about the common security threats your VPN might have to face. This part also discusses the various complementary security technologies that can strengthen you VPN solution.

The book's final chapters are dedicated to VPN management. Here, you'll also learn how to troubleshoot common problems that might hinder your VPN solution.

This book also includes five appendices. The appendices offer tips and recommendations that you can use when implementing your VPN, FAQs that give you relevant answers to questions about VPN technology, and an outline of future expected developments in the VPN arena. The appendices also includes information on creating a network security policy that compliments your security strategy and offers detailed lists of VPN hardware and software vendors and service providers.

How to Use This Book

This book has been organized to facilitate the understanding of a VPN novice, while offering easy-to-find answers for VPN veterans. Basic concepts integral to VPN functionality are covered toward the beginning; specific information regarding technology implementation and security concerns makes up the balance of the text.

◆ **Tips.** Tips have been used to provide special advice or unusual product shortcuts.

◆ **Notes.** Notes give additional information that may be of interest to the reader, but is not essential to performing the task at hand.

◆ **Cautions.** Cautions are used to warn users of possible disastrous results if they perform a task incorrectly.

◆ **New term definitions.** All new terms have been italicized and then defined as a part of the text.

PART I

VPN Basics

Chapter 1

Introduction to VPNs

In the last decade, the world has witnessed an explosive growth of the Internet. By no means has this growth stopped. In fact, industry pundits are continually astounded by the unprecedented expansion of technology. This growth is not simply a matter of the number of new members who join the Internet community by the hour, but a matter of the manner in which the Internet continues to invade every aspect of the modern life, reshaping business priorities, consumer requirements, and general commercial attitudes.

Initially, organizations all over the world were using the Internet to promote their products and services by providing access to their corporate Web sites. With time, the focus has shifted to e-commerce and e-business, which is all about providing secure, cost-effective, and global access to the business applications and related data stored on their systems. Moreover, due to their increasing global presence, many organizations have realized that instead of bearing the cost of Internet connectivity, they can effectively reduce the cost of implementation by outsourcing their Internet connectivity services to another organization that specializes in the field. As a result, they can also increase their profit margin considerably.

This growing demand for highly secure and cost-effective data transactions over a relatively "insecure" public media, such as the Internet, has given rise to the *Virtual Private Networks* (VPNs) of today. Because of the large number of benefits they offer, VPNs have emerged as the latest buzz in IT circles. You'll learn about their advantages and benefits as you progress through this chapter and the book.

In this chapter, you will learn the basics of VPN technology. Besides the whats and the whys of a VPN, you'll also learn about the types of VPNs and the role they play in advancing the existing network technology toward security and cost-effectiveness.

Understanding VPNs

The driving force behind the entire VPN technology is the use of the Internet and its global accessibility. However, because the Internet is a shared public medium that can be accessed by anyone, anytime, anyplace, the exchange of data across it is extremely prone to eavesdropping, unauthorized access, and damage while in transit. The primary intent of VPNs is to deliver the security, performance, and reliability of dedicated networks while ensuring that the overall setup justifies the cost of implementation.

So what exactly is a VPN?

According to the standard definition provided by the *Internet Engineering Task Force* (IETF), a VPN is *"An emulation of* [a] *private Wide Area Network (WAN) using shared or public IP facilities, such as the Internet or private IP backbones."*

In simpler terms, a VPN is an extension of a private intranet across a public network (the Internet) that ensures secure and cost-effective connectivity between the two communicating ends. The private intranet is extended with the help of private logical *"tunnels."* These tunnels enable the two ends to exchange data in a manner that resembles point-to-point communication. Figure 1-1 depicts a typical VPN setup.

Although the tunneling technology lies at the core of VPNs, elaborate security measures and mechanisms are also used to ensure safe passage of sensitive data across an unsecured medium. These safety mechanisms include the following:

◆ **Encryption.** Encryption is the process of changing data into a form that can be read only by the intended receiver. In order to read the message, the receiver of the data must have the correct decryption key. In traditional encryption schemes, the sender and the receiver use the same key to encrypt and decrypt data. Conversely, the public-key encryption scheme uses two keys. One of the keys is known as the *public key*, which anyone may use during encryption or decryption. Although the name of the key is "public key" it is owned by an entity. If a second entity needs to communicate with the owner of the key, it uses this public key to do so. The public key has a corresponding *private key*. The private key, as the name suggests, is private to the entity (or person) to which it is issued. As a result, with public-key encryption anyone may use the owner's public key to encrypt and send a message. However, only the owner

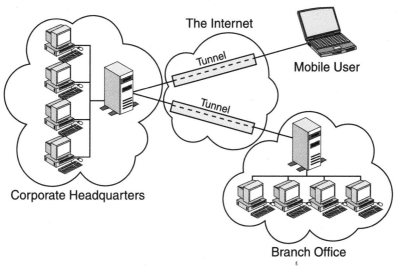

FIGURE 1-1 *The typical VPN setup.*

has the private key necessary to decrypt this message. In a communication, the sender uses its public key to encrypt the message. The recipient retrieves the message and decrypts the encoded message using the private key. *Pretty Good Privacy* (PGP) and *Data Encryption Standard* (DES) are two of the most popular public-key encryption schemes.

◆ **Authentication.** Authentication is the process of ensuring that data is delivered to its intended recipient. In addition, authentication also assures the receiver of the integrity of the message and its source. In its simplest form, authentication requires at least a username and password to gain access to the specified resource. In its complex form, authentication can be based on secret-key encryption or on public-key encryption.

◆ **Authorization.** Authorization is the process of granting or denying access to the resources located in a network after the user has been successfully identified and authenticated.

 NOTE

You'll learn more about encryption and decryption in Chapter 3, "Security Components of a VPN."

Now that you have a basic idea of what a VPN entails, in the next section you'll learn how VPN technology came into existence and its course of evolution.

Evolution of VPNs

VPNs are not exactly a new technology. Contrary to what most of us believe, the concept of VPNs has been around for the last 15 years and has undergone several generations to arrive in its latest form.

The first known VPNs were offered by AT&T in late eighties and were known as *Software Defined Networks* (SDNs). SDNs were long-distance WANs that were equally adept at making use of dedicated as well as switched connectivity and were strongly based on databases that were used to classify every access attempt as local or remote. Based on this information, the data packet was routed to its destination across the shared public switched infrastructure.

The second generation of VPNs came into existence with the emergence of X.25 and *Integrated Services Digital Network* (ISDN) technologies in the early nineties. These two technologies allowed transmission of packet streams across a shared public network. Therefore, the idea of low-cost transmissions across a public network gained popularity within the internetworking community very fast. For some time it seemed as though the X.25 protocol over ISDN would be established as the native VPN protocol. However, transmission rates failed to live up to the expected level of performance and the short-lived second generation of VPNs was passé.

After the second generation, the VPN market slowed until the emergence of cell-based *Frame Relay* (FR) and *Asynchronous Transfer Mode* (ATM) technologies. The third generation of VPNs was based on these ATM and FR technologies. These technologies, in turn, were based on the concept of virtual circuit switching, in which the data packets do not contain the source or destination addresses. Instead, they carry pointers to the virtual circuits where the source and destination nodes involved in the transaction are located.

 NOTE

Virtual Circuit switching technology offers much higher data transfer rates (160 Mbps and above) than its predecessors—SDN, X.25, and ISDN. However, the encapsulation of IP traffic into Frame Relay packets and ATM cells is considerably slower. Also, FR-based and ATM-based networks do not offer the packet-level end-to-end authentication and encryption required for high-end applications, such as multimedia. Another problem associated with VC-oriented networks is that they have limited capability to route across congested networks, which is a common phenomenon in shared public networks.

By the time e-commerce became *the* way to conduct business in the mid-nineties, the user requirements were clear. Users (and organizations) wanted a solution that was easy to implement, scale, and administer, globally accessible, and capable of providing a high level of end-to-end security. The current generation of VPNs—the *IP VPNs*—meets all these requirements by employing tunneling technology. Now, large-scale organizations *and* small organizations that once could ill-afford expensive leased lines-based solutions can mark their presence in the global market.

Tunneling is the technique of encapsulating a data packet in a tunneling protocol, such as *IP Security* (IPSec), *Point- to-Point Tunneling Protocol* (PPTP), or *Layer 2 Tunneling Protocol* (L2TP), and then finally packaging the tunneled packet into an IP packet. The resultant packet is then routed to the destination network using the overlying IP information. Because the original data packet can be of any type, tunneling can support multi-protocol traffic, including IP, ISDN, FR, and ATM. In the next section, you'll be introduced to the most commonly used VPN tunneling protocols.

VPN Tunneling Protocols

Three major tunneling protocols are prominently used in VPNs to ensure the safety aspects of VPN-based transactions. These include the following:

◆ **IP Security (IPSec).** Developed by IETF, IPSec is an open standard that ensures transmission security and user authentication over public networks. Unlike other encryption techniques, IPSec operates at the Network layer of the seven-layer Open System Interconnect (OSI) model. Therefore, it can be implemented independently of the applications running over the network. As a result the network can be secured without the need to implement and coordinate security for each individual application.

◆ **Point-to-Point Tunneling Protocol (PPTP).** Developed by Microsoft, 3COM, and Ascend Communications, PPTP was proposed as an alternative to IPSec. However, IPSec still remains the favorite tunneling protocol. PPTP operates at layer 2 (Data Link layer) of the OSI model and is used for secure transmission of Windows-based traffic.

◆ **Layer 2 Tunneling Protocol (L2TP).** Developed by Cisco Systems, L2TP was also intended to replace IPSec as the de facto tunneling protocol. However, IPSec still continues to be the dominant protocol for secure communication over the Internet. L2TP is a combination of *Layer 2 Forwarding* (L2F) and PPTP and is used to encapsulate *Point-to-Point Protocol* (PPP) frames to be sent over X.25, FR, and ATM networks.

 NOTE

L2F was an earlier proprietary protocol proposed by Cisco Systems to ensure secure transmissions over the Internet. However, it was later replaced by L2TP, which offered stronger encryption of data and also covered the Windows domain where L2F failed.

In the next section, you'll learn about the various advantages offered by VPNs and the various disadvantages associated with them.

Advantages and Disadvantages of VPNs

VPN offer a large number of benefits. These advantages follow:

◆ **Reduced cost of implementation.** VPNs cost considerably less than the traditional solutions, which are based on leased lines, Frame Relay, ATM, or ISDN. This is because VPNs eliminate the need for long-distance connections by replacing them with local connections to a carrier network, ISP, or ISP's *Point of Presence* (POP).

◆ **Reduced management and staffing costs.** By reducing the long-distance telecommunication costs, VPNs also bring down WAN-based network operation costs a considerable extent. In addition, an organization can bring down the overall cost of the network if the WAN equipment used in the VPN is managed by the ISP. The reason behind the lowered cost of operation is explained by the fact that the organization does not need to employ as many trained and expensive networking personnel as it would if the VPN were managed by the organization itself.

◆ **Enhanced connectivity.** VPNs employ the Internet for interconnectivity between remote parts of an intranet. Because the Internet is accessible globally, even the most far flung branch offices, users, and mobile users (such as salesmen) can easily connect to the corporate intranet.

◆ **Security of transactions.** Because VPNs use the tunneling technology to transmit data across "unsecured" public networks, data transactions are secure to an extent. In addition to the tunneling technology, VPNs use extensive security measures, such as encryption, authentication, and authorization to ensure the safety, confidentiality, and integrity of the data transmitted. As a result, VPNs offer a considerably high degree of transaction security.

◆ **Effective use of bandwidth.** In the case of Internet connectivity based on leased lines, the bandwidth is entirely wasted in the absence of an active Internet connection. VPNs, on the other hand, create logical tunnels to transmit data as and when required. As a result, the network bandwidth is used only when there is an active Internet connection. Therefore, there is considerably less chance of available network bandwidth waste.

◆ **Enhanced scalability.** Because VPNs are Internet-based, they allow a corporate intranet to evolve and grow as and when the business needs change, with minimal expenditures on extra equipment. This makes VPN-based intranets highly scalable and adaptive to future growth, without putting too much strain on the organization's network budget.

Despite the number of advantages offered by VPNs, a few disadvantages are also associated with them that have made a lot of users skeptical about their use. These disadvantages include the following:

- **High dependence on the Internet.** The performance of a VPN-based network is highly dependent on the performance of the Internet. Leased lines guarantee the bandwidth that is specified in a contract between the ISP and the organization. However, no one can guarantee the performance of the Internet. An overload of traffic and congestion can negatively affect the performance of the entire VPN-based network.

- **Lack of support to the legacy protocols.** Present-day VPNs are entirely based on IP technology. However, many organizations continue to use mainframes and other such legacy devices and protocols in their everyday transactions. As a result, VPNs are largely incompatible with legacy devices and protocols. This problem can be solved, to an extent, with the help of tunneling mechanisms. But, packaging SNA and other non-IP traffic within IP packets can slow down the performance of the entire network.

In the next section, you'll learn about the facts that need to be considered when implementing a VPN-based solution.

VPN Considerations

The most important considerations to keep in mind while implementing VPN-based networking solution are

- **Security.** Because sensitive and mission critical company data must travel across an extremely insecure network, such as the Internet, security is the top-most concern among organizations and network administrators. Proper measures should be taken to ensure that the data cannot be intercepted, eavesdropped, or damaged while in transit. Strong encryption mechanisms must be employed to encrypt data.

  Another major concern of selecting a VPN-based solution for your enterprise network is that the chosen solution must be compatible with the existing network infrastructure and security solutions, such as firewalls, proxies, anti-virus software, and other such intrusion detection systems. Another point to be kept in mind is that the entire solution must be manageable by using one single application.

- **Interoperability of devices from multiple vendors.** If there is the slightest lack of interoperability between devices used to implement the VPN, guaranteed *Quality of Service* (QoS) is difficult to deliver. Therefore, devices must be thoroughly tested for interoperability before implementing them in the VPN. Experts recommend that as far as possible, the devices used for the implementation of a VPN should be from one vendor. This ensures complete device interoperability and guaranteed high performance.

◆ **Centralized VPN management.** It should be possible to configure, manage, and troubleshoot VPN-related problems from one location or application. Also, it is important that the management software generates all the logs. These logs help a network administrator to proactively locate problems and solve them before the entire network performance is affected negatively.

◆ **Easy implementation.** The VPN solution must be easy to implement and configure. If you are implementing large-scale solutions, you must ensure that the management software is capable of recording and keeping track of the large number of tunnels that system implements.

◆ **Easy usability.** The VPN software, especially the VPN client software, must be simple and uncomplicated so that even end-users can implement it, if necessary. In addition, authentication processes and interfaces must be easy to understand and use.

◆ **Scalability.** The existing VPN must be capable of adapting to future demands and additions seamlessly and with minimal change to the existing infrastructure.

◆ **Performance.** Encryption, which is a very important aspect of VPNs, is a CPU-intensive operation. Therefore, it is necessary to select devices that are not only seamlessly interoperable, but also capable of performing tasks, such as data encryption, quickly and efficiently. If not, the low level of performance can bring down the overall performance of the VPN.

◆ **Bandwidth management.** To ensure high performance, high availability, and guaranteed QoS, it is essential to manage the bandwidth efficiently. Bandwidth management has many aspects. These include management of bandwidth by users, by groups, and applications, so that it is possible to prioritize users, groups, and applications per company policy.

◆ **Choosing an ISP.** The ISP you choose for your VPN must be reliable and must be capable of providing support to VPN users and network administrators anytime. This might even be more crucial if your ISP provides you managed services. You'll also want to ensure that your prospective ISP offers the kind of services you are looking for and, more importantly, can provide services immaterial to geographic location.

◆ **Protecting the network from unsolicited data.** Being directly connected to the Internet, VPNs can be clogged by unsolicited data preventing the network from performing properly. In extreme cases, this data can overwhelm the entire intranet leading to the disruption of connectivity and services. As a result, VPN tunnels should provide a mechanism to filter out non-VPN traffic. These mechanisms might include bandwidth reservation services or a policy of not assigning global IP addresses to the nodes located within the network, thus blocking the unauthorized access to these nodes from the public network.

The next section throws light on the various types of VPN-based solutions that are most commonly implemented.

Types of VPNs

The objective of VPN technology is to address three basic requirements. These include the following:

- Anytime access by remote, mobile, and telecommuting employees of an organization to the corporate network resources.
- Interconnectivity between remote branch offices.
- Controlled access to necessary network resources to customers, suppliers, and other external entities that are important to corporate business.

On the basis of the objectives specified above, present-day VPNs have evolved into the following three categories:

- Remote Access VPNs
- Intranet VPNs
- Extranet VPNs

You'll learn about these three types of VPNs in detail in the following sections.

Remote Access VPNs

As the name suggests, Remote Access VPNs provide anytime access by remote, mobile, and telecommuting employees of an organization to the corporate network resources. Typically, these remote access requests are issued by users who are constantly on the move or by small and remote branches that lack a permanent connection to the corporate intranet.

As shown in Figure 1-2, the switched remote access setup before the popularization of VPNs included the following major components:

- A *Remote Access Server* (RAS), which is located at the central site and authenticates and authorizes remote access requests.
- Dial-up connection to the central site, which can entail high charges in the case of long-distance requests.
- Support personnel who are responsible for configuring, maintaining, and managing RAS and supporting remote users.

By implementing Remote Access VPNs, remote users and branch offices only need to set up local dial-up connections to the ISP or the ISP's POP and connect to the corporate network across the Internet. The corresponding Remote Access VPN setup is depicted in Figure 1-3.

As you can infer from Figure 1-3, the major advantages of Remote Access VPNs over the traditional remote access approach are as follows:

- The need for RAS and its associated modem pool is entirely eliminated.
- The need for support personnel is eliminated because the remote connectivity is facilitated by the ISP.

◆ The need for long-distance dial-up connections is eliminated; instead, long-distance connections are replaced by local dial-up connections.

◆ The provision of inexpensive dial-up service for long-distance users.

◆ Because the dial-up access is local, modems perform at higher data rates as compared to long-distance access.

◆ VPNs provide better accessibility to the corporate site because they support a minimum level of access services despite the heavy increase in the number of simultaneous users accessing the network. As the number of connected users increases in a VPN setup, though services may be decreased, accessibility is not completely disrupted.

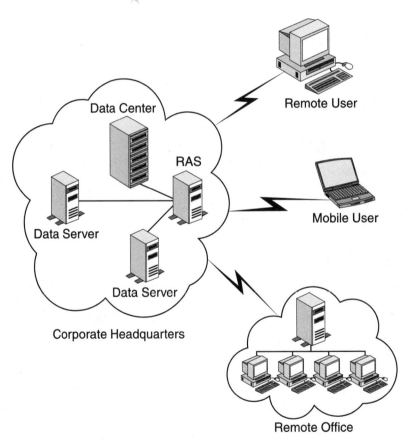

FIGURE 1-2 _The non-VPN remote access setup._

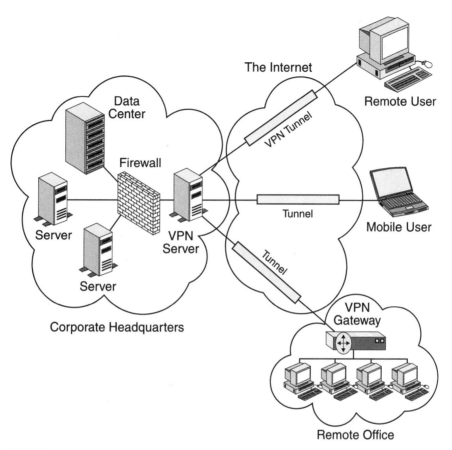

FIGURE 1-3 *The Remote Access VPN setup.*

Despite the number of advantages offered by Remote Access VPNs, a few inherent disadvantages are associated with them. These include the following:

◆ Remote Access VPNs do not offer a guaranteed QoS.

◆ The possibility of data loss is very high. In addition, packets can be delivered fragmented and out of order.

◆ Because of elaborate encryption algorithms, the protocol overhead is increased considerably. This leads to latency in the authentication process. In addition, IP- and PPP-based data compression is extremely slow and poor.

◆ Because of the underlying presence of the Internet, when transmitting high-end multimedia data across the Remote Access VPN tunnels, latency in transmission can be very high and throughput can be extremely low.

In the next section, you'll learn about the second type of VPNs—Intranet VPNs.

Intranet VPNs

Intranet VPNs are used to interconnect remote branch offices of an organization to the corporate intranet. In an intranet setup, without using the VPN technology each remote site must be connected to the corporate intranet (backbone router) using campus routers. This setup is shown in Figure 1-4.

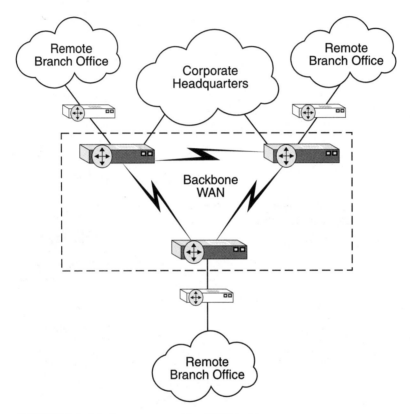

FIGURE 1-4 *The intranet setup using WAN backbone.*

The setup shown in Figure 1-4 is highly expensive because at least two routers are required to connect a remote campus to the organization's intranet. In addition, the implementation, maintenance, and management of intranet backbone can be an extremely expensive affair depending on the volume of network traffic that traverses it and the geographical extent of the entire intranet. For example, the cost of a global intranet can be up to several thousand dollars per month! The bigger the reach of the intranet, the more expensive it can be.

With the implementation of VPN solutions, the expensive WAN backbone is replaced by low-cost Internet connectivity, which can decrease the total cost of implementation of the entire intranet. A typical VPN-based solution is depicted in Figure 1-5.

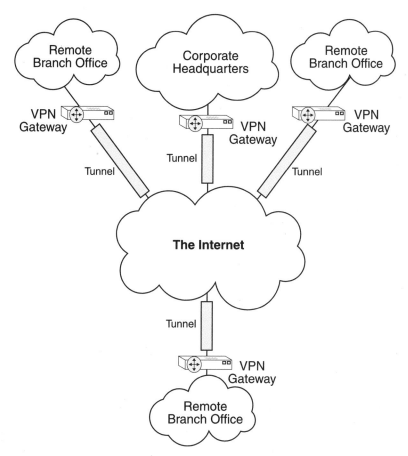

FIGURE 1-5 *The intranet setup based on VPN.*

The major advantages offered by the VPN-based setup shown in Figure 1-5 include the following:

◆ It is cost-effective due to the elimination of routers that are used to form the WAN backbone.

◆ It considerably reduces the number of support personnel required across the globe, stationed at various remote sites.

◆ Because the Internet acts as the connection medium, it is easier to accommodate new peer-to-peer links.

◆ A cost-effective backup facility can be achieved using the VPN tunnels in association with fast switching technology, such as FR.

◆ Because of the local nature of dial-up connectivity to the ISP, accessibility is faster and better. Also, the elimination of long-distance services further helps an organization reduce the cost of intranet operation.

The disadvantages associated with intranet VPN solutions are listed next:

◆ Because the data is still tunneled through a shared public network—the Internet—attacks, such as denial-of-service, can still pose serious security threats.

◆ The possibility of data packet loss while in transit is still very high.

◆ In case of transmission of high-end data, such as multimedia, latency in transmission can be very high and throughput can be extremely low due to the underlying presence of the Internet.

◆ Because of the underlying Internet connectivity, performance can be sporadic and QoS cannot be guaranteed.

In the next section, you'll learn about the third and the final type of VPNs—Extranet VPNs.

Extranet VPNs

Unlike intranet and remote access-based VPN solutions, Extranet VPNs are not entirely segregated from the "outer world." In fact, Extranet VPNs allow controlled access to necessary network resources to external business entities, such as partners, customers, and suppliers who play a major role in the organization's business.

The traditional approach of extranet connectivity is shown in Figure 1-6.

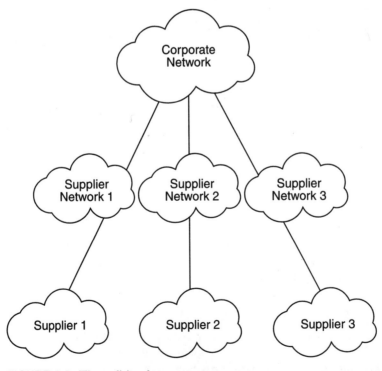

FIGURE 1-6 *The traditional extranet setup.*

As shown in Figure 1-6, the traditional setup is extremely expensive, because every separate network in the intranet must be tailored according to the external network. This typically results in complex implementation and management of various networks. Also, the need for qualified personnel to maintain and manage this extremely complex setup is very high. In addition, this type of setup cannot be easily extended because doing so would upset the entire intranet and might affect the other connected external networks. As a result of all the problems that you might encounter when connecting an intranet to external networks, implementation of extranets can be a network designer and administrator's nightmare.

The implementation of VPNs has made the task of setting up an extranet considerably easy and cost-effective. The Extranet VPN setup is shown in Figure 1-7.

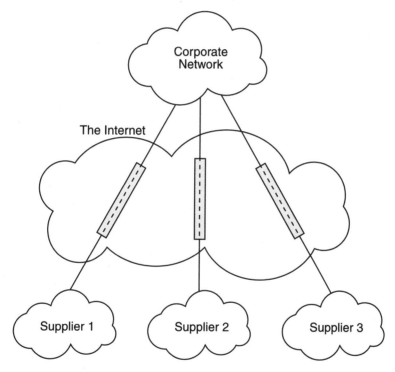

FIGURE 1-7 *The Extranet VPN setup.*

The major advantages of Extranet VPNs include the following:

◆ Fractional cost compared to the traditional setup.

◆ Easy implementation, maintenance, and ease of existing setup modification.

◆ Because of the underlying presence of the Internet, you have a bigger choice of vendors when selecting and tailoring solutions according to the needs of an organization.

◆ Because the Internet-connectivity part is maintained by the ISP, the need for support personnel is reduced considerably, thus bringing down the cost of operation of the entire setup.

A few disadvantages are associated with the Extranet VPN solution. These include the following:

◆ Security threats, such as denial-of-service, still exist.

◆ Increased risk of the penetration of the organization's intranet.

◆ Due to the underlying presence of the Internet, in the case of high-end data, such as multimedia, latency in transmission can be very high and throughput can be extremely low.

◆ Because of the underlying Internet connectivity, performance can be sporadic and QoS cannot be guaranteed.

Despite the disadvantages posed by VPN-based solutions, the number of advantages offered by VPNs far outweigh their disadvantages.

Summary

In this chapter, you were introduced to the current favorite in industry circles—VPN technology. Besides the basics of the technology, you learned about the advantages and disadvantages of VPNs. And, in addition to the whats and the whys of a VPN, you also learned about the types of VPNs, their common uses, and the role they have to play in advancing the existing network technology toward security and cost-effectiveness.

You'll learn about the VPN technology in greater details in the following chapters.

Check Your Understanding

Multiple Choice Questions

1. Which of the following is NOT a VPN protocol?

    a. X.25

    b. L2F

    c. PPTP

    d. IPSec

2. Which of the following statements are true?

    a. L2TP was a predecessor of L2F.

    b. PPTP is a proprietary Cisco protocol.

    c. L2TP is a combination of PPTP and L2F.

    d. IPSec functions at Layer 3 of the OSI model.

3. The three types of VPNs are _____, _____, and _____.

    a. Intranet

    b. Internet

    c. Extranet

    d. Remote Access

4. The term RAS stands for _____.

    a. Remote Access Standard

    b. Remote Access Storage

    c. Remote Access Server

    d. Remote Access Subsystem

5. Which of the following statements are true?

    a. Remote Access VPNs eliminate the need for a modem pool.

    b. Intranet VPNs are dependent on a WAN router backbone, which is why they are expensive solutions.

    c. Extranets are expensive and complex solutions that require efficient management.

    d. QoS cannot be guaranteed in the case of Intranet VPNs.

Answers

Multiple Choice Answers

1. **a**. X.25 is not a VPN protocol. Instead, it is a network technology.

2. **c**. L2TP is a combination of PPTP and L2F. L2TP is not the predecessor of L2F. Instead, L2F is the predecessor of L2TP. Also, PPTP is a proprietary Microsoft protocol. L2F and L2TP are Cisco protocols.

3. **a, c**, and **d**. Remote Access, Intranet, and Extranet VPNs are the three most popular categories of VPNs.

4. **c**. The term RAS stands for Remote Access Server.

5. **a ,c**, and **d**. Remote Access VPNs eliminate the need for a modem pool. Extranets are expensive and complex solutions that require efficient management. And, QoS cannot be guaranteed in the case of Intranet VPNs.

Chapter 2

VPN Requirements, Building Blocks, and Architectures

You learned in the previous chapter that a VPN is a secure and relatively simple method of establishing intranet connectivity across public networks. VPN technology not only reduces the cost of implementing a highly secure network environment, but also reduces management and staffing costs. In addition, it offers high availability, scalability, and effective use of network bandwidth.

What goes into the making of a VPN-based solution? What are the components and requirements of a VPN? What are the building blocks of a VPN? What are the possible VPN architectures? These are the questions that this chapter explores.

VPN Requirements

A VPN is a modified version of a private network that allows you to leverage the traditional LAN or intranet setup along with the Internet and other public networks to communicate securely and economically. As a result, most VPN requirements and the requirements of a traditional private network are essentially the same. However, the following requirements stand out clearly in the case of VPNs:

◆ Security
◆ Availability
◆ Quality of Service (QoS)
◆ Reliability
◆ Compatibility
◆ Manageability

Security

Private networks and intranets offer a high-security environment because the network resources are not accessible to the general public. Therefore, the probability of unauthorized people accessing the intranet and its resources is extremely low. However, this assumption might not hold true for VPNs as they use the Internet and other public networks, such as Public Switched Telephone Networks (PSTNs), for communication. The VPN setup offers would-be hackers and crackers a fair chance to gain access to a private network and the data flowing to it through public networks. As a result, security cannot be taken for granted. Comprehensive and advanced security measures must be implemented rigorously.

The data and the resources located within the network can be secured in the following ways:

◆ Implementation of peripheral defense mechanism(s) that allow only authorized traffic from trusted sources into the network and block all the other traffic. Firewalls and Network Address Translation (NAT) are examples of defense mechanisms that are implemented at the point where a private network or intranet is connected to a public network. Firewalls scrutinize not only the incoming traffic but also the outgoing traffic, thus ensuring a high level of security. NATs, on the other hand, do not reveal the real IP addresses of the resources located within the network. As a result, hackers and other attackers cannot target a specific resource located within the intranet and, consequently, the data stored there.

◆ Implementation of user and packet authentication to establish the identity of the user and determine if he or she should be allowed access to the VPN-accessible resources within the network. The Authentication Authorization Accounting (AAA) model is an example of one such comprehensive user authentication system. First, it authenticates the user accessing the network. After the user is authenticated successfully, the user can then access only those resources that he or she is authorized to use. In addition, a detailed log of activities of all network users is also maintained, which allows network administrators to track unauthorized activities.

◆ Implementation of data encryption mechanisms to ensure the authenticity, integrity, and confidentiality of data while the data is being transmitted across an untrusted internetwork. Internet Protocol Security (IPSec) has emerged as one of the most powerful data encryption mechanisms. It not only encrypts the data being transmitted, but also enables the authentication of each user and each packet individually.

> **NOTE**
>
> Refer to Chapter 11, "VPN Security Technologies," for detailed information on firewalls and the AAA model. Various data encryption schemes including Diffie-Hellman and RSA algorithms are covered in Chapter 3, "Security Components of a VPN." You can learn about IPSec in detail in Chapter 6, "An Introduction to IPSec."

VPN security methods should be chosen with care. They should not only be easy to implement and manage, but also should withstand any access violations from internal users as well. In addition, the user login process should be fast and easy so that users do not face difficulties while accessing the VPN.

Availability and Reliability

Availability refers to the total uptime of the network setup. In private networks and intranets, uptime is relatively high because the entire infrastructure is proprietary and in complete control of the organization. However, VPNs use intermediate internetworks in the form of the Internet and PSTNs. Therefore, VPN-based setups are highly dependent on the intermediate internetwork. In this scenario, the availability factor is highly dependent on the Internet Service Provider (ISP) you use.

Generally, ISPs ensure availability in the form of a *Service Level Agreement (SLA)*. An SLA is a written agreement between the ISP and the user (an organization or corporation) that guarantees the network uptime. Though expensive, some ISPs offer network uptime as high as 99 percent.

If your organization is looking for very high availability, look for a service provider who offers a highly resilient backbone switching infrastructure. This includes:

◆ Powerful routing capability, which allows the rerouting of traffic through an alternative path in case the main path fails or is congested. In order to ensure maximum efficiency, this routing capability must also support options to designate routing preferences as and when required.

◆ Redundancy of access lines, which can be used to accommodate increased demand on the network bandwidth.

◆ Fully redundant infrastructure with complete automatic failover. This infrastructure should not only include hot-swappable devices (servers and access and storage devices), but also power supplies and cooling systems.

Reliability is another major requirement of VPNs and it is tightly woven into the availability factor. Reliability of transactions in VPNs ensures end-to-end delivery of data in all situations. Like most other network setups, reliability in a VPN-based environment can be achieved by switching packets to a different path, if the given link or device within the path should fail. This entire process is transparent to the end user and can be achieved by implementing redundancy in links as well as hardware.

Quality of Service

Quality of Service (QoS) is the ability of a network to respond to critical situations by assigning a higher percentage of network bandwidth and resources to mission critical and delay sensitive applications. Applications, such as financial transactions and order processing, are more important from the business perspective than user activities that include Web surfing. Similarly, applications such as videoconferencing are extremely delay sensitive and require enough bandwidth to avoid the poor quality of transmission and jitters. It is the responsibility of QoS to allocate sufficient bandwidth to these applications without delay.

QoS is comprised of two critical dimensions—*latency* and *throughput*. Latency is the delay in an ongoing communication and is extremely important to audio and video applications. Throughput refers to the availability of appropriate bandwidth to all applications, especially mission-critical and bandwidth-intensive applications.

Like availability, QoS is also dependent on an SLA. With the help of an SLA, a service provider promises a certain level of latency and throughput to the subscriber. If at any time the level of latency and throughput supplied by the service provider is lower than that promised in the SLA, the agreement is violated. In this manner, an organization can ensure that it receives the promised level of the service.

Depending on the level of latency and throughput that is promised by the service provider, QoS can be divided into following three categories:

◆ **Best Effort QoS.** This class of service, at best, indicates the absence of QoS because the service provider assures neither latency nor throughput. Because of this, Best Effort QoS is the least expensive class of service and should not be used for bandwidth-intensive or delay-sensitive traffic.

◆ **Relative QoS.** This class of service is capable of prioritizing data traffic. Therefore, at least the throughput is assured. However, this assurance is not absolute and depends on the load on the network and the percentage of traffic that needs to be prioritized at a given point of time. In addition, this class of service has no provisions for minimizing latency. This is a moderately expensive class of service meant for bandwidth-intensive applications.

◆ **Absolute QoS.** This class guarantees both throughput as well as latency. Therefore, it is the most expensive class of service and supports both bandwidth-intensive and delay-sensitive applications.

Best effort QoS is offered to individual Internet-users that need the connectivity to surf the Web (generally from home). Absolute QoS, on the other hand, is meant for real-time audio and video transactions. Relative QoS is best suited for extranets and remote accesses that neither demand extremely high throughput nor minimal latency. In the real world, organizations generally use a combination of all the three classes of service to meet their enterprise networking needs in a cost-effective manner.

In VPNs, QoS provides predictable performance and policy implementation to various applications that run on the VPN. Within the VPN structure, a policy is used to categorize applications, individual users, or user groups on the basis of designated priority.

Manageability

Complete control of network resources and operations, along with proper management, have been very important issues for all organizations with networks spread across the globe. In this scenario, most organizations are connected to their world-wide resources with the help of service providers. As a result, end-to-end control of an organization's intranet is not possible because of the intermediate presence of the ISP's intranet. In this situation, organizations manage their own resources as far as their enterprise networks, while service providers manage their own network setup.

With the availability of the current breed of VPN devices and agreement between the ISP and the organization, it has become possible to eliminate the traditional boundaries of resource management and manage the entire private and public part of the VPN end-to-end. An organization can now manage, monitor, troubleshoot, and maintain its own networks as in the traditional paradigm. The organization has complete control of network access and has the right to monitor real-time status, performance of the VPN setup, and the allocated budget. In addition, an organization can also supervise the public portion of the VPN. In a similar manner, the service provider manages and controls the proprietary part of its infrastructure. However, if required, the ISP can also manage the entire infrastructure, including the subscriber organization's VPN infrastructure.

 CAUTION

Despite the boundless management that VPNs allow, it is very important for organizations to tightly control the access to its intranet resources because the services of an ISP are not restricted to one client (or subscriber) exclusively. Therefore, it is essential to ensure that no other organization that subscribes to the same service provider can interfere with your organization's VPN setup. RADIUS and TACACS, which are located within the premises of your intranet, offer an effective solution to this problem.

You'll learn more about RADIUS and TACACS later in this chapter. Chapter 11, "VPN Security Technologies," also discusses these topics in further detail.

Compatibility

As you already know, VPNs use public networks "as is" for long-distance connectivity. These intermediate internetworks can either be IP-based, such as the Internet, or can be based on other networking technologies, such as Frame Relay (FR) and Asynchronous Transfer Mode (ATM). As a result, VPNs should be able to make use of all types of underlying technologies and protocols.

In the case of IP-based intermediate internetworks, VPNs must be capable of using IP addressing and IP applications. To ensure compatibility with an IP-based infrastructure, the following methods can be integrated into VPNs:

♦ **Use of IP gateways.** IP gateways convert (or translate) non-IP protocols to IP and vice versa. These devices can be either dedicated network devices or can be software-based solutions. As hardware devices, IP gateways are generally implemented at the edges of an organization's intranet. As software-based solutions, IP gateways are installed on every server and are used to convert traffic to and from non-IP protocol to IP. Novell's IP Gateway for NetWare is one such example. It converts IPX traffic to IP and vice versa.

NOTE

IPX, or Internetwork Packet eXchange, is a proprietary Novell LAN protocol.

♦ **Use of Tunneling.** Tunneling, as you learned in the previous chapter, is the technique of encapsulating non-IP data packets into IP packets for transmission across IP-based infrastructure. The other end, on receiving these tunneled packets, processes and removes the IP header to retrieve the original information, which is referred to in tunneling terminology as the payload.

♦ **Use of Virtual IP Routing (VIPR).** As shown in Figure 2-1, *VIPR* works by logically partitioning a physical router located at the service provider end (as a part of the ISP's infrastructure). Each partition is configured and managed as a physical router and can support an individual VPN. In simpler terms, each logical partition is treated as a complete router with full router functionality. As a result, these logical router partitions can support multiple protocols and are capable of handling private IP addresses.

In case of non-IP protocols and technologies, such as Frame Relay and ATM, *Virtual Private Trunking* (VPT) technology is used. VPT technology is depicted in Figure 2-2. VPT is compatible with a wide range of protocols and is based on packet switching technologies. Therefore, it makes use of Permanent Virtual Circuits (PVCs) and Switched Virtual Circuits (SVCs) for data transmissions. For successful transactions, VPT requires a WAN device, such as a

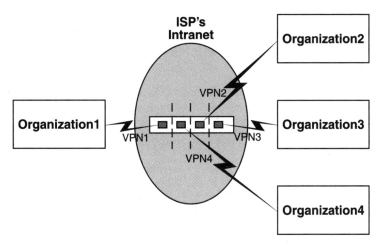

FIGURE 2-1 *A generic representation of VIPR.*

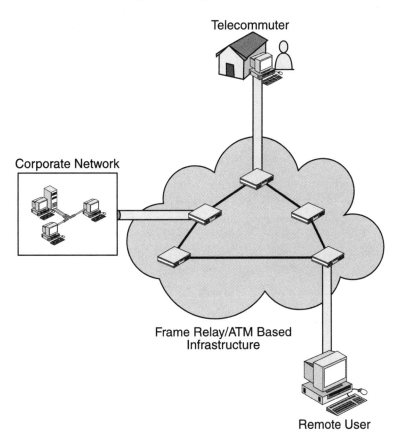

FIGURE 2-2 *A generic representation of VPT.*

router, that also supports FR and ATM capabilities. To ensure cost effective transactions, PVCs are generally used for linking sites within a private network or an intranet. SVCs, on the other hand, are used to link sites within an extranet.

> **NOTE**
>
> PVC is a virtual path through a network in which the end points of the connection are defined by the administrator. An SVC is also a virtual path through a network; however, in contrast to PVCs, the end points of the communication are defined by the user at the time of the call initiation.

Now that you are familiar with the basic requirements of a VPN, consider what elements (components or building blocks) go into the making of a physical VPN.

Building Blocks of a VPN

As shown in Figure 2-3, six fundamental elements (or building blocks) make up a complete VPN-based solution. These VPN building blocks are listed below.

- ◆ **VPN hardware**, which includes VPN servers, clients, and other hardware devices, such as VPN routers, gateways, and concentrators
- ◆ **VPN software**, which includes server and client software and VPN management tools
- ◆ **Security infrastructure of the organization**, which typically includes RADIUS, TACACS, NAT, and AAA-based solutions
- ◆ **Service provider's supporting infrastructure**, which includes the service provider's network access switching backbone and the Internet backbone
- ◆ **Public networks**, which include the Internet, Public Switched Telephone Networks (PSTNs), and Plain Old Telephone Services (POTS)
- ◆ **Tunnels**, which might be PPTP-based, L2TP-based, or based on L2F

Of the above-mentioned building blocks, you were introduced to tunnels and tunneling technology in Chapter 1, "Introduction to VPNs." Tunneling technology is also discussed in detail in Chapter 4, "Understanding Tunneling Technology." Therefore, to avoid unnecessary repetition of concepts, tunnels are not discussed here.

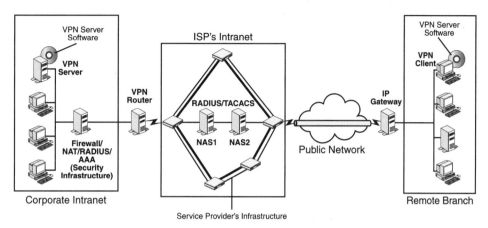

FIGURE 2-3 *The six building blocks of a VPN.*

VPN Hardware

As mentioned earlier, VPN hardware is mainly made up of VPN servers, VPN clients, and other hardware devices, such as VPN routers and concentrators.

VPN Servers

Generally, VPN servers are dedicated network devices running server software. Depending on the organization's requirements, there might be one or more VPN servers. Because a VPN server must provide services for remote as well as local VPN clients, they are always operational and ready to accept requests.

The main functions of VPN servers include the following:

◆ Listening for VPN connection requests.

◆ Negotiating connection requirements and parameters, such as encryption and authentication mechanisms .

◆ Authentication and authorization of VPN clients.

◆ Accepting data from the client or forwarding data requested by the client.

◆ Acting as the end point of the VPN tunnel and connection. The other end point is supplied by the end user requesting the VPN session.

VPN servers might support two or more network adapter cards. One or more adapter cards are used for connecting them to the organization's intranet, while other are used to link them to the Internet. in the latter case, VPN servers also act as VPN gateways or routers.

CAUTION

A VPN server that might also act as a gateway or a router is acceptable only if the number of requests or the number of users is small (up to 20). If the VPN server must support a large number of users and act as a router or a gateway, the burden of tunneling, encryption, authentication, firewalling, and routing will result in the slowdown of the server, thus bringing down overall performance. In addition, it would be extremely difficult to secure the information stored on the server. Therefore, VPN servers must be dedicated to serving VPN clients and requests only.

VPN Clients

VPN clients are remote or local machines that initiate a VPN connection to a VPN server and log on to the remote network after they have been authenticated at the remote-network end. Only after a successful login can the VPN server and client communicate with each other. Generally, a VPN client is software-based. However, it can also be a dedicated hardware device. A VPN hardware router with dial-on-demand routing capability that dials in to another VPN hardware router is an example of dedicated VPN hardware device.

With the increase in the mobile workforce of an organization, a lot of users (VPN clients) may have roaming profiles. These users might use a VPN to communicate securely to the organization's intranet. Typical VPN client profiles, as shown in Figure 2-4, include the following:

♦ Telecommuters who use the Internet or a public network to connect to their organization's resources from home.

♦ Mobile users with laptops, palmtops, and notebooks who use a public network to connect to their organization's intranet in order to access email and other such intranet resources.

♦ Remote administrators who use the intermediate public network, such as the Internet, to connect to a remote site in order to manage, monitor, troubleshoot, or configure services and devices.

VPN Routers, Concentrators, and Gateways

In the case of a small VPN setup, the VPN server can take on the onus of routing. However, this practice is not effective in the case of large-scale VPNs that entertain a huge number of requests. In such cases, a separate VPN routing device is required. Generally, a router is the end point of a private network unless it is behind a firewall. The role of a VPN router is to make remote parts on the intranet reachable. Therefore, routers are primarily responsible for finding all possible paths to the destination network and choosing the shortest path of the available set of routes, as is the case in traditional networks.

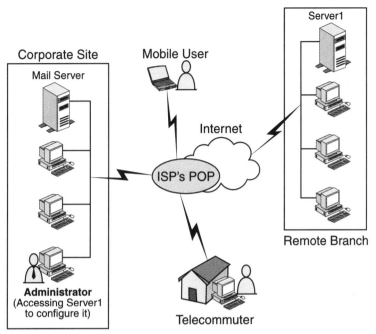

FIGURE 2-4 *Typical VPN client profiles.*

Although normal routers can be used in VPNs, experts suggest the use of VPN-optimized routers. These routers, in addition to routing, also provide security, scalability, and QoS in the form of redundancy in paths. Cisco's 1750 Modular Access router is one such popular example.

 NOTE

Add-ons to routers are also quite popular in VPNs. Router add-ons are not true routers, but an enhancement to traditional routers that make them work seamlessly in a VPN-based environment. Router add-ons are installed either at the LAN or WAN interface of a normal router and provide tunneling and/or IPSec encryption and authentication capabilities to the router. Use of these add-ons can reduce the cost of VPN setup considerably because the organization can leverage its existing routers. However, initially it is a little difficult and time-consuming to install, configure, and troubleshoot them.

Like hubs used in traditional networks, VPN concentrators are used to set up a small-scale remote access VPN. Besides increasing the capacity and throughput of the VPN, these devices also provide high availability performance, and advanced encryption and authentication capabilities. Cisco's Series 3000 and 5000 concentrators and Altiga's VPN concentrators are some commonly used concentrators.

IP gateways, as discussed earlier, translate non-IP protocols to IP and vice versa. As a result, these gateways allow a private network to support IP-based transactions. These devices can be either dedicated network devices or software-based solutions. As hardware devices, IP gateways are generally implemented at the edges of the organization's intranet. As software-based solutions, IP gateways are installed on every server and are used to convert traffic to and from non-IP protocol to IP. Novell's Border Manager IP Gateways are one such example.

VPN Software

Software solutions used in VPNs can be divided into three broad categories. These include the following:

◆ **VPN server software.** Microsoft's Windows 2000 and versions of Windows NT, Novell's NetWare, and Linux are operating systems that are generally installed on a VPN server. In other words, any machine that has these Network Operating Systems (NOSs) and is used to serve VPN client requests is referred to as a VPN server.

◆ **VPN client software.** Any networked computer that issues a request to a VPN server is referred to as a VPN client. Operating systems, such as Windows 95/98 or any other operating system that resides on a VPN client is termed VPN client software. It is interesting to note that VPN clients are not available as separate hardware devices like VPN servers. However, in case of dial-on-demand routing, VPN hardware may have a built-in VPN client.

◆ **VPN management applications and tools.** These are the applications and tools that are used for the management of a VPN-based setup. These applications are used to manage, monitor, configure, and troubleshoot problems. Novell's Border Manager and Cisco Secure Policy Manager are the best-known examples of VPN management tools. Microsoft's Windows 2000 also offers various tools, such as RRAS snap-in for MMC for the purpose of VPN management.

 NOTE

Over time, software-based VPN solutions are less expensive and are easy to configure and fine tune. However, they are difficult to initially set up and manage. Today, hardware-based VPN solutions are also available. "In-the-box solutions," as they are commonly called, offer all-in-one functionality and therefore are more expensive. However, they are easy to set up and offer high performance. Nortel's Contivity is one such example of a hardware-based in-the-box solution.

Security Infrastructure of the Organization

The security infrastructure of the organization is another important element of the overall VPN design. A well-designed and well-planned security infrastructure can protect an organization's intranet from many future disasters. The VPN security infrastructure often boasts all or a combination of some of the following security mechanisms:

◆ Firewalls

◆ Network Address Translation (NAT)

◆ Authentication servers and databases

◆ AAA architecture

◆ IPSec protocol

Firewalls

A firewall, as mentioned earlier, acts as a security blanket and serves as an effective barrier to all unauthorized attempts to access the resources located in the organization's intranet. In addition to this primary role of securing an intranet or a private network from external security threats, firewalls are also responsible for preventing the after-effects of a serious attack from affecting the entire intranet. Firewalls can operate on the basis of specific IP addresses, ports used, packet types, application types, and even data content.

Figure 2-5 depicts the position of firewalls in the overall intranet setup.

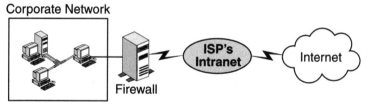

FIGURE 2-5 *Position of firewalls in an organization's intranet.*

Network Address Translation (NAT)

NAT-based devices allow you to connect to remote resources and networks without revealing the IP address of the internal hosts of a private network or intranet. As shown in Figure 2-6, NATs are also implemented at the periphery of an intranet and every communication is routed through them. In addition to providing basic security, NATs also allow you to economize on IP addresses.

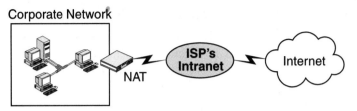

FIGURE 2-6 *Position of NATs in an organization's intranet.*

Authentication Servers and Databases

Remote Access Dial-In User Services (RADIUS) and Terminal Access Controller Access Control System (TACACS), as shown in Figure 2-7, are some of the most commonly implemented authentication servers and databases. They offer strong authentication and authorization mechanisms for remote authentication. These devices are most effective when they are located within the premises of an organization's intranet and receive every authentication request from the service-provider end.

 NOTE

TACACS is Cisco proprietary, but there's another AAA protocol that offers compatibility with RADIUS. This protocol is called Diameter. Go to http://www.diameter.org for further information about Diameter.

When a RADIUS- or a TACACS-based server receives an authentication request, it is authenticated only if the related information is stored locally. Otherwise, the query is forwarded to a central database that is dedicated to storing information related to remote users. Upon receiving the response of the query, RADIUS- or TACACS-based servers communicate the same to the Network Access Server (NAS) at the ISP end to establish a VPN connection or reject the connection request. In this manner, an organization can exercise complete control over all the remote access attempts despite the presence of intermediate service provider's intranet.

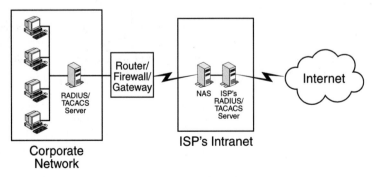

FIGURE 2-7 *Possible implementations of RADIUS and TACACS in an organization's intranet.*

AAA Architecture

Authentication Authorization Accounting (AAA) is another popularly-implemented authentication mechanism and is implemented in almost all remote access as well as local access scenarios. This security mechanism can be implemented as a complementary technology to RADIUS/TACACS, thus adding another layer of authentication.

AAA provides answers to most fundamental questions related to remote access. These include the following:

♦ Who is accessing the network?

♦ What services and resources is the user allowed to access?

♦ What are the user activities and when were they performed?

When a NAS located at the ISP end receives a remote connection request, it proxies the request to the AAA server at the organization end. This server authenticates the client and, on successful authentication, determines the resources and services the user is allowed to access. If the user attempts to access a service or resource that is prohibited, the AAA mechanism prevents the access and notifies the user. AAA also tracks the user's attempts to access various resources.

 NOTE

Refer to Chapter 11, "VPN Security Technologies," for detailed information on firewalls, NAT, RADIUS, TACACS, and AAA. You'll also be introduced to other VPN security mechanisms, such as SSL, SOCKS, and TLS.

IPSec Protocol

IPSec is the latest security technology in the field of VPNs. Unlike the other security technologies discussed previously, IPSec should not be an optional measure. It must be an integral part of VPNs because it provides highly-secure and advanced security mechanisms that offer extremely resilient encryption algorithms and comprehensive user and individual data packet authentication. However, systems at both communicating ends must be IPSec compliant to support these encryption and authentication techniques. In addition, if the VPN setup uses firewalls as a complementary security technology, the security policies that are set on the firewalls must be same as IPSec Security Associations (SAs).

IPSec provides data encryption and authentication between the following elements of a VPN setup:

♦ Client to server

♦ Client to router

♦ Firewall to router

♦ Router to router

NOTE

Refer to Chapter 6, "An Introduction to IPSec," for detailed information about IPSec and its security associations.

Service Provider's Supporting Infrastructure

Another important building block in VPN design is the service provider's infrastructure because the service provider's infrastructure is the point of access between an organization's intranet and a comparatively unsecured public network. If the infrastructure at the service provider end is not resilient, high-performing, and secure, it can cause major bottlenecks. If security measures are not stringent at the service provider end, the subscriber organization's intranet may be extremely vulnerable to all sorts of security threats, such as spoofing or Denial-of-Service. Because of this, the service provider's infrastructure should not only be high-availability and high-performance, but also extremely secure.

 NOTE

Refer to Chapter 10, "VPN Security Issues," for detailed information on the various VPN security threats.

The reliability of the service provider's infrastructure is dependent on two elements—the network access switching backbone and the Internet backbone of the ISP.

The features that you should look for in a service provider's switching backbone, which lies at the core of a service provider's Point Of Presence (POP), follow:

◆ It should be capable of supporting a varied range of technologies, such as Frame Relay, ATM, IP, IP multicast, Voice over IP (VoIP), and so on. For this purpose, the service provider's switching backbone must support both Virtual IP Routing (VIPR) and Virtual Private Trunking (VPT).

◆ It should be able to support all the popular tunneling options, such as PPTP, L2TP, and L2F.

◆ It should be scalable and adaptable to fast-changing networking scenario. In addition, it should be able to support emerging tunneling and security standards.

◆ It should offer high QoS at cost-effective rates. To maximize QoS levels, the service provider's network access switching backbone must offer the capability of dynamic bandwidth management, built-in compression to increase the overall throughput, and high-level resiliency to disasters in the form of link, power supply, and device redundancy.

◆ It should ensure a high-level of security measures, such as IPSec, RADIUS, and certification with local carriers.

The features to look for in the second component of service provider's infrastructure—the WAN (or Internet) backbone—include the following:

◆ It should offer a wide range of WAN access options, such as ISDN lines, X.25, leased lines, and T1.E1 lines.

◆ It should be capable of handling traditional router and switches in addition to VPN routers, switches, gateways, concentrators, and other VPN hardware devices.

◆ It should be capable of handling a large number of LAN and WAN ports.

◆ It should offer high throughput, low latency, and high uptime.

◆ It should be capable of supporting anticipated growth in the field of VPNs as well as the Internet.

◆ It should be compliant to all routing industry standards, such as Routing Information Protocol (RIP), Open Shortest Path First (OSPF), Exterior Gateway Protocol (EGP), and Border Gateway Protocol (BGP).

Public Networks

It is a popular opinion that the Internet is the public network. That perception is not correct because there are various types of public networks that exist today. The major categories of public networks include the following:

◆ **POTS (Plain Old Telephone Service).** POTS refers to the standard telephone services you use at home and work. The main difference between POTS and non-POTS services is based on the speed of communication. POTS supports speeds up to 56Kbps. Note that high-speed telephone services, such as Frame Relay, ATM, FDDI, and so on, do not belong to the POTS category.

◆ **PSTN (Public Switched Telephone Network).** PSTN refers to interconnected voice-oriented public telephone networks, which might be used for commercial purposes or belong to the government. Although they started as copper-based voice systems for carrying analog signals, they have rapidly progressed to high-speed digital technology, such as ADSL, DSL, ISDN, FDDI, Frame Relay, and ATM, which in turn are based on packet and circuit switching. PSTNs provide the mainstay of connectivity for the Internet.

◆ **Internet.** The Internet is perhaps the best-known public network today. It refers to a global connection of computer networks and individual computers that initially began as a connection of merely four networks. Today, the Internet is a self-sustaining phenomenon that is not governed by any body—commercial or governmental—and is accessible by virtually anybody from anywhere in the world. The Internet is based on existing POTS and PSTNs, but is slightly different from both because it uses two main protocols, TCP/IP, for controlling and managing all communications.

Public networks use various technologies for fast and successful transactions. The main technologies include the following:

◆ **Asymmetric Digital Subscriber Line (ADSL)**. ADSL allows high-speed digital transmissions while using the existing PSTN infrastructure. ADSL provides leased-line-like connections that can accommodate analog as well as digital signals simultaneously. ADSL offers data rates ranging between 64Kbps, 128Kbps, 512Kbps, and 6Mbps.

◆ **Fiber Distributed Data Interface (FDDI)**. FDDI is a LAN technology used for transmitting digital signals across fiber-optic cabling. FDDI is a token-passing technology, where a special token frame is used to transmit data. It can be single-ringed like Token ring as well as dual-ringed. A typical single ring FDDI-based network supports data rates up to 100Mbps, extends to 124 miles and can support a few thousand users. A dual-ring infrastructure is far more stable and extends to 62 miles. Because of these reasons, FDDI is commonly used for the WAN-access backbone. The latest version of FDDI called FDDI-2 can support data as well as audio and video signals on the same infrastructure. Another version of FDDI, known as FDDI Full Duplex Technology (FFDT), can support data rates up to 200Mbps.

◆ **Integrated Services Digital Network (ISDN).** ISDN is the transmission technology that allows transmission of voice, video, and data signals across copper as well as fiber-optic cables. ISDN-based implementations use an ISDN adapter (also known as CSU/DSU) at both ends instead of traditional modems. ISDN uses two types of services—Basic Rate Interface (BRI) and Primary Rate Interface (PRI). BRI is used for individual users working from home, while PRI is used for organizations and enterprises. A complete ISDN-based solution is comprised of two types of channels: B-channels and D-channels. B-channels are used for carrying data, voice, and other signals. D-channels carry control and signaling information. The original version of ISDN was baseband, which allowed a single signal over the B-channel. Today, a broadband version of ISDN called B-ISDN is available, which allows many signals to be multiplexed on the same channel and supports data rates up to 1.5Mbps.

◆ **Frame Relay.** Based on X.25 packet switching technology, Frame Relay is a cost-effective technology that carries data traffic from LANs to WANs. In Frame Relay, the frames used for data transactions are of variable size. In addition, any error-control mechanism is the responsibility of only the sender and the recipient end, which results in high-speed data transmissions. Frame Relay uses two types of circuits for transmitting data: Permanent Virtual Circuits (PVCs) and Switched Virtual Circuits (SVCs). PVCs, which are used more often, allow the end user to use dedicated connections without having to invest in more expensive options, such as leased lines. In the U.S., Frame Relay networks operate at T1 (1.544Mbps) and T3 (45Mbps). Service providers such as AT&T offer Frame Relay services. However, some telephone companies also provide rates as low as 56 Kbps. In Europe, Frame Relay transmission rates range from 64Kbps to 2 Mbps.

◆ **Asynchronous Transfer Mode (ATM).** ATM is a PVC-based digital switching technology that can support audio, video, and data signals over digital transmission mediums at rates of 155.5Mbps, 622Mbps and up to 10Gbps. ATM uses frames or packets of fixed size for this purpose. These packets are better known as cells, which are 53-byte long. Because of the small size of cells and the fact that every type of signal is framed in a cell of fixed size, no signal—audio, video, or data—can congest the line. In addition, all cells are queued before transmission and processed asynchronously irrespective of other related cells, which makes the ATM transmission faster than other switching technologies. ATM provides four types of services: Constant Bit Rate (CBR), Available Bit Rate (ABR), Variable Bit Rate (VBR), and Unspecified Bit Rate (UBR). CBR provides fixed bit rates and are analogous to leased lines. ABR provides a guaranteed minimum capacity even in case of congestion. VBR guarantees specified throughput and is commonly used for videoconferencing. UBR guarantees no throughput and is used for normal data transfers.

 NOTE

The ISDN BRI service supports two 64Kbps B-channels and one 16Kbps D-channel. Therefore, in aggregate the Basic Rate service offers up to 128Kbps service. The Primary Rate, on the other hand, consists of 23 B-channels and one 64 Kbps D-channel in the United States. In Europe, the Primary Rate service is comprised of 30 B-channels and 1 D-channel.

VPN hardware, software, tunnels, security infrastructure of the subscriber organization, infrastructure at the service provider site, and the intermediate public network all are important parts of the VPN design. You can control all these elements except the intermediary public networks and the Internet. Therefore, you must be careful when you choose the other VPN building blocks. You must also establish a balance between the two most sensitive issues of any network implementation—cost of implementation and security. For this reason, you should carefully and thoroughly analyze the requirements of your organization and the budget constraints that you face. The best solution might be to mix and match the available technologies. This will help you reduce the total cost of VPN implementation, especially if you're working within a small budget. You must also be very careful when choosing the service provider and analyze the SLA thoroughly before you accept the agreement.

Now that you know the basic building blocks of a VPN, you can now consider the various ways and architectures of implementing VPNs using these elements.

VPN Architectures

VPNs can be implemented in many ways. For example, depending on which end (the service provider or the subscriber organization) implements the basic VPN requirements (security, availability, QoS, and so on), VPNs can be organized into three categories. Similarly, depending on the security requirements of the setup, VPNs can be divided into four categories. Again, depending on the layer of the OSI model on which the overall VPN infrastructure functions, VPNs can be divided into two major groups. Finally, depending on the scale and the complexity of the VPN setup, VPNs can also be classified into five classes. What follows is a consideration of each individual type of VPN architecture category.

Implementer-based VPN Architectures

Depending on which communication end is responsible for implementing the VPN and taking care of the security requirements, VPNs can be categorized into three categories. These include:

- Dependent or Outsourced VPNs
- Independent or In-house VPNs
- Hybrid VPNs

Dependent or Outsourced VPNs

In the case of dependent VPNs, the service provider is responsible for providing the complete VPN solution. Therefore, it is the responsibility of the service provider to implement the tunneling infrastructure and provide security and performance while ensuring the manageability of the setup. As a result, the subscriber organization has the smallest role to play in this type of VPN implementation. Because of this, the organization does not need to change its existing infrastructure. Figure 2-8 depicts the dependent VPN architecture.

Because the complete VPN implementation and management is done by the service provider, the tunneling process is transparent to end users. When a user tries to access a remote resource or service, the NAS located at the ISP's POP authenticates the user. If the NAS stores the information related to member profiles, privileges, and tunneling parameters, it can authenticate the users itself. However, the NAS can also query a RADIUS, AAA, or TACACS server for the relevant information. After being authenticated, the end user (who initiated the VPN session) sends and receives non-tunneled data packets. These packets are tunneled or de-tunneled at the service provider end.

As is evident from the description, a dependent architecture is not a safe bet from the organization's point of view. Therefore, elaborate measures must be taken by the organization to ensure the safety of internal resources. As a result, RADIUS, AAA, and TACACS are not optional in this scenario. It is essential to implement these safety measures and preferably to do so at the organization's intranet, no matter how trusted the service provider is. Implementation of firewalls is also very important here, as they serve to keep unauthorized access from the organization's intranet.

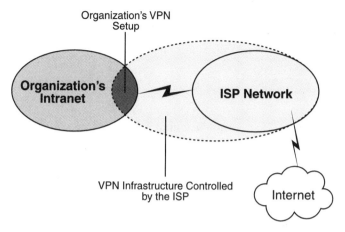

FIGURE 2-8 *The dependent VPN architecture.*

Independent or In-house VPNs

Independent VPNs are the opposite of dependent VPNs. Here, the entire responsibility of establishing the VPN is handled by the subscriber organization. The role of service provider in this scenario is negligible and is relegated to handling Internet traffic. Tunneling/de-tunneling and data encryption/decryption occurs within the organization's intranet. Figure 2-9 depicts the independent VPN architecture.

Independent VPNs, as evident, offer a high level of security and allow the organization to maintain complete control over VPN-based transactions. Most administrators consider this approach to be an ideal approach toward security because the organization does not have to

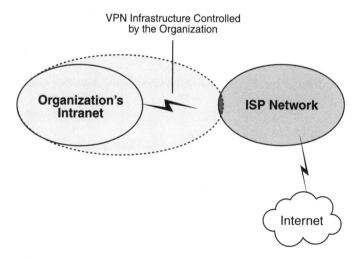

FIGURE 2-9 *The independent VPN architecture.*

hand over the responsibility of the VPN architecture to an external entity. Moreover, the total cost of implementation of in-house VPNs is not much higher than the cost of dependent VPNs. However, this approach does add additional onus and overhead related to management on the network administrator(s).

Hybrid VPNs

The Hybrid VPN architecture offers a combination of the dependent and independent VPN approaches. This approach is used when the organization does not outsource the complete VPN solution to a service provider. Instead, some part of the VPN solution is implemented and controlled by the organization while the rest is implemented and managed by the service provider, as shown in Figure 2-10.

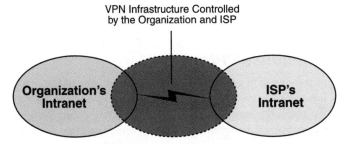

FIGURE 2-10 *The hybrid VPN architecture, jointly controlled by the organization and the service provider.*

Another approach to hybrid VPNs, as shown in Figure 2-11, is that the organization outsources the VPN solution to multiple service providers instead of a single service provider controlling the entire setup as in dependent architecture. As a result, none of the service providers can wholly control the complete architecture and in this manner, the organization is able to implement an outsourced VPN without the onus of VPN management. Though this approach is little complex in terms of management, it allows the organization to eliminate the monopoly of one service provider. The biggest advantage of this approach is that it establishes availability—if one ISP's links go down, you still have the other.

Security-based VPN Architectures

Although VPNs themselves are security solutions, the following VPN categories offer an organization's intranet enhanced security:

- ◆ Router-to-router VPNs
- ◆ Firewall-to-firewall VPNs
- ◆ Client-initiated VPNs
- ◆ Directed VPNs

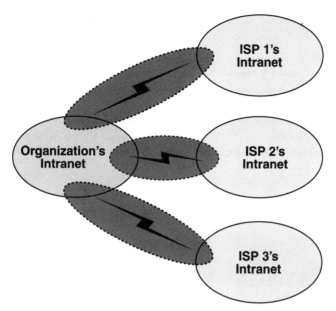

FIGURE 2-11 *The hybrid VPN architecture, controlled by multiple service providers.*

Router-to-router VPNs

Router-to-router VPNs allow secure connectivity between organization sites across the Internet. Router-to-router VPNs allow the following implementations:

◆ **VPN-on-demand tunnels.** In this implementation of VPNs, a secure tunnel is established between the routers that are attached to the client-side and the server-side of the connection, as shown in Figure 2-12. These types of tunnels can support multiple connections simultaneously and persist until the last connection is terminated. For a successful implementation of VPN-on-demand router-to-router tunnels, the routers at both ends must support VPN capabilities, such as key exchange

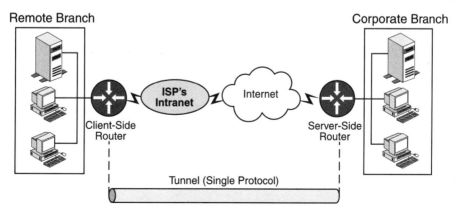

FIGURE 2-12 *VPN-on-demand router-to-router tunnels.*

and encryption algorithms. A big disadvantage of this approach is that these router-to-router tunnels are specific to the chosen service provider intranet or tunneling protocol.

◆ **VPN-on-demand multi-protocol tunnels.** This implementation is a logical extension of VPN-on-demand tunnels as it supports multiple tunneling protocols between the two sites across the Internet. When a non-IP client issues a request for a VPN session, a "transparent" tunnel, which is not specific to any tunneling protocol, is established between the routers at the two ends, as shown in Figure 2-13. The non-IP data is then tunneled across the Internet or any other public network to the destination router.

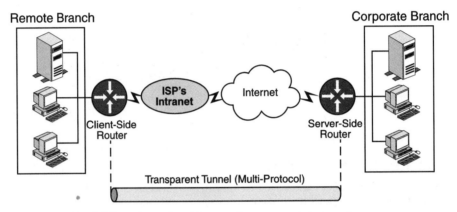

FIGURE 2-13 *VPN-on-demand multi-protocol router-to-router tunnels.*

◆ **VPN-on-demand encrypted sessions.** In this implementation, a separate tunnel for each request is established between the routers at the two ends, despite the fact that multiple connection requests are issued for the same remote site. Figure 2-14 depicts VPN-on-demand encrypted sessions between two routers. As a result of multiple separate tunnels existing simultaneously between two sites, each session is individually encrypted, hence the name. The major disadvantage of this VPN architecture is that it generates large overheads.

Firewall-to-firewall VPNs

Unlike a router-to-router VPN architecture, firewall-to-firewall VPNs are established between two firewalls. Firewall-to-firewall VPNs can be implemented in the following two manners:

◆ **VPN-on-demand tunnels**. As shown in Figure 2-15, this firewall-to-firewall implementation is very similar to router-to-router VPN-on-demand tunnel implementation except that because firewalls are used at both ends, it provides increased security. In addition, when required network administrators can impose more stringent restrictions. With the help of firewalls, traffic can also be more strictly audited.

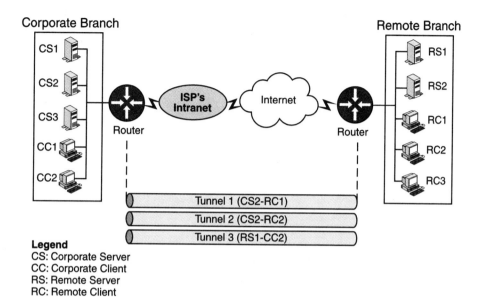

FIGURE 2-14 *VPN-on-demand router-to-router encrypted sessions.*

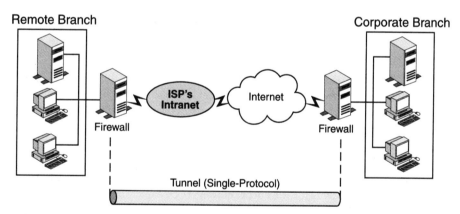

FIGURE 2-15 *VPN-on-demand firewall-to-firewall tunnels.*

◆ **VPN-on-demand multi-protocol tunnels.** This firewall-to-firewall implementation addresses the problem associated with the dissimilarity of firewalls at the two communicating ends: dissimilar firewalls cannot communicate successfully in a VPN-based environment. Firewalls at both ends must support similar protocols for filtering traffic belonging to different protocols. Generally, IPSec is used for the purpose because it supports multi-protocol tunnels as well as firewalls. However, the requirement in this case is that the other end must be IPSec-compliant. Figure 2-16 depicts VPN-on-demand multi-protocol firewall-to-firewall tunnels.

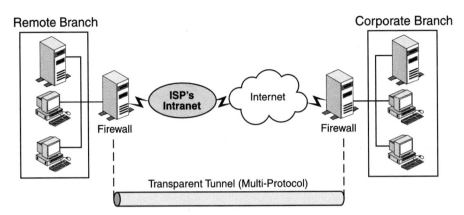

FIGURE 2-16 *VPN-on-demand multi-protocol firewall-to-firewall tunnels.*

Client-initiated VPNs

In client-initiated VPNs, unlike the two previous types of VPNs, the encryption and tunnel management mechanism is installed on the VPN client itself. As a result, VPN clients play an important role in the establishment of the tunnels—hence the name client-initiated VPNs. These VPNs can be further categorized into the following two types:

◆ **Client-to-firewall/Router VPNs.** In this implementation, the VPN session is nego-tiated between the client and the firewall, as shown in Figure 2-17. The firewall in this case must support the handling of client-initiated requests for a VPN session. This approach imposes a huge processing burden on the client because key distribu-tion, management, and security entail highly complex processing. In addition, the client must face the added onus of being able to communicate with a large variety of operating systems and platforms.

◆ **Client-to-server VPNs.** In this firewall-to-firewall implementation an end-to-end VPN session is established between the originator of the request and the processor of the request, as shown in Figure 2-18. Once again, this approach imposes huge processing onus for the client. However, it is much more secure than a client-to-firewall VPN because the intermediary service provider, whose services the client avails to connect to the remote server, remains ignorant about the tunnel. This reduces the chances of tunnel attacks.

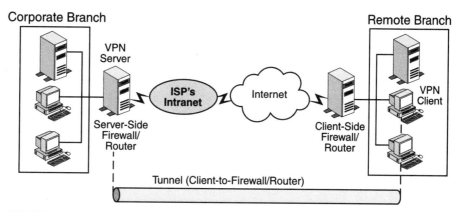

FIGURE 2-17 *Client-to-firewall VPN architecture.*

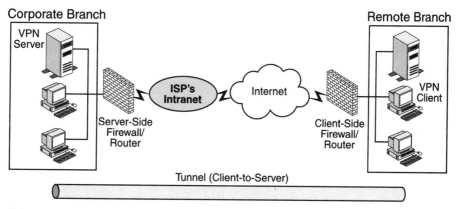

FIGURE 2-18 *Client-to-server VPN architecture.*

Directed VPNs

Unlike all other VPN architectures, directed VPNs do not make use of bi-directional tunnels for secure communication. Instead, a unidirectional tunnel is established between the two communicating ends, as shown in Figure 2-19. Directed VPNs are different from other VPN architectures in one more way. Data is encrypted in directed VPNs at layer five of the OSI model—Session layer. The protocol most commonly used for this purpose is SOCKS v5.

 NOTE

Refer to Chapter 11, "VPN Security Technologies," for more information about SOCKS v5.

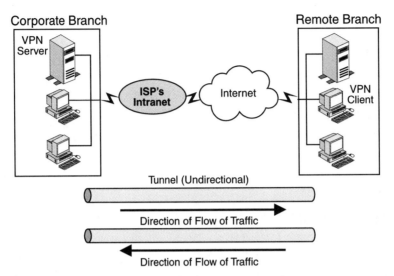

FIGURE 2-19 *Directed VPN architecture.*

When compared to bi-directional tunneling, directed VPN architecture provides enhanced security in the following ways:

◆ In a two-way trust relationship, when a hacker gains access to a network, all other connected networks can be affected because the hacker can gain access to these connected networks with the help of the two-way tunnel. This is not the case with directed VPNs. Due to the fact that traffic flow is unidirectional in directed VPNs, two-way trust is not assumed. As a result, even if a hacker gains access to a communicating side, the probability of this security threat is reduced by half because of the use of one-way tunnels.

◆ Access control in a bi-directional tunnel approach is based on source and destination addresses. In contrast, access control in directed VPNs can be based not only on source and destination addresses, but also on the basis of other parameters, such as user ID, time, and application. Directed VPNs can also base the access control on the content of the data packets.

◆ User authentication is more stringent in directed VPNs because in addition to the RADIUS servers, routers, gateways, and firewalls that authenticate a remote user, the VPN server (as well as the client) is also capable of authenticating the other end. However, this is not the case with other VPN architectures. In their case, VPN requests are tunneled across a series of intermediate devices—NASs, series of routers, firewalls, and so on—which base their authentication on source and destination IP addresses. This bi-directional approach used in other architectures makes it very easy for the hacker to spoof an IP address.

◆ Encryption in directed VPNs is based on Session layer, which can support a wide range of encryption mechanisms. As a result, encryption in directed VPNs is much more elaborate than in other VPN architectures.

Layer-based VPN Architectures

Depending on the layer of the OSI model on which the VPN setup functions, VPNs can be categorized in one of the following two broad categories:

◆ Link-layer VPNs

◆ Network-layer VPNs

Link-layer VPNs

As the name suggests, Link-layer VPNs use Link-layer connectivity. Link-layer VPN transactions are limited to a local network because they use MAC addresses; therefore, Link-layer VPNs are functionally similar to private networks.

Based on Link-layer technologies, Link-layer VPNs are of the following four types:

◆ **Frame Relay virtual connections**. Frame Relay-based virtual connections use the switching infrastructure of the private networks, which they connect. The main difference between virtual connections and dedicated connections is that in virtual connections, the two ends use adaptive clocking of data during transmissions. As a result, the transmission rate is adjusted according to the application and signaling requirements. The main advantage of this VPN technology is that it is inexpensive and guarantees Committed Information Rate (CIR).

◆ **ATM virtual connections.** ATM-based virtual connections are quite similar to Frame Relay-based virtual connections. However, these connections use the underlying ATM infrastructure of the private networks. These virtual connections also boast a lack of data clock synchronization. ATM virtual connections are relatively faster and offer better performance. Therefore, ATM virtual connections are more expensive than Frame Relay virtual connections.

◆ **Multi-Protocol Over ATM (MPOA).** MPOA-based VPN connections are based purely on ATM infrastructure. However, they can support multiple protocols because they are dependent on routers located at the edge of the private network to determine the forwarding path within the ATM network. This approach hasn't gained much popularity because the underlying infrastructure is ATM, which might not be acceptable in a hybrid intranet that uses various networking technologies.

◆ **Multi-Protocol Label Switching (MPLS).** MPLS provides an effective means of deploying IP-based VPNs across ATM-based WAN backbones. In MPLS, the VPN MPLS router builds up the VPN-specific routing table using the VPN routing protocols that include BGP, and so on. Each route is then assigned a label. This labeled routing information is then forwarded to all attached routers. During a transmission, the first MPLS device that receives these IP packets encapsulates these IP packets using the MPLS labels. Subsequently, the MPLS label, and not the IP header, is used for routing the packets through the ATM-based infrastructure. On the edge of the intranet, when the packet is about to access the IP-based infrastructure (such as the Internet), the MPLS label is removed. Figure 2-20 depicts the workings of MPLS.

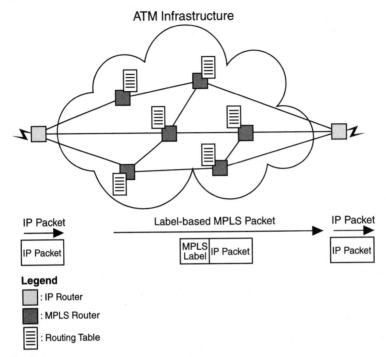

ATM Infrastructure

IP Packet   Label-based MPLS Packet   IP Packet

| IP Packet |
| MPLS Label | IP Packet |
| IP Packet |

Legend

◻ : IP Router

◼ : MPLS Router

▤ : Routing Table

FIGURE 2-20 *An MPLS Link-layer VPN.*

Network-layer VPNs

Network-layer VPNs, also known as Layer 3 VPNs, use the functionality of the Network layer and can be organized into the following two categories:

◆ **Peer-VPN model.** In the peer-VPN model, the Network-layer forwarding path is computed on a hop-to-hop basis. More simply, the path is considered at each router in the path to the destination network. Therefore, all the routers in the data transit path are considered as peers, as shown in Figure 2-21. VPNs in traditionally routed networks are an example of the Peer-VPN model, as each router in the path is a peer of all the routers that are directly attached to it.

◆ **Overlay VPN model.** Unlike the peer-VPN model, overlay VPN models do not compute the network path to the destination network on a hop-to-hop basis. Instead, the intermediate internetwork infrastructure is used as a "cut-through" to the next router in the data transit path. ATM-based VPNs, Frame Relay VPNs, and VPNs using tunneling technology are some examples of the overlay VPN model.

Layer 3 VPN networks are also popularly referred to as *Virtual Private Dial Networks* (VPDNs). Layer 3 VPNs commonly use two Layer 2 technologies—PPTP and L2TP—for tunneling. You will learn more about these Layer 2 tunneling technologies in Chapter 5,

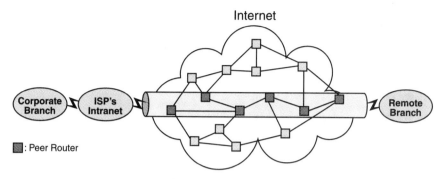

FIGURE 2-21 *Peer-VPN architecture.*

"Tunneling Protocols at Layer 2." VPDNs also use IPSec, which has already been established as the de facto VPN standard because it offers comprehensive authentication and encryption capabilities.

Class-based VPN Architectures

According to a classification proposed in a white paper by VPNet Technologies Inc., VPNs can be divided into five classes—Class 0 through Class 4—depending upon the purpose, size, scope, and complexity of the VPN setup.

Class 0 VPNs

VPNs that belong to Class 0 are meant for small organizations with an intranet limited to a single site. Also, the number of remote users who access the organization's network is limited to 50 or less. As a result, Class 0 VPNs are the easiest to implement and the least expensive.

The minimum requirements of a Class 0 VPN include the following:

◆ A VPN server with at least Windows 2000

◆ A VPN client with at least Windows 95/98

◆ A tunneling protocol, such as PPTP

◆ Packet filtering capabilities offered by a router, gateway, or firewall

◆ An access option, such as DSL or T1

The main disadvantage of this approach is that VPNs belonging to this class are meant for local tunnels only and cannot support site-to-site VPN connectivity. In addition, Class 0 VPNs take longer than any other class to locate and troubleshoot a problem.

Class 1VPNs

Class 1 VPNs are best suited for the requirements of small- to medium-scale organizations with an intranet consisting of two to 20 remote branch networks. In addition, on average at least 250 remote users can be expected to access the intranet. These VPNs are much more secure than those of Class 0 and offer IPSec security to tunneled data as well as a strong remote user authentication mechanism.

The minimum requirements of Class 1 VPNs include the following:

◆ DES-based data encryption

◆ IKE-based key management

◆ A user authentication mechanism

◆ At least one VPN gateway

◆ Remote dial access and remote access client software

◆ A fast access option, such as T1 or T3

VPNs of this class are easy to install and are cost-effective. They also offer enhanced security to data during transit. An added advantage of this approach is that site-to-site and remote access VPNs are possible (unlike Class 0 VPNs). However, because Class 1 VPNs are strongly based on IPSec, extranet connectivity might be a problem because extranets might not support IPSec.

Class 2 VPNs

Class 2 VPNs are best suited for medium-scale organizations with an intranet spread across 10 to 100 remote sites. VPNs that belong to this class can support up to 500 remote users. In addition, this class offers stronger security than Class 1 and is still considered to be a cost-effective solution. Like Class 1 VPNs, Class 2 VPNs also support site-to-site and remote connectivity.

The main requirements of a Class 2 VPNs include the following:

◆ IPSec and 3DES-based data encryption

◆ IKE-based key management

◆ A native user authentication mechanism, such as soft tokens

◆ At least two to five VPN gateways, or one gateway that can support 500 simultaneous sessions

◆ Additional security mechanisms, such as AAA, RADIUS, TACACS, NAT, and/or firewalls

◆ Remote dial access and remote access client software

◆ Fast access options, such as T1 or T3

Although this class offers greater security and connectivity, its disadvantages include a lack of support to extranets, as they need to be IPSec-compatible. In addition, the infrastructure does not support real-time applications, such as audio and video. The use of additional security measures, such as AAA, RADIUS, and NAT does make the intranet more secure; however, it entails an additional management onus for the network administrator(s).

Class 3 VPNs

Class 3 VPNs are best suited for medium- to large-scale organizations with an intranet spread across several hundred remote sites. VPNs that belong to this class can support to up to a few thousand remote users. The security offered by this class is comparable to Class 2 security. Class 3 VPNs also support extranets in addition to site-to-site and remote connectivity. The most important benefit offered by this class is support to delay-sensitive and mission-critical traffic and applications, such as videoconferencing. VPNs that belong to this class are expensive.

The minimum requirements of Class 3 VPNs include the following:

- ISP connectivity with a well-defined SLA
- Centralized directory service, such as X.500 or LDAP
- IPSec and 3DES-based data encryption
- IKE-based key management
- A native user authentication mechanism, such as soft tokens and smart cards
- At least ten to 20 VPN gateways, or one gateway that can support up to 1000 simultaneous sessions
- Additional security mechanisms, such as AAA, RADIUS, TACACS, NAT, and/or firewalls at the main site and all large remote branches
- In-house certificate services
- A well-defined remote access policy
- Remote dial access and remote access client software
- Fast access options, such as ISDN and xDSL along with T1 or T3

The main disadvantage of this class is that VPNs that belong to this class are difficult to manage, monitor, configure, and implement because the organization's resources are scattered across the globe. In addition, it is very important to have a well-defined and thoroughly planned design, else this expensive solution might not live up to expectations.

Class 4 VPNs

Class 4 VPNs are best suited for large-scale organizations with an intranet spread across several thousand remote sites. VPNs that belong to this class can support tens of thousands of remote users. The security offered by this class is the maximum. In addition, this class is the most scalable and adaptable to future growth. As a result, VPNs that belong to Class 4 are very expensive. Class 4 VPNs support extranets and site-to-site and remote connectivity. Because of the fast access options that are used in Class 4 VPNs, they can support e-commerce transactions as well as real-time audio and video transactions.

The minimum requirements of Class 4 VPNs include the following:

- ISP connectivity with a well-defined SLA
- Centralized directory service, such as LDAP
- IPSec and 3DES-based data encryption

◆ IKE-based key management

◆ A native user authentication mechanism, such as soft tokens and smart cards

◆ At least ten to twenty VPN gateways, or one gateway that can support more than 5000 simultaneous sessions

◆ High redundancy and bandwidth management capabilities

◆ A well-defined remote access policy

◆ Additional security mechanisms, such as AAA, RADIUS, TACACS, NAT, and/or firewalls at the main site and all large remote branches

◆ In-house certificate services

◆ Remote dial access and remote access client software

◆ Fast access options, such as ISDN and xDSL along with T3 and OC3

The main disadvantage of this class is that it is extremely complex and the most difficult to manage. Only highly trained professionals can handle the management task. Also, large traffic overhead is another major problem associated with these VPNs, despite measures to control and manage it.

Summary

In this chapter, you learned about the requirements, elements and various architectures of present-day VPNs. You started with the fundamental requirements of VPNs, which include security, availability, Quality of Service (QoS), reliability, compatibility, and manageability.

Next, you learned about the six building blocks of VPN design. These include VPN hardware, VPN software, an organization's security infrastructure, the service provider's supporting infrastructure, public networks, and tunnels. You explored each of these elements in detail and the role they play in VPNs.

Finally, you learned about the various VPN architectures in which a typical VPN-based solution can be implemented. For example, depending on which end (service provider or subscriber organization) implements the basic VPN requirements, such as security, availability, QoS, and so on, VPNs can be categorized into three categories—dependent, independent, and hybrid. Similarly, depending on the security requirements of the setup, VPNs can be divided into four categories. These include router-to-router VPNs, firewall-to-firewall VPNs, client-initiated VPNs, and directed VPNs. Depending on which layer of the OSI model the overall VPN infrastructure functions, VPNs can be divided into two major groups, Link-layer VPNs and Network-layer VPNs. Finally, depending on the scale and the complexity of the VPN setup, VPNs can also be classified into five classes, Class 0 through Class 4.

In the next chapter, you will learn about the security components of a VPN. These include user authentication and access control schemes. The chapter also focuses on various data encryption techniques, such as symmetric and asymmetric cryptography. The chapter also discusses the basics of PKI and its implementation in VPNs.

Check Your Understanding

Multiple Choice Questions

1. Which of the following is NOT a valid QoS class?
   a. Relative QoS
   b. Available QoS
   c. Best Effort QoS
   d. Absolute QoS

2. Which of the following options are types of a public network?
   a. POT
   b. POTS
   c. PSTN
   d. ATM

3. Which of the following protocols offers key management capability?
   a. IPSec
   b. PPTP
   c. L2TP
   d. IKE

4. Which of the following options belong to Security-based VPN architectures?
   a. Dependent
   b. Directed
   c. Hybrid
   d. Client-initiated

5. Which of the following statements is true?
   a. MPLS technology stores labels instead of standard routes in the routing tables.
   b. VPDN is a Link-layer VPN.
   c. Frame Relay virtual connections offer better performance than ATM virtual connections.
   d. Tunneling-based VPNs belong to the Peer-VPN architecture.

Short Questions

1. ABC Inc. is a well-established organization that has recently undergone a large-scale expansion. They are now targeting the South-east Asian market and have established remote branches in 20 major South-east Asian cities. In addition, they are aggressively expanding in Europe. Their plan is to establish branch offices in 70 cities on the continent. Keeping their expansion plans in mind, what class of VPNs should they choose? What are the minimum requirements of this class of VPNs?

2. WebSafe Inc. is a Virginia-based small organization that has recently established remote branch offices on the west coast and in the Midwest. Because their main network did not support large number of users (53 to be exact), before their growth they used private addresses within the network. To connect to the Internet, they depended mainly on their proxy server. Now that they have remote branches, they plan to use VPNs for secure data transfers across the Internet. What options will allow them to continue using a private addressing scheme in the main network and still connect to remote branches through their VPNs?

Answers

Multiple Choice Answers

1. **b**. The three classes of QoS include Best effort QoS, Relative QoS, and Absolute QoS.

2. **b** and **c**. Plain Old Telephone Service (POTS), and Public Switched Telephone Network (PSTN), are two types of public networks. The Internet is a third.

3. **d**. Internet Key Exchange (IKE) is a protocol used by IPSec and offers key management capability.

4. **b** and **d**. Client initiated and directed are two of the four types of security-based VPN architectures. The other two are router-to-router and firewall-to-firewall.

5. **a** and **c**. MPLS technology stores labels instead of standard routes in the routing tables. Frame Relay virtual connections offer better performance than ATM virtual connections. VPDN is a Network-layer VPN. Tunneling-based VPNs belong to the Overlay VPN Network-layer architecture.

Short Answers

1. They should use Class 3 VPNs. The minimum requirements of a Class 3 VPN include the following:

   ◆ ISP connectivity with a well-defined SLA

   ◆ Centralized directory service, such as X.500 or LDAP

   ◆ IPSec and 3DES-based data encryption

   ◆ IKE-based key management

   ◆ A native user authentication mechanism, such as soft tokens and smart cards

   ◆ At least ten to twenty VPN gateways, or one gateway that can support up to 1000 simultaneous sessions

   ◆ Additional security mechanisms, such as AAA, RADIUS, TACACS, NAT, and/or firewalls at the main site and all large each remote branches

   ◆ In-house certificate services

   ◆ A well-defined remote access policy

   ◆ Remote dial access and remote access client software

   ◆ Fast access options, such as ISDN and xDSL along with T1 or T3

2. They can implement one of the following schemes:

   ◆ Use IP gateways to convert non-IP-based traffic into IP-based traffic.

   ◆ Use tunneling to encapsulate non-IP data packets into IP datagrams for successful routing of these tunneled packets.

   ◆ Use Virtual IP Routing (VIPR) to allow a router located at the ISP site to support multiple VPNs.

Chapter 3

Security Components of a VPN

The Internet has always been considered an "unsecured" medium of transmission; data traversing through it is highly susceptible to unauthorized or malicious access. The emergence of VPN technology, which is based on tunneling, has lowered this security risk considerably. So, what guarantees the safe transmission of data through VPN tunnels? How is sensitive and mission-critical data prevented from unauthorized and malicious access? This chapter attempts to answer these questions.

In this chapter, you will learn about two basic security components of a secure VPN setup: access control and encryption. You'll also be introduced to the basics of Public Key Infrastructure (PKI), which is fast emerging as the de facto methodology to safeguard data transactions across unsecured and untrustworthy media.

User Authentication and Access Control

The data stored on various network resources is susceptible to various types of attacks. The generic categories of these attacks include the following:

◆ **Network service interruptions.** Sometimes, due to malicious attacks from outside as well as from within the network, various network resources and services can be rendered unusable for long intervals. In the case of severe attacks, the entire network might become inaccessible to its users.

◆ **Data interception.** While in transit, the data might be intercepted by an unauthorized individual. As a result, the confidentiality of the data is lost. In such cases, an organization stands to lose much (in terms of business and money) if sensitive data falls into the wrong hands.

◆ **Data modification.** Interception of data can also lead to its modification. In the case of such attacks, the destination user receives falsified or tampered data. This can cause the organization to lose considerable money, especially if the data is of high importance.

◆ **Data fabrication.** In such attacks, an unauthorized user can pose as an authorized and trusted network user. After gaining access to the network, this individual can then disseminate spurious and harmful messages to other users in the network. This can ultimately lead to the shutdown of part or all of the network, disrupting services.

User authentication and access control are the two most basic steps you can take towards preventing these security threats and securing the sensitive data stored in the network. The process of verifying user identity is known as *user authentication*. Allowing access to certain network resources while denying access to others is referred to as *access control*. Together these two mechanisms can, to a certain extent, lessen the security threats just noted.

Figure 3-1 depicts a generic implementation of user authentication and access control in the typical VPN scenario.

The next two sections discuss user authentication and access control mechanisms in further detail.

Authenticating Users

The user authentication mechanism is implemented at the VPN point of access and is used to authenticate the user accessing a resource within the network. As a result, only authorized users can access network resources, thus reducing the possibility of unauthorized access to the data stored in the network.

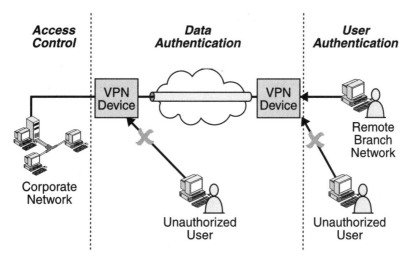

FIGURE 3-1 *Generic implementation of user authentication and access control in VPNs.*

The authentication schemes that are implemented separately or in combination with other schemes include the following:

◆ **Login ID and password.** This scheme uses the operating system-based login ID and password to verify the identity of the user accessing the VPN node.

◆ **S/Key password.** In this scheme, the user initializes S/KEY by selecting a secret password and an integer, *n*. This integer denotes the number of times a secure hash function (currently MD4) will be applied to the secret password. The result is then stored on the corresponding server. When the user attempts to log in, the server issues a challenge. Software on the user's client machine prompts for the secret password, applies *n-1* iterations of the hash function to it, and sends this response to the server. The server applies the hash function to this response. If the result it obtains is the same as the value it stored earlier, the user is authenticated successfully. The user is allowed in, and the server replaces the stored value with the response obtained from the client and decrements the password counter.

◆ **Remote Access Dial-In User Service (RADIUS).** RADIUS is an Internet security protocol that is strongly based on the client/server model, where the machine accessing the network is the client and the RADIUS server at the network-end authenticates the client. Generally, a RADIUS server authenticates a user using an internal username/password list that it maintains.

RADIUS can also act as a client to authenticate the users of operating systems, such as UNIX, NT and NetWare. In addition, RADIUS servers can act as clients to other RADIUS servers. To further secure the data during transit, transactions between the client and the RADIUS server can be encrypted using authentication mechanisms, such as Password Authentication Protocol (PAP) and Challenge Handshake Authentication Protocol (CHAP).

◆ **Two-factor token-based technique.** As the name suggests, this scheme implements dual authentication to verify a user's credentials. It combines the use of a token and a password. During the authentication process, a hardware-based electronic device serves as the token and a unique identification, such as Personal Identification Number (PIN) is used as the password. Traditionally, the token has been a hardware device (possibly a card), but now some vendors are now offering software-based tokens.

 NOTE

You can compare the use of two-factor token-based authentication with withdrawing money from Automated Teller Machine (ATM). You can successfully withdraw money from ATM only if you supply your identity. You do this using an ATM card to access your account (hardware-based identification) and also with a secret password or a PIN. Only with these two factors together can you access your account.

Controlling Access

After a user has been successfully authenticated, by default he/she gains access to all the resources, network services, and applications located in the network. This can prove to be a major security threat because the user, even though trusted, can knowingly or unknowingly tamper with the data stored on various devices. By screening resources that store highly sensitive data or data that is nonessential to a user in his/her everyday work, you can effectively prevent this. For example, technical support personnel do not need to deal with financial or HR-related data. As a result, access can be restricted to the storage devices that store this data.

Controlling access rights is also an integral part of controlling access. The security threat can be further reduced by providing limited access rights to the users. For example, data can further be safeguarded by allowing normal users to only read the data. Only trusted users and administrators can have rights to write, modify, or delete data.

Access control is based on user identification. However, other parameters, such as source and destination IP addresses, port addresses, and group affiliations also play a major role in traditional access control methods. Modern-day advanced access control mechanisms are also based on parameters such as time, day, date, application, service, authentication method, URL, and encryption mechanism.

Refer back to Figure 3-1 to see how user authentication and access control serve as end-point security implementations. But, how is data protected from prying eyes during transit? You'll learn more about that in the following section.

Encrypting Data

Data encryption or *cryptography* is one of the most important components of VPN security and plays major role in securing data during transit. It is the mechanism of converting data into an unreadable format, known as *ciphertext*, so that unauthorized access to the data can be prevented as the data is transmitted across an unsecured transmission medium.

Data encryption prevents the following:

◆ Data interception and viewing.

◆ Data modification and stealth stealing.

◆ Data fabrication.

◆ Data non-repudiation.

◆ Interruption of network services.

On receiving the message, the recipient decrypts the data back into its original format. Even if the ciphertext is intercepted during the transmission, to make sense of it the intercepting party has to know the method used to convert plain data into the scrambled format. Otherwise, the text is useless. This traditional encryption model is depicted in Figure 3-2.

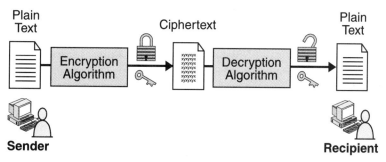

FIGURE 3-2 *The traditional encryption model.*

The sender and the recipient, along with the process of encryption, form a *cryptosystem*. Cryptosystems are one of two types:

◆ Symmetric

◆ Asymmetric

A cryptosystem is categorized by the number of *keys* it uses. A key might be a number, a word, or even a phrase that is used for the purpose of encryption and decryption.

Symmetric Cryptosystems

Symmetric cryptosystems are based on a single key, which is a bit string of fixed length. Therefore, this encryption mechanism is also referred to as *single-key encryption*. The key is private (or secret) and is used for encryption as well as decryption.

NOTE

In some literature, symmetric cryptosystems are also referred to as *private* or *secret key cryptosystems* and the technique is referred to as private key cryptography or secret key cryptography.

Before two parties can exchange data, the key must be shared between them. The sender then encrypts the original message using this private key and sends the message to the recipient. On receiving the encrypted message, the recipient uses the same key to decrypt it.

The process of symmetric cryptography is depicted in Figure 3-3.

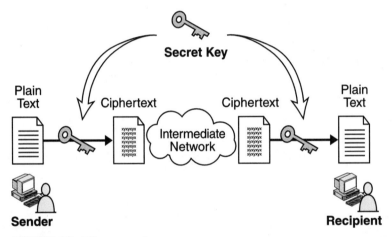

FIGURE 3-3 *The symmetric cryptosystem.*

As recently noted, the sender as well as the recipient must share the same key. One method of sharing the key entails that the sender provide the secret key to the recipient in person. However, this can not only be time-consuming, but also defeats the entire purpose of networks. Another method of conveying the key to the recipient would be via the phone. But, this method is susceptible to phone tapping and eavesdropping. Yet another method would be to send it to the recipient through snail mail or e-mail. However like the previous methods, this method is also extremely susceptible to interception by an unauthorized individual.

Because practically all methods of key exchange are unsecured, a viable solution to the problem is to make the length of the key sufficiently long. Any interceptor would need to "break" or decode the key before the original message can be viewed. Therefore, the longer the length of the key, the stronger the encryption and the greater the effort needed to break or decode the cryptosystem.

Depending on the length of the key, many symmetric encryption algorithms have been developed over the years. Some of the most commonly used symmetric algorithms in VPN solutions include the following:

◆ **Data Encryption Standard (DES).** The original DES proposal suggested a key-length of up to 128 bits. However, the key size was reduced to 56 bits by the US government in an effort to make the algorithm faster. This reduction in the key length, along with the availability of faster computer processing systems, has served to make DES a relatively "weak" algorithm susceptible to *Brute Force attacks*. In a Brute Force attack, keys are randomly generated and are applied to the original text until the correct key is determined. The smaller the key-size, the easier it is to generate the correct key and break the cryptosystem.

 NOTE

The official name of DES is Federal Information Processing Standard (FIPS) 46-3.

◆ **Triple Data Encryption Standard (3DES).** Like its predecessor—DES—3DES also uses a 56-bit key. However, it is much more secure because three different keys are used to encrypt the data. The process proceeds like this: The first key encrypts the data. Then, the second key decrypts the newly encrypted data. Finally, the third key encrypts the data for a second time. This entire process makes 3DES a highly secure algorithm. But, because of the complexity of this algorithm, it is three times slower than DES.

◆ **Ron's Code 4 (RC4).** Developed by Ron Rivest, this algorithm uses keys whose length can vary to up to 256 bytes. Because of this key length, RC4 is categorized as a strong encryption mechanism. It is also relatively fast. RC4 creates a stream of random bytes and XORs them with the original text. Because bytes are generated randomly, RC4 requires a new key for each outgoing message.

 NOTE

eXclusive OR (XOR) is a Boolean operator that returns True (1) if both the operands are different. Else it returns False (0). For example, 1 XOR 0 and 0 XOR 1 returns 1. However, 1 XOR 1 and 0 XOR 0 return False (0). Therefore, 100 XOR 110 returns 010.

Symmetric cryptosystems pose two main problems. First, because just one key is used for the encryption as well as decryption purposes, if it becomes known to the intruder, all communication using that key is jeopardized. As a result, the key should be changed periodically.

The other problem with symmetric cryptosystem is that if the number of communications is large, key management becomes a complicated task. In addition, the overhead associated with the initial key-pair setup, distribution, and periodic key replacement is both expensive and time-consuming.

Asymmetric cryptosystems overcome the problems posed by symmetric cryptosystems. In addition, they also offer enhanced security during transactions. You'll learn more about asymmetric cryptosystem in the following section.

Asymmetric Cryptosystems

Instead of the single key used in symmetric cryptography, asymmetric cryptosystems use a pair of mathematically related keys. One of the keys is private and is known only to the owner of the pair. The second key is public and is freely distributable. The public key is used for encryption purposes whereas the private key is used for decrypting messages. This asymmetry in encryption and decryption is the reason behind the name, asymmetric cryptosystem.

 NOTE

Asymmetric cryptosystems are also popularly referred to as *public key cryptosystems* and the technique is referred to as public key cryptography.

In VPN solutions, two asymmetric cryptographic systems are used most commonly. These include the *Diffie-Hellman* (*DH*) algorithm and the *Rivest Shamir Adleman* (*RSA*) algorithm.

The Diffie-Hellman Algorithm

In the Diffie-Hellman algorithm, every communicating entity receives a pair of keys, one of which is distributed to other communicating entities while the other is kept private. The Diffie-Hellman algorithm works in the following manner:

1. The sender retrieves the recipient's public key, which is available to all communicating parties.
2. The sender then performs a calculation that involves the private key and the recipient's public key. The calculation results in a shared secret key.
3. The message is encrypted using the resulting shared secret key.
4. The encrypted message is then forwarded to the recipient.
5. On receiving the encrypted message, the recipient generates the shared secret key by performing a similar calculation involving its own private key and the sender's public key.

The basic assumption of this algorithm is that if anyone intercepts the encrypted message, that person cannot retrieve the original information because he or she does not possess the recipient's private key. A data exchange based on the Diffie-Hellman algorithm is depicted in Figure 3-4.

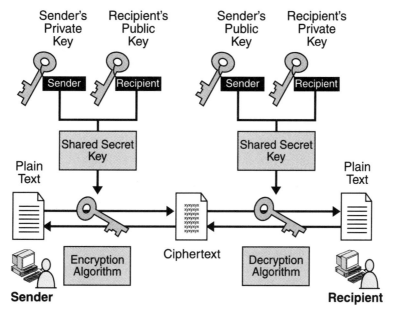

FIGURE 3-4 *Data exchange as defined by the Diffie-Hellman algorithm.*

The data exchange based on the Diffie-Hellman algorithm is considerably secure because there is little possibility that the data can be eavesdropped or modified during transmission. In addition, because no secret (private) key exchange is involved during the VPN session, the probability that the private key of any entity involved in communication will become known to intruders is very low. Also, key management is not as time-consuming as it is with symmetric cryptosystems—despite a large number of communications.

Although the Diffie-Hellman algorithm does offer more security than symmetric cryptosystems, there is one inherent problem associated with it—ensuring that the public keys exchanged before the actual data transmission are genuine. For example, if the two communicating ends exchange their public keys over an unsecured medium, such as the Internet, it's possible that an early intruder could intercept the request for the public keys and send its own public key to both communicating ends. In this case, the intruder can easily tap into the communication because the two ends will now exchange the data using the intruder's public key. This type of intrusion is known as a Man-in-the-Middle attack.

The Rivest Shamir Adleman (RSA) algorithm, which is discussed in the following section effectively addresses the threat posed by Man-in-the-Middle attacks that crop up in the Diffie-Hellman algorithm. As a result, the RSA algorithm has emerged as one of the strongest asymmetric encryption mechanisms.

The Rivest Shamir Adleman (RSA) Algorithm

Due to its strong encryption mechanism, RSA has emerged as the de facto standard in asymmetric cryptosystems. Unlike Diffie-Hellman, the original message is encrypted using the recipient's public key. The recipient retrieves the original message using the sender's public key.

The RSA algorithm is implemented for authentication using digital signatures as follows:

1. The sender's public key is requested by the intended recipient and is then forwarded.

2. The sender uses a hash function to reduce the size of the original message. The resultant message is known as the *message digest* (*MD*).

3. The sender encrypts the message digest with its private key resulting in the generation of a unique digital signature.

4. The message and the digital signature are combined and forwarded to the recipient.

5. Upon receiving the encrypted message, the recipient regenerates the message digest using the same hash function as the sender.

6. The recipient then decrypts the digital signature using the sender's public key.

7. The recipient then compares the regenerated message digest (step 5) and the message digest retrieved from the digital signature (step 6). If the two match, data was not intercepted, fabricated or modified during transmission. Otherwise, the data is rejected.

The data exchange based on the RSA algorithm is shown in Figure 3-5.

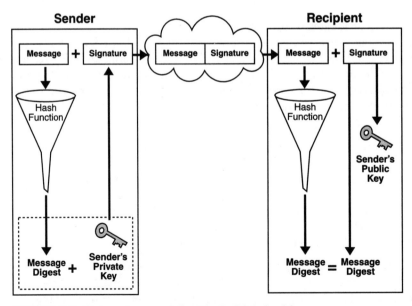

FIGURE 3-5 *Data exchange as defined by the RSA algorithm.*

RSA guarantees safe and secure passage of data because the recipient checks the correctness of the data three times (steps 5, 6, and 7). RSA also simplifies the task of key management. In symmetric cryptography, n^2 keys are required if n entities are involved in a transaction. By comparison, asymmetric cryptography only requires $2*n$ keys.

As you might have noticed, both symmetric as well as asymmetric transactions are based on a one-way trust relationship. *Public Key Infrastructure* (*PKI*), on the other hand, came into existence to enhance the trust between two communicating entities, to ensure the authenticity of the entities involved, and to ensure the security of Internet-based (VPN) data exchange sessions.

Public Key Infrastructure

PKI is a framework of policies for managing keys and establishing a secure method for data exchange. The data exchanges that use PKI can take place within an organization, country, industry, or zone. To enhance key management and ensure highly secure data transactions, a PKI-based framework includes policies and procedures that are supported by hardware and software resources. The major functions of PKI follow:

- Generate private and public key pairs for PKI clients.
- Create and authenticate digital signatures.
- Register and authenticate new users.
- Issue certificates to users.
- Track issued keys and maintain a history of each key (used for future reference).
- Revoke invalid and expired certificates.
- Authenticate PKI clients.

Before attempting to understand the working of PKI, let us first understand the components that go into the making of the PKI framework.

PKI Components

The key components that constitute the framework of PKI are

- The PKI client.
- The Certification Authority (CA).
- The Registration Authority (RA).
- Digital certificates.
- The Certificate Distribution System (CDS).

PKI Client

A *PKI client* is the entity that requests a digital certificate from the assigned CA or RA. Before a PKI client can participate in data transactions, it must obtain a digital certificate. To do this, the client issues a request for a certificate from the CA or RA assigned to the organization. When the client is authenticated successfully, it receives the certificate it requested. After receiving the certificate, the client uses it to identify itself. However, it is the sole responsibility of the client to safeguard the certificate.

Certification Authority (CA)

The CA is a trusted third party that issues digital certificates to PKI clients. Before issuing a digital certificate, the CA verifies the identity and authenticity of the PKI client.

The CA follows its own procedures and guidelines for issuing digital certificates. As you might expect, the certification process varies depending on the validation infrastructure supported by the CA, its organization policies, and the level of certification requested. The process may even require pieces of identification, such as drivers' licenses, notarization, or fingerprints.

An example of a well-known CA is Verisign, Inc.

Registration Authority (RA)

Before entertaining a request for a digital certificate, the CA must authenticate and validate the request. However, because of the sheer number of requests for digital certificates, the CA delegates the request verification responsibility to the RA. The RA receives all certification requests and validates them.

After an RA validates a request successfully, it forwards the request to the CA. The CA issues the required certificate and passes the certificate to the RA. The RA then forwards the certificate to the client that originally issued the certificate request. In this manner, the RA acts as the middleman between PKI clients and CAs.

Digital Certificates

A digital certificate is the electronic equivalent of an ID card and is used to uniquely identify an entity during a transmission. Besides establishing the identity of the owner, digital certificates also eliminate the chance of impersonation, thus reducing the threat of data fabrication. In addition, digital certificates effectively prevent senders from disowning information.

 NOTE

Digital certificates are also sometimes referred to as digital IDs, digital passports, X.509 certificates, or public key certificates.

A digital certificate consists of information that helps validate the sender and includes the following information:

◆ The certificate's serial number

◆ The certificate's date of expiration

◆ The CA's digital signature

◆ The owner's (PKI client's) public key

During a transaction, the sender must send his or her digital certificate along with an encrypted message to authenticate himself or herself. The recipient uses the public key of the CA (that issued the digital certificate) to validate the sender's public key, which is attached to the received message. As in case of public keys, the CA's public key is widely publicized and is available to all. When the recipient is sure of sender's true identity, the recipient uses the sender's public key to decrypt the actual message.

Certificate Distribution System (CDS)

The Certificate Distribution System is a repository of certificates issued to users and organizations. In addition, CDS generates and stores key pairs, signs public keys after validating them, and stores and revokes expired and lost keys. CDS is also responsible for publishing public keys to directory service servers.

PKI-based Transactions

As has been mentioned previously, PKI offers four main security functions—confidentiality, integrity, authenticity, and non-repudiation. Each step in a PKI-based transaction reiterates one or more of these security features. The steps in a PKI-based transaction are as follows:

1. **Key pair generation.** Before the sender can forward data to the intended recipient, it intimates to the recipient its intention of data exchange. As a result, both ends generate a key pair made up of a private and a public key. First, the private key is generated. Then, the corresponding public key is created by applying a one-way hash function to the private key.

 NOTE

In PKI transactions, as in RSA-based transactions, the private key is used to sign the message. The public key, on the other hand, serves to verify the signature.

2. **Digital Signature generation.** After the key pair has been created, a unique digital signature is created. This digital signature serves to identify the sender of the data. To generate the digital signature, first the original message is hashed. In other words, a hash function is applied to the original message. This process of hashing results in a

message digest, which is then encrypted with sender's private key. The result is known as the digital signature.

3. **Message encryption and digital signature application.** After a digital signature is generated, the original message is encrypted with the sender's public key. Next, the digital signature that was created earlier is attached to the encrypted message.

4. **Encrypted message and sender's public key forwarded to the recipient.** The encrypted message is then transmitted to the recipient, along with the sender's public key. Instead of forwarding the public key in cleartext, the public key is first encrypted with the receiver's public key. In order to decode the encrypted public key, the recipient must use its own private key. Because the recipient's private key is known only to the recipient, the chances that an intruder will break the public key and, hence, the cryptosystem, are very small. The sender's public key is also referred to as a *session key*.

5. **Message reception and sender identity verification.** Upon receiving the encrypted message and the public key, the recipient might request the corresponding CA to verify the sender's identity. The CA does so by verifying the digital signature attached to the message and notifying the recipient of the result. If the digital signature is verified successfully (that is, the sender is who he or she claims to be), the recipient continues with the process of decrypting the message. Otherwise, the received message is rejected and the transaction (VPN session) is terminated.

6. **Message decryption.** After the sender's identity is verified successfully, the recipient decrypts the message. To do so, the recipient must first decode the sender's public key using its own private key. When the sender's public key is successfully retrieved, the recipient uses it to decrypt the message.

7. **Message content verification.** Finally, the recipient verifies the content of the received message. First, the digital signature is decrypted using sender's public key and the message digest is retrieved. The decrypted message is then hashed through a hash function and a new message digest is extracted. The received message digest and the newly generated message digest are then compared. If they match, the data was not intercepted or tampered with while in transit.

Figure 3-6 depicts a PKI-based transaction.

In the next section, you'll learn about the various PKI implementations that are predominantly employed by organizations all over the world.

Implementing PKI

As you already know, CAs help establish the true identity of communicating entities. However, CAs not only certify PKI clients, but also other CAs by issuing digital certificates to them. The verified CAs, in turn, can verify other CAs and this chain continues until every entity can trust the other entity involved in a transaction. This certification chain is known as the *certification path* and the arrangement of CAs in this certification path is referred to as *PKI architecture*.

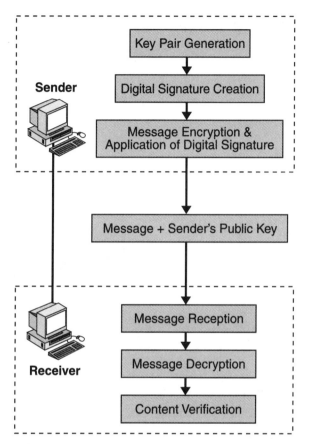

FIGURE 3-6 *A generic representation of a PKI-based transaction.*

The main categories of PKI architecture include the following:

- Single CA architecture
- Trust List architecture
- Hierarchical architecture
- Mesh architecture
- Hybrid architecture

Single CA Architecture

Single CA architecture is the simplest PKI architecture. As the name suggests, this architecture is based on a Single CA, which issues certificates, verifies PKI clients, and, when necessary, revokes certificates. All the underlying entities have a trust relationship with this CA. Because of the absence of other CAs in the model, this architecture does not support the CA trust relationship.

Figure 3-7 depicts the Single CA architecture.

Single CA architecture works well for small organizations because the number of PKI clients is relatively low and management of these clients is not a time-consuming task.

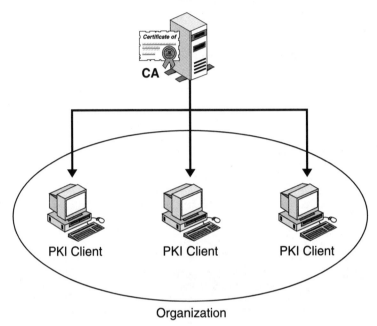

FIGURE 3-7 *The Single CA architecture of a PKI framework.*

Trust List Architecture

As the number of PKI clients in an organization grows, certificate management and identity verification becomes complicated and time-consuming for a Single CA. This situation can be simplified by introducing multiple CAs into the architecture.

With multiple CAs, a single PKI client can request certificates from more than one CA. As a result, each client must maintain a list of trust relationships with all the CAs in the infrastructure—hence the name *Trust List architecture*. Figure 3-8 depicts the Trust List architecture.

As you might have noticed in Figure 3-8, this architecture does not support CA trust relationships.

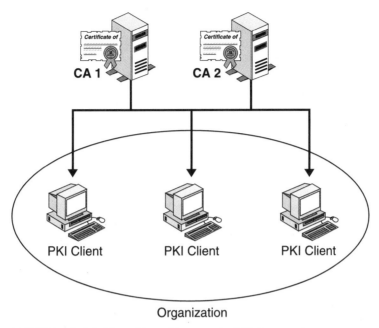

FIGURE 3-8 *The Trust List architecture of a PKI framework.*

Hierarchical Architecture

Hierarchical architecture is the most commonly implemented PKI architecture and is employed in large-scale organizations. Unlike the previous architectures, this model is based on trust relationships between various CAs within the model.

As the name suggests, CAs are arranged hierarchically and share a "superior-subordinate" type of trust relationship. The top-most CA is referred to as the *root CA* and is considered the starting point of the model. It issues certificates and verifies the identity of its subordinate CAs. The subordinate CAs, in turn, can issue certificates to their subordinates and PKI clients. However, they cannot issue certificates to their superiors.

Figure 3-9 depicts the Hierarchical architecture.

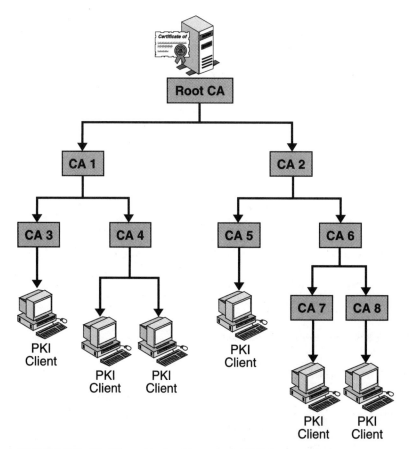

FIGURE 3-9 *The Hierarchical architecture of a PKI framework.*

Mesh Architecture

Unlike the Hierarchical architecture, in a *Mesh architecture* CAs share a peer-to-peer trust relationship with each other. As a result, they can issue digital certificates to each other, which means that the trust relationship between the CAs is bi-directional. The CAs also issue certificates to their PKI clients.

Figure 3-10 shows the PKI Mesh architecture.

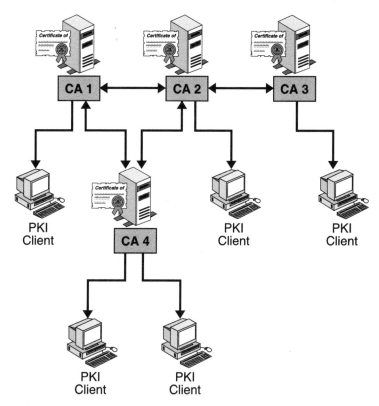

FIGURE 3-10 *The Mesh architecture of a PKI framework.*

Hybrid Architecture

The previous architectures cater to the requirements of a single organization. However, the scenario and the implementation of PKI infrastructure become complicated when one organization must interact with other organizations, as is the case with most organizations today. The problem lies in the possibility of differences in each organization's PKI architectures. For example, one organization might use Mesh architecture while the other uses the Single CA architecture. In such situations, a *Hybrid architecture* proves helpful as it allows successful interaction between the two organizations.

There are three Hybrid architectures. These include:

◆ **Extended Trust List architecture.** In this architecture, all PKI clients maintain an extended list of all *trust points* in the other organization's architecture—in addition to trust points in their own. A trust point in another organization's architecture can either be a Single CA, more than one CA, or all the CAs of the other organization. Figure 3-11 depicts the Extended Trust List architecture between three organizations.

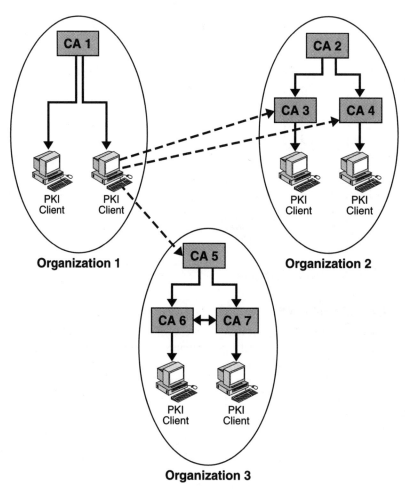

FIGURE 3-11 *The Extended Trust List architecture of a PKI framework.*

◆ **Cross-certified architecture.** In this hybrid architecture, the root CA of one organi-zation's infrastructure maintains a peer-to-peer relationship with the root CAs of other organizations. Figure 3-12 depicts the Cross-certified architecture.

◆ **Bridge CA architecture.** Unlike the Cross-certified architecture, where a direct peer-top-peer relationship exists between the root CAs of each organization's infra-structure, a new entity called a Bridge CA (BCA) maintains the peer-to-peer rela-tionship between the root CAs. Figure 3-13 depicts the Bridge CA architecture.

The five categories of PKI architecture—Single CA, Trust List, Hierarchical, Mesh, and Hybrid—allow for the establishment of VPN sessions and allow for the safe and secure trans-mission of data across VPN tunnels.

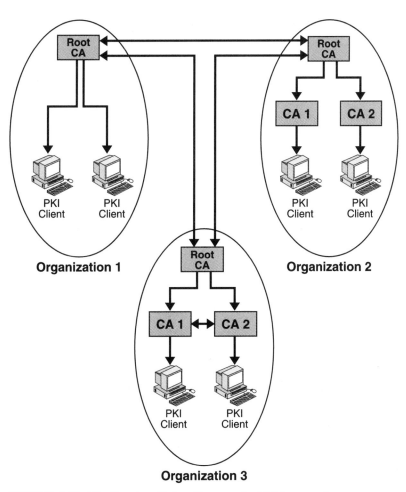

FIGURE 3-12 *The Cross-certified architecture of a PKI framework.*

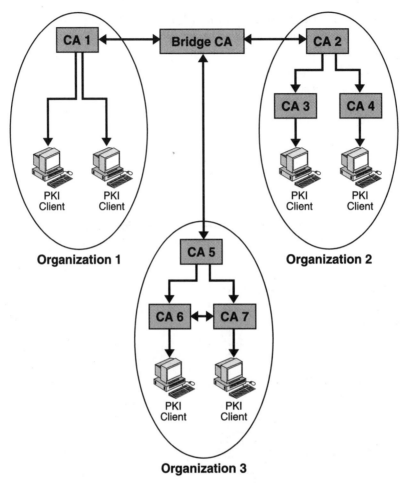

FIGURE 3-13 *The Bridge CA architecture of a PKI framework.*

Summary

In this chapter, you learned about the basic security components of a secure VPN setup: user authentication, access control, and encryption. The process of verifying that users are who they claim to be is known as user authentication. Allowing access to certain network resources while denying access to others is referred to as access control. Together these two mechanisms can, to a certain extent, reduce the security threats to the network resources.

While user authentication and access control are basically used to secure data that is stored within the network, encryption is used to ensure the safe passage of data across unsecured media. Encryption is the mechanism of converting data into an unreadable format, known as ciphertext, so that while the data is being transmitted to the recipient unauthorized access to the data can be prevented. The two types of encryption mechanisms are symmetric encryption and asymmetric encryption. Symmetric cryptography is based on the exchange of a single key that is used to encrypt as well as decrypt the data. However, this mechanism is highly susceptible to Man-in-the-Middle attacks. Asymmetric cryptography overcomes the problems posed by symmetric cryptography and is based on two different keys to encrypt data and another to decrypt data. Asymmetric cryptography uses two algorithms for data exchange: Diffie-Hellman (DH) and Rivest Shamir Adleman (RSA).

Finally, you were introduced to the basics of Public Key Infrastructure (PKI), which is fast emerging as the de facto methodology used to safeguard data transactions across unsecured and untrustworthy media. You learned about the components of PKI, the way PKI works, and PKI implementation and its accompanying architectures—Single CA, Trust List, Hierarchical, Mesh, and Hybrid.

Check Your Understanding

Multiple Choice Questions

1. Which of the following statements about data fabrication is true?
   a. Malicious attacks from "outside" as well as from within the network can render part or all of the network or unusable for long intervals.
   b. The destination user receives falsified or tampered data.
   c. After gaining access to the network by posing as an authorized and trusted network user, an unauthorized user disseminates spurious and harmful messages to other users in the network.
   d. After intercepting a message, an eavesdropper changes the content of the message.

2. The S/Key password authentication mechanism is based on _____.
   a. MD4
   b. DES
   c. IDEA
   d. CAST

3. Which of the following is (are) asymmetric encryption mechanisms?
   a. RC4
   b. Diffie-Hellman algorithm
   c. RSA
   d. MD5

4. In which of the PKI architectures do CAs share a bi-directional trust relationship with each other?

   a. Bridge CA architecture

   b. Trust List architecture

   c. Mesh architecture

   d. Hierarchical architecture

5. Which of the following statements about Extended Trust List architecture is true?

   a. A direct peer-top-peer relationship exists between the root CAs of each organization's infrastructure.

   b. All PKI clients in an organization's network can request and receive certificates from any CA in the other organization.

   c. A "superior-subordinate" relationship exists between CAs.

   d. This is the simplest PKI architecture.

6. RADIUS stands for _____.

   a. Remote Access Dial Internet User Service

   b. Reserved Access Dial-In User Service

   c. Reserved Access Dial Internet User Service

   d. Remote Access Dial-In User Service

Short Questions

1. How does the RSA algorithm guarantee data safety during transmission?

2. Alice has been communicating with Bob for some time. However, she has positive evidence that Arthur is eavesdropping on their communications—despite the fact that they use the opposite party's public key and their one private key to encrypt and decrypt the data.

   A. How can the third party intrude into their communication?

   B. What should be done to entirely remove the possibility of any intrusion?

3. ABC, Inc. is a wholesale supplier of canned food products all over US, Canada, and some countries in Latin America. The company has an elaborate network setup, which allows them 24x7x365 interaction with their suppliers as well as their clients. Their clients and their suppliers range in size from small- to large-scale operations. To ensure maximum data safety they have reached an agreement with most of their clients and suppliers to implement PKI infrastructure. Which PKI architecture would best suit this situation?

Answers

Multiple Choice Answers

1. **c.** In attacks related to data fabrication, an unauthorized user can pose as an authorized and trusted network user. After gaining access to the network, this individual can then disseminate spurious and harmful messages to other users in the network. This can ultimately lead to the shutdown of part or all of the network.

2. **a.** The S/Key password authentication mechanism is based on the MD4 hash function.

3. **b** and **c.** The Diffie-Hellman algorithm and the RSA algorithm are asymmetric algorithms. RC4 and MD5 are symmetric encryption algorithms (hash functions).

4. **c.** In Mesh-based PKI architectures CAs share a bi-directional trust relationship with each other because they can issue certificates to each other.

5. **b.** All PKI clients in an organization's network can request and receive certificates from any CA in the other organization. In the Extended Trust List architecture, all PKI clients maintain an extended list of all *trust points* in the other organization's architecture—besides the trust points in their own. A trust point in another organization's architecture can be a Single CA, more than one CA, or all the CAs of the other organization.

6. **d.** The acronym RADIUS stands for Remote Access Dial-In User Service.

Short Answers

1. RSA guarantees safe and secure passage of data because the recipient checks the correctness of data three times. Upon receiving an encrypted message, the recipient regenerates the message digest using the same hash function as the sender. The recipient then decrypts the digital signature using the sender's public key. Finally, the recipient compares the regenerated message digest to the message digest retrieved from the digital signature. If the two match, data was not intercepted, fabricated or modified during transmission. Otherwise, the data is rejected.

2. A. They are probably using the Diffie-Hellman encryption algorithm to encrypt/decrypt data. If the two communicating ends exchange their public keys over an unsecured medium, such as the Internet, there is a possibility that an early intruder can intercept the request for the public keys and sends his or her own public key to both communicating ends. In this case, the intruder can easily tap into the communication because the two ends will now exchange the data using intruder's public key. This type of intrusion is known as a Man-in-the-Middle attack.

   B. They should switch to the RSA encryption algorithm.

3. The scenario and the implementation of PKI infrastructure becomes extremely complicated when one organization must interact with other organizations. The problem lies in the possibility of differences between each organization's PKI architectures. For example, a large-scale organization might use Mesh architecture while a small-scale organization might use the Single CA architecture. In such situations, Hybrid architecture proves helpful as it allows successful interaction between two (or more) organizations.

PART II

VPN Protocols

Chapter 4

Basics of Tunneling Technology

As you learned in the previous chapter, tunneling lies at the core of VPN technology. While the cost effectiveness of VPNs is attributed to the use of the Internet, the safety and security that VPNs offer are the direct result of tunneling.

In this chapter, you'll learn about the basics of tunneling technology and the role it plays to ensure the safety of transactions across a widely heterogeneous internetwork, such as the Internet. You'll learn about the components of tunneling, the working of tunneling technology, and the format of a tunneled packet. You'll also learn about the different types of tunnels and tunneling protocols.

Understanding Tunneling Technology

Tunneling is the most significant component of VPN technology. It allows organizations to create virtual networks across the Internet and other public networks. This virtual network cannot be accessed by "outsiders"—users or computers that are not a part of the organization's intranet.

 NOTE

The most commonly used intermediate internetwork is the Internet. However, any other public or private network can serve as the intermediate internetwork during a long-distance data transmission.

Tunneling is the technique of encapsulating an entire data packet in the packet of another protocol format. In other words, the header of the tunneling protocol is appended to original packet. The resultant packet is then transferred to the destination node or network across the intermediate infrastructure.

The most important aspect of tunneling is that the original data packet, also referred to as the *payload*, can belong to an unsupported protocol. Instead of transferring the original packet, which might not be routable across the intermediate infrastructure, the underlying tunneling protocol appends its header to the tunneled packet. This header provides the requisite routing information so that the packet can be successfully delivered across the internetwork.

 NOTE

Tunneling is analogous to sending a letter. After you write a letter, you place it in an envelope. This envelope displays the address of the recipient. When you post this letter, it is delivered to the recipient according to the address on the envelope. The recipient then needs to open the envelope to read the letter. In tunneling technology, the letter is equivalent to the original payload and the envelope represents the packet of the routable protocol in which the payload is encapsulated. The address on the envelope represents the routing information that is appended to the packet.

When a tunneled packet is routed to the destination node, it travels across the internetwork through a logical path. This logical path is referred to as a *tunnel*. Upon receiving a tunneled packet, the recipient returns the packet to its original format. Figure 4-1 depicts the process of tunneling.

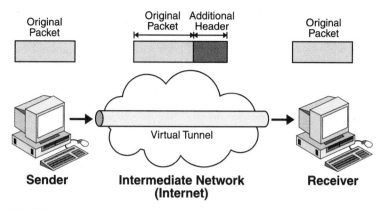

FIGURE 4-1 *The tunneling process.*

Tunneling technology offers a number of advantages that have played a major role in its popularity. The next section throws light on these advantages.

Advantages of Tunneling

Tunneling offers a few advantages that have made a significant impact on networking technology. These advantages are listed below:

♦ **Simplicity and ease of implementation.** Because the basic idea behind tunneling is simple, the technology itself is simple and easy to implement. Moreover, there is no need to change the existing infrastructure to accommodate tunneling technology, which makes tunneling a viable and lucrative solution for large- as well as medium-scale organizations.

♦ **Security.** An organization's tunnel access is prohibited to unauthorized users. As a result, data traveling through the tunnels is relatively safe—despite the fact that the data is being transmitted across an unsafe and public medium, such as the Internet.

♦ **Cost-effectiveness.** Tunneling uses public networks as the intermediate internetworks to transfer data to a destination. This makes tunneling an extremely cost-effective solution, especially when you compare it to the cost of implementing private intranets that span the globe or long-distance leased lines. In addition, an organization can save the considerable amount of money that it would have to spend annually on the administration and maintenance of these expensive solutions.

♦ **Protocol indifference.** Data belonging to non-routable protocols, such as Network Basic Input/Output System (NetBIOS), and NetBIOS Enhanced User Interface (NetBEUI) is not compatible with the Internet protocols TCP and IP. Therefore, these data packets cannot be routed as-is across the Internet. However, tunneling allows you to route such non-IP packets successfully to the destination by "enveloping" them within IP packets.

◆ **IP address savings.** As mentioned earlier, tunneling allows protocols with non-routable non-IP addresses to be inserted within a packet that uses a globally unique public IP address. As a result, instead of having to buy and assign a globally unique IP address (also known as a public IP address) for each node within the network, the network can buy a small block of globally unique IP addresses. When a node within this private network establishes a VPN connection, any of the available IP addresses from the block can be appended to the non-IP data packets. Thus, the private network can reduce an organization's need for globally unique IP addresses.

 NOTE

For the purpose of cost reduction, convenient administration, and complete control of the addressing scheme, many organizations implement their own IP addresses. These addresses need not be globally unique and therefore need not be bought from authorized agencies, such as InterNIC. This addressing scheme is known as *private IP addressing* and it works effectively within an organization's network. However, a globally unique IP address is required for successful communication across the Internet and other such public networks.

Now that you have the basic ideas of tunneling technology, you're ready to move to a discussion of tunneling components.

Components of Tunneling

To successfully establish a tunnel between the two communicating ends, four tunneling components are required.

◆ **Target network.** The network that contains the resources that needs to be accessed by the remote client, which initiated the VPN session request. (The target network is also referred to as *home network* in some VPN-related documentations.)

◆ **Initiator node.** The remote client or server that initiates the VPN session. The initiator node can be a part of a local network or can be a mobile user using a laptop.

◆ **HA (*Home Agent*).** The software interface that generally resides at the network access node (router) in the target network. However, a destination node, such as a dial-up access server, can also host the HA. The HA receives and authenticates the incoming requests to verify that they are from trusted hosts. Upon successful initiator authentication, the HA allows the establishment of a tunnel.

◆ **FA (*Foreign Agent*).** The software interface that resides either at the initiator node or at the network access node (router) of the network to which the initiator node belongs. The initiator node uses the FA to request a VPN session from the HA at the target network.

Now that you are familiar with the tunneling components, the next section discusses how these components contribute to the successful tunneling process.

Tunnel Technology Operations

For the purpose of easy comprehension, tunneling technology operations can be divided into two phases.

♦ **Phase I.** The initiator node (or remote client) requests a VPN session and is authenticated by the corresponding HA.

♦ **Phase II.** The actual data transfer occurs across the tunnel.

In Phase I, a connection request is initiated and session parameters are negotiated. (This phase can also be referred to as the *tunnel establishment phase*.) If the request is accepted and session parameters are negotiated successfully, a tunnel is established between the two communicating ends. This occurs in following manner:

1. The initiator sends the connection request to the FA located in the network.

2. The FA authenticates the request by validating the login name and the password supplied by the user. (The FA generally uses the services of a Remote Access Dial-Up Services (RADIUS) server to authenticate the identity of the initiator node.)

3. If the login name and the password supplied by the user are not valid, the request for the VPN session is rejected. However, if the FA authenticates the identity of the initiator successfully, it forwards the request to the target network HA.

4. If the request is accepted by the HA, the FA sends the encrypted login ID and the corresponding password to it.

5. The HA verifies the supplied information. If the verification is successful, the HA sends Register Reply, along with a tunnel number, to the FA.

6. A tunnel is established when the FA receives Register Reply and the tunnel number.

 NOTE

If the two ends do not use the same tunneling protocol, tunnel configuration variables such as encryption, compression parameters, and the tunnel maintenance mechanism are also negotiated.

With the establishment of the tunnel, Phase I is considered to be over and Phase II, or the *data transfer phase*, begins. The transactions in the data transfer phase occur as follows:

1. The initiator starts forwarding data packets to the FA.

2. The FA creates the tunnel header and appends it to each data packet. The header information of a routable protocol (that was negotiated in Phase I) is then appended to the packet.

3. The FA forwards the resulting encrypted data packet to the HA using the supplied tunnel number.

4. On receiving the encrypted information, the HA strips off the tunnel header and the header of the routable protocol, thus bringing the packet back to its original format.

5. The original data is then forwarded to the intended destination node in the network.

Figures 4-2 and 4-3 depict the two phases of tunneling.

Phase 1

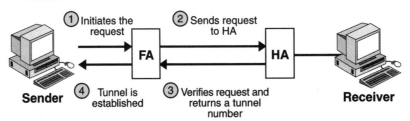

FIGURE 4-2 *The process of establishing a tunnel.*

Phase II

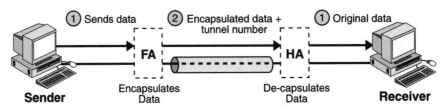

FIGURE 4-3 *The process of transferring data across a tunnel.*

The next section discusses the format of the tunneled packet.

Tunneled Packet Format

As described earlier, before it is delivered to the target network across the tunnel, the original data packet is encrypted by the FA. This encrypted packet is referred to as the tunneled packet. The format of a tunneled packet is shown in Figure 4-4.

As shown in Figure 4-4, a tunneled packet consists of three parts. These parts follow:

◆ **Header of the routable protocol.** This header field contains the addresses of the source (FA) and the destination (HA). Because transactions over the Internet are predominantly IP-based, this header is generally the standard IP header and contains the IP addresses of the FA and HA involved in the transaction.

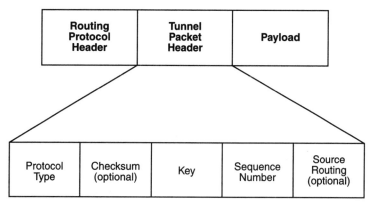

FIGURE 4-4 *The format of a tunneled packet.*

◆ **Tunnel packet header.** This header contains the following five fields:

- ◆ **Protocol type.** This field indicates the type of the original data packet (or payload) protocol.
- ◆ **Checksum.** This field contains the checksum that is used to check whether the packet was corrupted during the transmission. This information is optional.
- ◆ **Key.** This information is used to identify or authenticate the actual source of data (initiator).
- ◆ **Sequence number.** This field contains a number that indicates the sequence number of the packet in the series of packets that are being transmitted.
- ◆ **Source routing.** This field contains additional routing information. This field is optional.

◆ **Payload.** The original packet sent by the initiator to the FA. It also contains the original header.

There are two types of tunnels that are used to tunnel information during a VPN session. The next section discusses these tunnel types along with the protocols that are used to tunnel information during a VPN session.

Tunnel Types

Based on the manner in which a tunnel is created, it can be either voluntary or compulsory.

Voluntary Tunnels

Also known as *end-to-end tunnels*, *voluntary tunnels* are created at the request of a user (client) computer. As a result, the initiator node acts as the tunnel endpoint. Therefore, a separate tunnel is created for each communicating pair. After the communication between the two ends is over, the tunnel is terminated. Figure 4-5 depicts a voluntary tunnel.

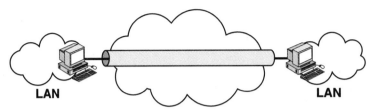

FIGURE 4-5 *A voluntary tunnel.*

In the case of a remote client using a dial-up connection, the client first needs to establish a dial-up connection to the internetwork. This is a preliminary step for establishing tunnels and is not accomplished by tunneling protocols. Only after a dial-up connection is established can the initiator set the tunnel up to the intended destination node. However, the situation is less complex in the case of a client that is a permanent part of the local network. In this case, the client is already connected to the internetwork. Therefore, it doesn't need to establish a separate dial-up connection to the internetwork.

Compulsory Tunnels

Unlike voluntary tunnels that are requested and created by client nodes, *compulsory tunnels* are created and configured by an intermediate device. Network Attached Storages (NASs) or dial-up servers are such intermediate devices. This type of tunneling is referred to as compulsory tunneling because the initiator must use the tunnel created by the intermediate device.

 NOTE

The intermediate device that is used to set up the tunnels during VPN sessions is known differently by different tunneling protocols. For example, in L2TP terminology an intermediate device is referred to as an L2TP Access Concentrator (LAC). Similarly, in PPTP terminology the device is known as a Front End Processor (FEP). In a typical IPSec setup, the intermediate device that sets up a tunnel during a VPN communication session is commonly referred to as an IP Security Gateway.

In the case of compulsory tunneling, as shown in Figure 4-6, both the remote client as well as the LAN-attached client must connect to the intermediate device, which is generally located at the ISP's POP. After the connection is established successfully, the intermediate device creates the tunnel.

Because the initiator node has no part in the creation or configuration of the tunnel, it does not act as the tunnel endpoint. In this case, the intermediate devices that are responsible for the tunnel serve as the tunnel endpoints. Also, unlike voluntary tunneling, in which a separate

FIGURE 4-6 *A compulsory tunnel.*

tunnel is allocated to each pair of communicating nodes, compulsory tunnels can be shared by multiple communications. As a result, the tunnel is not terminated until the last communication is complete.

 NOTE

Some experts define two types of tunnels based on a tunnel's period of activity—*static tunnels* and *dynamic tunnels*. Static tunnels remain active until they are terminated, regardless of data transmission. As a result, these tunnel types are expensive and are primarily seen in site-to-site VPNs. Dynamic tunnels, on the other hand, are activated only when data needs to be transferred. These tunnels are more secure than static tunnels.

Table 4-1 summarizes the difference between the two types of tunnels.

Table 4-1. Compulsory and Voluntary Tunnel Comparison

Voluntary tunnels	Compulsory Tunnels
The initiator node acts as the tunnel endpoint.	The intermediate device acts as the tunnel endpoint.
A separate tunnel is provided for each ongoing communication.	The same tunnel is shared by multiple ongoing communications.
A tunnel is terminated when the data exchange between the two ends is complete.	The tunnel is not terminated until the last communicating pair completes data transaction.
Data exchange between the two ends is faster.	Data exchange between the two entities is comparatively slow because the same tunnel is shared by multiple communications.
These are short-term tunnels.	These tunnels are comparatively long-term tunnels.

Tunneling Protocols

Tunneling technology makes use of three types of protocols.

◆ **Carrier protocol.** These protocols are used to route tunneled packets to their intended destination across the internetwork. The tunneled packets are encapsulated within the packets of this protocol. Because it must route the packets across a heterogeneous internetwork, such as the Internet, this protocol must be widely supported. As a result, if tunnels are created across the Internet, the carrier protocol that is used predominantly is IP. However, in the case of private intranets, native routing protocols can also serve as carrier protocols.

◆ **Encapsulating protocol.** These protocols are used to encapsulate the original payload. In addition, the encapsulating protocol is also responsible for the creation, maintenance, and termination of the tunnel. Today, PPTP, L2TP, and IPSec are the most commonly used encapsulating protocols.

◆ **Passenger protocol.** The original data that needs to be encapsulated for the purpose of transmission across the tunnel belongs to this protocol. PPP and SLIP (*Serial Line Internet Protocol*) are commonly used passenger protocols.

Figure 4-7 maps the tunneled packet format discussed earlier in the chapter to the three types of tunneling protocols.

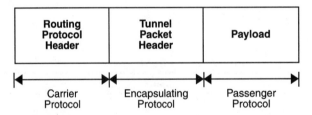

FIGURE 4-7 *Mapping the tunneled packet format to tunneling protocols.*

Summary

In this chapter, you learned about the basics of tunneling technology and the role it plays to ensure the safety of transactions across a widely heterogeneous internetwork, such as the Internet. You learned about the various components of tunneling, the working of tunneling technology, and the format of a tunneled packet. Finally, you also learned about the two types of tunnels and the three types of tunneling protocols.

Tunneling protocols can function at Layer 2 as well as Layer 3 of the OSI model. In the next chapter, you'll learn about the three tunneling protocols—PPTP, L2F, and L2TP—that function at Layer 2. Chapter 6 deals with IPSec, which functions at Layer 3 of the same model.

Check Your Understanding

Multiple Choice Questions

1. Which of the following is not a tunneling component?

    a. Home Agent

    b. Initiator node

    c. Tunneled packet

    d. Target agent

2. Which of the following is a Phase I operation?

    a. The FA authenticates the request by validating the login name and password supplied by the user.

    b. The initiator starts forwarding data packets to the FA.

    c. The FA creates the tunnel header and appends it to each data packet. The header information of a routable protocol (that was negotiated in Phase I) is then appended to the packet.

    d. The FA forwards the resulting encrypted data packet to the HA using the supplied tunnel number.

3. Which of the following statements about compulsory tunnels are true?

    a. These tunnels are known as end-to-end tunnels.

    b. The number of tunnels depends on the number of communicating pairs.

    c. An intermediate device plays an important role in these tunnels.

    d. The tunnel is terminated on completion of the data transaction between the last communicating pair.

4. Which of the following fields is not a part of the tunnel packet header?

    a. Protocol type

    b. Checksum

    c. Source routing

    d. Header of the routable protocol

Answers

Multiple Choice Answers

1. **c** and **d.** A tunneled packet and a target agent are not valid tunneling components. The components of tunneling include a target network, the initiator node, a home agent, and a foreign agent.

2. **a.** The authentication of the remote client (or the initiator node) is a Phase I activity. In this phase, the initiator node starts the tunneling process by requesting a VPN session. After the remote client is authenticated by the corresponding HA, a tunnel is established between the two communicating ends.

3. **a, c,** and **d.** Compulsory tunnels are known as end-to-end tunnels and are established with the help of an intermediate device. However, the same tunnel is shared by multiple ongoing communications. As a result, multiple tunnels are not supported. In addition, because a single tunnel is used, the tunnel is terminated on completion of the data transaction between the last communicating pair.

4. **d.** The tunneled packet header is made up of the protocol type, checksum, key, sequence number, and source routing fields. The header of the routable protocol is not a part of the tunneled packet header.

Chapter 5

In the previous chapter, "Basics of Tunneling Technology," you learned about tunneling and how it helps secure confidential transactions across unsecured intermediate internetworks. In this chapter, you will learn about tunneling protocols that enable and support this tunneling technology. As you might guess, these tunneling protocols are fundamental for building VPNs and securing transmissions across VPNs. Some of the most commonly implemented VPN tunneling protocols function at the second layer—Data Link layer—of the (OSI) Open System Interconnect model, which is depicted in Figure 5-1.

This chapter focuses on popular tunneling protocols that function at Layer 2 of the OSI model, as shown in Figure 5-1. These include the *Point-to-Point Tunneling Protocol* (*PPTP*), *Layer 2 Forwarding* (*L2F*), and the *Layer 2 Tunneling Protocol* (*L2TP*). Before these protocols can be discussed, however, an understanding of *Point-to-Point Protocol* (*PPP*) is essential as all tunneling protocols at Layer 2 use PPP inherently.

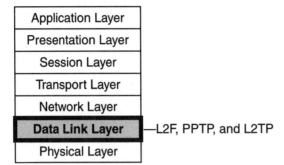

FIGURE 5-1 *The position of Layer 2 tunneling protocols in the OSI model.*

Point-to-Point Protocol (PPP)

PPP is an encapsulation protocol that facilitates the transportation of network traffic across serial point-to-point links. The biggest advantage of PPP is that it can operate any Data Terminal Equipment (DTE) or Data Connection Equipment (DCE) including EIA/TIA-232-C and ITU-T V.35. Another point in favor of PPP is that it does not restrict transmission rates. During transmission, the only transmission-based restrictions are imposed by the DCE/DTE interface in use. Finally, the only requirement of PPP is the availability of a duplex (two-way) connection, which can be either synchronous or asynchronous and can operate either in a switched or dedicated mode.

 NOTE

EIA/TIA-232-C was formerly known as RS-232C.

Besides the encapsulation of IP and non-IP data and its transportation across serial links, PPP is also responsible for the following functions:

◆ Assignment and management of IP addresses to non-IP datagrams.

◆ Configuration and testing of the established link.

◆ Asynchronous and synchronous encapsulation of datagrams.

◆ Error detection during a transmission.

◆ Multiplexing of multiple Layer 2 network protocols.

◆ Negotiation of optional configuration parameters, such as data compression and addressing.

PPP realizes this functionality with the use of three standards.

◆ A standard for encapsulating data packets over point-to-point links

NOTE

This standard for encapsulating data packets over point-to-point connections is loosely modeled on the High-Level Data Link Control (HDLC) protocol. However, there are differences between the two standards. For example, HDLC divides data packets into frames; PPP does not.

◆ A standard for establishing, configuring, and testing the point-to-point connection with the help of the Link Control Protocol (LCP)

◆ A standard for establishing and configuring various Network-layer protocols and detecting errors during transmission in the form of the Network Control Protocol (NCP) suite

PPP Operation

As depicted in Figure 5-2, PPP operations are carried out in the following way:

1. After the data packets are encapsulated, the source (or initiator) node sends LCP frames over the point-to-point link to the destination node.

2. These frames are used to configure the link per the parameters specified and test the established link, if required.

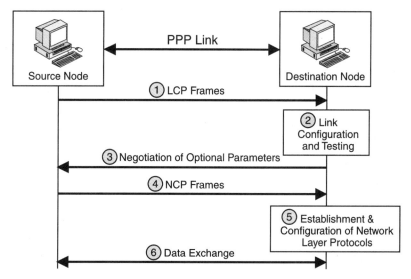

FIGURE 5-2 *Establishing a PPP link and exchanging data.*

3. After the destination node accepts the connection request and a link is successfully established, optional facilities are negotiated, if specified by the LCPs.

4. The source node then sends NCP frames to choose and configure Network-layer protocols.

5. After the required Network-layer protocols have been configured, the two ends start exchanging data.

When a PPP link is established, it exists until LCP or NCP frames signal the link termination. The link may also be terminated in the case of link failure or user intervention.

PPP Packet Format

Six fields constitute a PPP frame, as illustrated in Figure 5-3. A description of the fields that make up a PPP frame follows:

◆ **Flag.** This field indicates the beginning and the end of a frame. The length of this field is one byte.

◆ **Address.** Because it uses point-to-point links, PPP does not use the addresses of individual nodes. Therefore, this field contains the binary sequence 11111111, which is a standard broadcast address. The length of the field is one byte.

◆ **Control.** This field contains the binary sequence 00000011, which denotes that the frame carrying the user data is an unsequenced frame indicating the connection-less nature of PPP transmissions. The length of the field is one byte.

◆ **Protocol.** This field identifies the protocol of the data that is encapsulated in the frame's data field. The protocol in this field is specified per the assigned numbers in RFC 3232. The length of the field is two bytes. However, this is negotiable to one byte if both peers agree.

◆ **Data.** This field contains the information being exchanged between the source and the destination nodes. The length of the field varies, though the maximum length of the field can be up to 1500 bytes.

◆ **FCS (Frame Check Sequence).** This field contains the check sequence that helps the recipient verify the accuracy of the information received in the Data field. Generally, the length of this field is two bytes. However, PPP implementations can negotiate a 4-byte FCS for the purpose of improved error detection.

 NOTE

RFC 3232 is available at http://www.armware.dk/RFC/rfc/rfc3232.html.

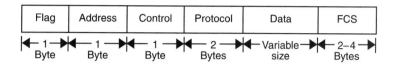

FIGURE 5-3 *The format of a typical PPP frame.*

PPP Link Control

In addition to successful data exchange between two nodes, PPP is also responsible for controlling the link that is established between the two communicating ends. PPP uses LCP for this purpose, where LCP is responsible for the following functions:

- ◆ Helping establish the PPP link.
- ◆ Configuring the established link to satisfy the requirements of the communicating parties.
- ◆ Performing regular maintenance of an established PPP link.
- ◆ Terminating the link if the data exchange between the two ends is complete.

 NOTE

In the case of PPP, the term "link" refers to the point-to-point connection.

LCP-based link control occurs in four phases—the *Link establishment and negotiation phase,* the *Link quality determination phase,* the *Network-layer protocol negotiation phase,* and the *Link termination phase.* The following description summarizes the four link control phases:

- ◆ **Link establishment and negotiation.** Before any PPP-based exchange is possible between the source and the destination nodes, LCP must establish (open) a connection between the two ends and negotiate configuration parameters. LCP uses Link-establishment frames for this purpose. When each end responds back with its own Configuration-Ack frame, this phase is completed.
- ◆ **Link quality determination.** This is an optional phase in which the quality of the established link is determined to verify that the link is ready for the negotiation of Network-layer protocols.
- ◆ **Network-layer protocol negotiation.** In this phase, the underlying Network-layer protocol of the data that is encapsulated in the Protocol field of the PPP frame is negotiated.

◆ **Link termination.** This is the final phase of LCP and serves to terminate the established PPP link between the two ends. The termination of the link can be graceful or abrupt. Graceful link termination occurs after data exchange between the two ends is complete, or at the request of either end. A physical event, such as the loss of carrier or the expiration of an idle-period timer, results in abrupt link termination. Link-termination frames are exchanged between the involved parties before the link is disconnected.

In addition to Link-establishment and Link-termination frames, PPP uses a third category of frames called Link-maintenance frames. These frames, as the name suggests, are exchanged in case of link-related problems and are used to manage and debug PPP-based links.

 NOTE

You might refer to RFC 1661 for detailed information on PPP. This RFC is available at http://www.freesoft.org/CIE/RFC/1661/.

Although not used in present-day VPNs "as-is," PPP technology is fundamental to other tunneling protocols used extensively in VPNs today. In fact, all popular tunneling protocols are based on PPP and encapsulate PPP frames into IP or other datagrams for transmission across the intermediate internetwork

Point-to-Point Tunneling Protocol (PPTP)

PPTP is a proprietary solution that enables secure data transfers between a remote client and an enterprise server by creating a VPN across an IP-based internetwork. Developed by the PPTP Consortium (Microsoft Corporation, Ascend Communications, 3COM, US Robotics, and ECI Telematics), PPTP offers on-demand VPNs across unsecured internetworks. PPTP not only facilitates secure transmissions across public TCP/IP-based internetworks, but also across private intranets.

 NOTE

As Microsoft Corporation played a key role in the development of PPTP, all Microsoft networking products, such as Windows NT 4.0 (server and workstation editions) and Windows 2000, support PPTP natively.

Historically, two phenomenons have played a major role in the success of PPTP in secure long-distance connections. These include:

◆ **The use of PSTNs (Public Switched Telephone Networks).** PPTP allows the use of PSTNs for the implementation of VPNs. As a result, the process of VPN deployment is remarkably simple and the total cost of implementation is significantly small. The reason for this is simple—the need for enterprise-wide connectivity solutions based on leased lines and dedicated communication servers is totally eliminated.

◆ **Support to Non-IP protocols.** Although meant for IP-based networks, PPTP also supports other commonly-implemented network protocols, such as TCP/IP, IPX, NetBEUI, and NetBIOS. Therefore, PPTP has proven to be as successful in the deployment of VPNs across a private LANs as in the deployment of VPNs across public networks.

PPP plays a major role in PPTP-based transactions. The next section discusses this role in further detail.

Role of PPP in PPTP Transactions

PPTP is a logical extension of PPP as PPTP does not change the underlying PPP technology. It only defines a new way of transporting PPP traffic across unsecured public internetworks. Quite like PPP, PPTP also does not support multiple connections. All PPTP supported connections must be point-to-point. In addition, PPP fulfills the following functions in PPTP-based transactions:

◆ Establishes and terminates the physical connections between communicating ends.

◆ Authenticates PPTP clients.

◆ Encrypts IPX, NetBEUI, NetBIOS, and TCP/IP datagrams to create PPP datagrams and secure the data exchange between the involved parties.

 NOTE

PPP may use cleartext, encrypted, or Microsoft-encrypted authentication mechanisms for authenticating PPTP clients. You'll learn more about these encryption and authentication mechanisms later in this chapter.

Figure 5-4 depicts the role of PPP in PPTP-based transactions.

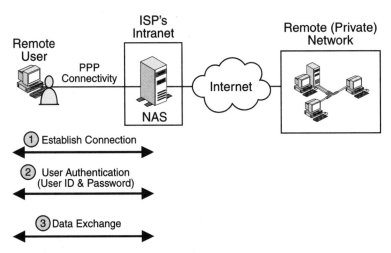

FIGURE 5-4 *The three responsibilities of PPP in a PPTP transaction.*

 NOTE

The role of PPP is very similar in L2F and L2TP transactions.

Components of PPTP Transactions

Any PPTP-based transaction implements at least three components, as shown in Figure 5-5. These PPTP components are

◆ A PPTP client
◆ A Network Access Server (NAS)
◆ A PPTP server

PPTP Clients

A PPTP client is a network node that supports PPTP and can request another node for a VPN session. If the connection is requested from a remote server, the PPTP client must use the services of an ISP's NAS. For this, the client must be connected to a modem, which is used to establish a dial-up PPP connection to the ISP. The PPTP client must also be connected to a VPN device so that it can tunnel the request (and the subsequent data, if the request is accepted) to the VPN device on the remote network. The link to the remote VPN device uses the first dial-up connection to the ISP's NAS in order to establish a tunnel between the VPN devices across the Internet or other such intermediate internetwork.

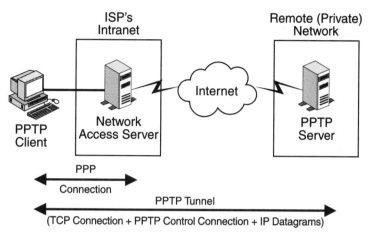

FIGURE 5-5 *A PPTP tunnel and the three components of PPTP-based transactions.*

Unlike remote requests for VPN sessions, the requests for a VPN session to a local server do not require a connection to the ISP's NAS. Both the client and the server are physically connected to the same network (LAN), making a connection to the ISP's NAS unnecessary. The client, in this case, only requires a dial-up networking session with the VPN device on the server.

As the routing requirements of PPTP packets for a remote request and a local request are different, the packets associated with the two requests are processed differently. The PPTP packets to a local server are placed on the physical medium attached to the network adapter of the PPTP client. Conversely, the PPTP packet to a remote server is routed through the physical media attached to a telecommunication device, such as a router. The placement of PPTP packets on the network media is illustrated in Figure 5-6.

PPTP Servers

PPTP Servers are network nodes that support PPTP and are capable of servicing requests for VPN sessions from other nodes—remote or local. In order to respond to remote requests, these servers must also support routing capabilities. A Remote Access Server (RAS) and any other Network Operating System (NOS) that supports PPTP, such as Windows NT Server 4.0, can act as a PPTP server.

PPTP Network Access Servers (NASs)

PPTP NASs are located at the ISP site and provide Internet connectivity to clients that dial-in using PPP. As the probability of many clients requesting a VPN session simultaneously is high, these servers must be capable of supporting multiple clients concurrently. Also, PPTP clients are not restricted to Microsoft NOSs only. Therefore, PPTP NASs must be capable of handling a wide range of clients including Microsoft's Windows-based clients, Unix machines, and Apple's Macintosh clients. However, it is important that these clients support PPTP connectivity to NASs.

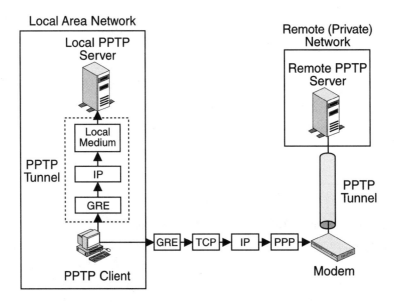

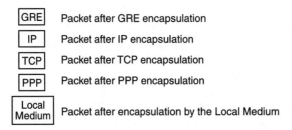

GRE	Packet after GRE encapsulation
IP	Packet after IP encapsulation
TCP	Packet after TCP encapsulation
PPP	Packet after PPP encapsulation
Local Medium	Packet after encapsulation by the Local Medium

FIGURE 5-6 *Transmitting the PPTP packet to the destination node.*

PPTP Processes

PPTP employs three processes to secure PPTP-based communication over unsecured media. These processes are

◆ PPP-based connection establishment

◆ Connection control

◆ PPTP tunneling and data transfer

PPTP Connection Control

After a PPP-based physical connection is established between the PPTP client and the server, PPTP connection control commences, as shown in Figure 5-7. PPTP connection control is established based on the IP addresses of the PPTP client and server, which use a dynamically

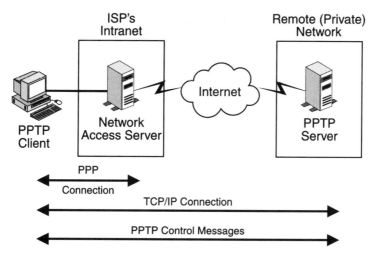

FIGURE 5-7 *Exchanging PPTP control messages over a PPP connection.*

allocated TCP port and the reserved TCP port number 1723, respectively. After the connection control is established, control and management messages are exchanged between the communicating parties. These messages are responsible for maintenance, management, and termination of the PPTP tunnel. These messages include periodic transmission of "PPTP-Echo-Request, PPTP-Echo-Reply" messages that help detect a connectivity failure between the PPTP server and the client.

Some commonly used PPTP control messages are listed in Table 5-1.

Table 5-1. Common PPTP Control Messages

Name	Description
Start-Control-Connection-Request	Request from the PPTP client to establish control connection.
Start-Control-Connection-Reply	Response from the PPTP server to the client's Start-Control-Connection-Request message.
Outgoing-Call-Request	Request from the PPTP client to the server to establish a PPTP tunnel.
Outgoing-Call-Reply	Response from the PPTP server to the client's Outgoing-Call-Request message.
Echo-Request	Keep-alive mechanism from either server or client. If the Opposite party does not answer this message, the tunnel is terminated

Table 5-1. Continued

Name	Description
Echo-Reply	Response to the Echo-Request message from the opposite end.
Set-Link-Info	Message from either side to set PPP-related options.
Call-Clear-Request	Message from the PPTP client initiating the termination of the tunnel.
Call-Disconnect-Notify	Response from the PPTP server to the client's Call-Clear-Request. It also serves as a message from the server initiating tunnel termination.
WAN-Error-Notify	Message from the PPTP server to all connected PPTP clients to notify of errors in server's PPP interface.
Stop-Control-Connection-Request	Message from the PPTP client or server notifying the other end of the termination of control connection.
Stop-Control-Connection-Reply	Response from the opposite end to the Stop-Control-Connection–Request message.

As depicted in Figure 5-8, PPTP control messages are encapsulated in TCP datagrams. Therefore, after the establishment of a PPP connection with the remote server or client, a TCP connection is established. This connection is subsequently used to exchange PPTP control messages.

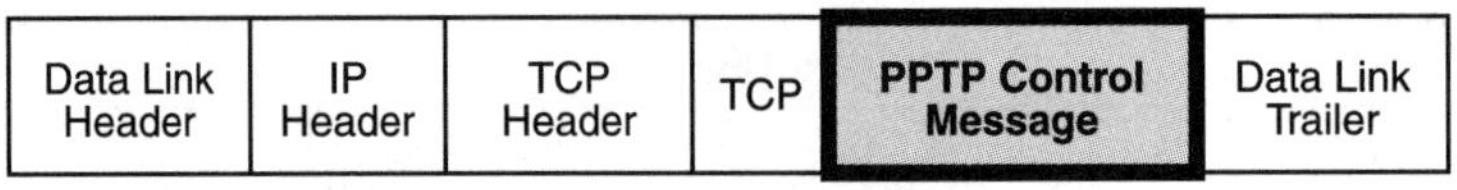

Data Link Header	IP Header	TCP Header	TCP	**PPTP Control Message**	Data Link Trailer

FIGURE 5-8 *PPTP control in the TCP datagram.*

PPTP Data Tunneling and Processing

A PPTP data packet undergoes multiple encapsulation stages, which include the following:

1. **Encapsulation of data.** The original information (payload) is encrypted and then encapsulated within a PPP frame. A PPP header is added to the frame.

2. **Encapsulation of PPP frames.** The resultant PPP frame is then encapsulated within a modified Generic Routing Encapsulation (GRE). The modified GRE header contains a 4-byte Acknowledgement field and a corresponding Acknowledgement bit that notifies the presence of the Acknowledgement field. In addition, the Key field in

the GRE frame is replaced with a 2-byte long field called Payload length and a 2-byte long field called Call ID. The PPTP client sets this field when it creates the PPTP tunnel.

3. **Encapsulation of GRE packets.** Next, an IP header is added to the PPP frame, which is encapsulated within the GRE packet. This IP header contains the IP addresses of the source PPTP client and the destination server.

4. **Data Link layer encapsulation**. As you already know, PPTP is a Layer 2 tunneling protocol. Therefore, the Data Link layer header and trailer play important roles in tunneling the data. Before being placed on the transmission medium, the Data Link layer adds its own header and trailer to the datagram. If the datagram has to travel through a local PPTP tunnel, the datagram is encapsulated with a LAN-technology (such as Ethernet) header and trailer. On the other hand, if the tunnel is rendered across a WAN link, the header and trailer that are added to the datagram is invariably once again PPP.

Figure 5-9 depicts the process PPTP data tunneling.

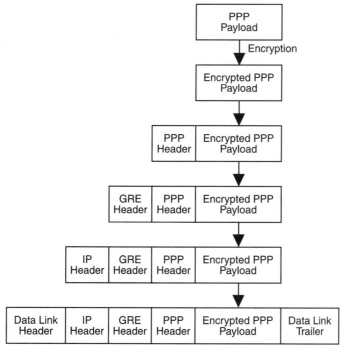

FIGURE 5-9 *The process of PPTP data tunneling.*

NOTE

GRE is a simple, lightweight, general-purpose encapsulation mechanism for IP-based data. GRE is generally used by ISPs to forward routing information within their intranets. However, the Internet backbone routers of the ISP intranet filter this GRE-based traffic. Therefore, the established PPTP tunnels can securely and privately carry data to the recipient.

When the PPTP data is transferred successfully to the intended recipient, the recipient must process the tunneled packet to extract the original data. The processing of PPTP-tunneled data extraction is exactly the reverse of PPTP data tunneling. As shown in Figure 5-10, in order to retrieve the original data the recipient PPTP node follows these steps:

1. The recipient end processes and removes the Data Link header and trailer that were added by the sender.
2. Next, the GRE header is removed.

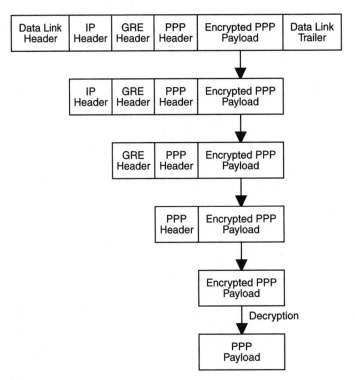

FIGURE 5-10 *Processing PPTP-tunneled data at the recipient end.*

3. The IP header is processed and removed.

4. The PPP header is processed and removed.

5. Finally, the original information is decrypted (if required).

PPTP Security

PPTP offers various built-in security services to PPTP clients and servers. These security services include the following:

♦ Data encryption and compression

♦ Authentication

♦ Access control

♦ Packet filtering

In addition to the native security mechanisms mentioned above, PPTP can be used in conjunction with firewalls and routers.

PPTP Data Encryption and Compression

PPTP does not provide a built-in encryption mechanism to secure data. Instead, it uses the encryption services offered by PPP. PPP, in turn, uses *Microsoft Point-to-Point Encryption (MPPE)*, which is based on the shared-secret encryption method.

The shared secret used for encryption purposes in the case of PPP is the user ID and its corresponding password. The 40-bit session key used to encrypt the user ID and password is derived from the hashed algorithm that is stored on both client and the server. The hashed algorithm that is used to generate the key is RSA RC4. This key is used to encrypt all the data that is transferred through the tunnel. However, a 40-bit key is too short and hence too weak for today's advanced hacking techniques. Therefore, a 128-bit key version is also available. In addition to decreasing the security risk, Microsoft recommends that the key be refreshed after every 256th packet.

PPTP Data Authentication

PPTP supports the following Microsoft authentication mechanisms natively:

♦ **MS-CHAP (Microsoft Challenge Handshake Authentication Protocol).**
MS-CHAP is Microsoft's customized version of CHAP, and is used for PPP-based authentications. Because of its strong resemblance to CHAP, the functionality of MS-CHAP is quite similar to that of CHAP. The main difference between the two is that while CHAP is based on the RSA MD5 hash algorithm, MS-CHAP is based on RSA RC4 and DES. Due to the fact that MS-CHAP was solely developed for Microsoft products (Windows 9x and various versions of Windows NT), it is not supported by other platforms.

◆ **PAP (Password Authentication Protocol)**. PAP is the simplest and the most commonly implemented dial-in authentication protocol. It is also used to authenticate PPP-based connections. However, it sends the user ID and password in an unencrypted format across the link. Therefore, it offers no protection from playback or repeated trial and error attacks. Another PAP loophole is that the communicating ends are authenticated only once—at the establishment of the connection. Hence, if a hacker successfully takes over the connection once, he or she would not have to worry about further authentication. Because of these reasons, PAP is considered the least sophisticated authentication protocol and is not the preferred authentication mechanism for VPNs.

 NOTE

Refer to Chapter 3, "Security Components of a VPN," for more information on RC4 and DES algorithms.

PPTP Access Control

After a remote PPTP client is authenticated successfully, its access to the resources within the network might be restricted for the purpose of enhanced security. This objective is achieved by the implementation of access control mechanisms, such as:

◆ Access rights
◆ Permissions
◆ Workgroups

You might want to refer to Chapter 3, "Security Components of a VPN," for more information on Access control.

PPTP Packet Filtering

PPTP packet filtering allows a PPTP server on a private network to accept and route packets from only those PPTP clients that have been successfully authenticated. As a result, only authorized PPTP clients can gain access to the specified remote network. In this manner, PPTP not only provides authentication, access control, and encryption mechanisms, but it also increases the network security.

PPTP with Firewalls and Routers

PPTP devices (clients and servers) accept TCP and IP (GRE) traffic at ports 1723 and 47, respectively. However, when PPTP is used in conjunction with routers and firewalls, the traffic destined for these ports is routed through the firewall or router, which filters the traffic on the basis of Access Control Lists (ACLs) and other native security strategies. In this manner, PPTP further enhances the security services it offers.

You should now have the basic idea of PPTP and its functionality. The next section familiarizes you with the pros and cons of implementing PPTP in your VPNs.

PPTP Pros and Cons

The main advantages offered by PPTP are as follows:

◆ PPTP is shipped as a built-in solution with Microsoft products, which are widely used.

◆ PPTP can support non-IP protocols.

◆ PPTP is supported by various platforms, such as Unix, Linux, and Apple's Macintosh. Other platforms that do not support PPTP can also avail the services of PPTP by using the built-in router PPTP client capability.

PPTP implementation also has a flipside. Major disadvantages of PPTP include the following:

◆ PPTP is a weaker option security-wise. L2TP and IPSec are far more secure technologies.

◆ PPTP is platform-dependent.

◆ PPTP requires extensive configuration on the PPTP server as well as the client.

◆ Although PPTP is shipped as a built-in VPN solution, a Routing and Remote Access Server (RRAS) may also need to be configured, in case of Dial-on-Demand routing solutions.

The biggest disadvantage associated with PPTP is its weaker security mechanism due to its use of symmetric encryption in which the key is derived from the user's password. This is far more risky because passwords are sent in the clear for authentication. The next tunneling protocol—Layer 2 Forwarding (L2F)—was developed while keeping enhanced security in mind.

Layer 2 Forwarding (L2F)

As mentioned earlier, traditional dial-up network services were realized across the Internet and therefore were based on IP technology. This is why popular tunneling solutions, such as PPP and PPTP, proved to be more successful with the IP infrastructure than other contemporary networking technologies, such as ATM, Frame Relay, and so on. Security was another issue. Despite Microsoft's claims of secure transactions, PPTP was based on MS-CHAP, which, as you learned in a previous section, is not very secure. These issues made industry organizations and experts search for alternative solutions that would offer secure seamless multi-protocol virtual dial-up services.

Cisco Systems, along with Nortel, was one of the leading vendors that started working toward a solution that would:

◆ Enable secure transactions.

◆ Provide access through the underlying infrastructure of the Internet and other intermediate public internetworks.

◆ Support a wide range of networking technologies, such as ATM, FDDI, IPX, NetBEUI, and Frame Relay.

The long-sought alternative that Cisco presented after extensive research was L2F. Besides fulfilling the main objectives mentioned above, L2F offered another major advancement in remote access technology: L2F tunnels can support more than one session simultaneously within the same tunnel. In simpler terms, more than one remote user can access a private intranet using a single dial-up connection. L2F achieved this by defining multiple connections within a tunnel where each connection represents a single PPP stream. In addition, these streams can either originate from a single remote user or from multiple users. Because one tunnel can support multiple connections simultaneously, fewer connections are required from a remote site to the ISP and from the ISP's POP to the gateway of a private network. This feature is especially useful in reducing user costs. Figure 5-11 depicts L2F tunneling.

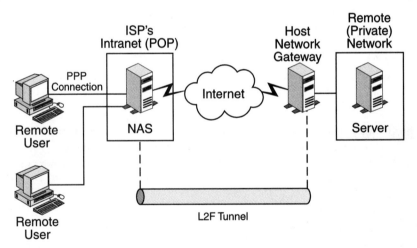

FIGURE 5-11 *L2F tunnel from the ISP's POP to the gateway of a private network.*

L2F Processes

When a remote dial-up client initiates a connection to a host located in a private intranet, the following processes are executed sequentially:

1. The remote user initiates a PPP connection to its ISP. If the remote user is part of a LAN setup the user may employ ISDN or other such connectivity to connect to the ISP. Alternatively, if the user is not a part of any intranet, he or she will need to use the services of the underlying PSTN.

2. If the NAS present at the ISP's POP accepts the connection request, the PPP connection is established between the NAS and the user.

3. The user is authenticated at the ISP end. Either CHAP or PAP is used for the purpose.

4. If no tunnel exists to the gateway of the desired destination network, one is initiated.

5. After a tunnel is established successfully, a unique multiplex ID (MID) is allocated to the connection. A notification message is also sent to the host network's gateway. This message notifies the gateway about the request for connection from a remote user.

6. The gateway may either accept the connection request or reject it. If the request is rejected, the user is notified about the request failure and the dialup connection is terminated. On the other hand, if the request is accepted, the host gateway sends initial setup notification to the remote client. This response may also include the authentication information, which is used by the gateway to authenticate the remote user.

7. After the user is authenticated by the host network gateway, a virtual interface is established between the two ends.

 NOTE

If CHAP is used for user authentication, as specified in step 6, the response includes the challenge, username, and raw response. For PAP-based authentications, the response includes username and password in cleartext. In the case of PPP, the initial setup notification also includes CONFACK messages that are exchanged between the two ends after a successful TCP negotiation. These acknowledgements allow the host network's gateway to initialize its own PPP state, thus eliminating the need for an additional LCP negotiation phase.

Figure 5-12 depicts the entire process of establishing an L2F tunnel between two communicating ends.

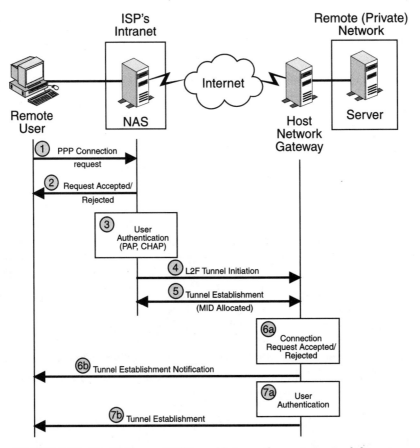

FIGURE 5-12 *Establishing an L2F tunnel between the remote user and the server.*

L2F Tunneling

When a remote user is authenticated and the connection request is accepted, a tunnel is established between the ISP's NAS and the remote host network's gateway, as shown in Figure 5-13.

After a tunnel between the two ends is in place, Layer 2 frames can be exchanged over the tunnel as follows:

1. The remote user forwards normal frames to the NAS located at the ISP.

2. POP strips the Data Link layer information or transparency bytes and adds the L2F header and trailer to the frame. The newly encapsulated frame is then forwarded to the destination network via the tunnel.

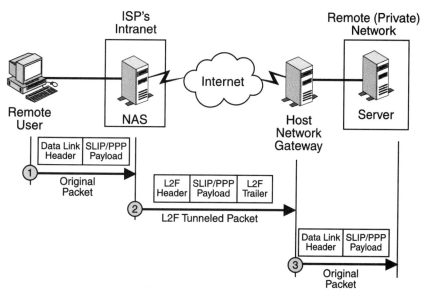

FIGURE 5-13 *The L2F-based data tunneling process.*

3. The host network gateway accepts these tunneled packets, strips the L2F header and trailer and forwards the frames to the destination node within the intranet.

4. The destination node processes the received frames as non-tunneled frames.

NOTE

L2F tunnels are also known as "virtual interfaces."

Any response from the destination host in the host network undergoes the reverse process. That is, the host sends a normal Data Link layer frame to the host gateway, which encapsulates the frame in an L2F packet (shown in Figure 5-14), and forwards it to the NAS located at the ISP site. NAS strips the L2F information from the frame and adds appropriate Data Link layer information to it. The frame is then forwarded to the remote user.

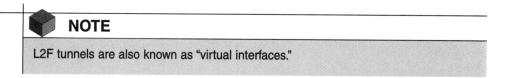

FIGURE 5-14 *The L2F packet format.*

L2F Security

L2F provides the following services:

◆ Data encryption

◆ Authentication

L2F Data Encryption

L2F uses MPPE (Microsoft Point-to-Point Encryption) for basic encryption purposes. However, MPPE is not a safe bet against today's enhanced hacking techniques. As a result, L2F also uses encryption based on *Internet Protocol Security* (*IPSec*) to ensure that the data is secure during transmissions. IPSec uses two protocols for encryption purposes—*Encapsulating Security Payload* (*ESP*) and *Authentication Header* (*AH*). In addition, to ensure enhanced key security during the key-exchange phase, IPSec also uses a third party protocol called *Internet Key Exchange* (*IKE*).

The biggest advantage of IPSec-based encryption technology is that IPSec forces authentication of each packet individually instead of the common practice of per-user authentication. In per-user authentication mechanisms, each user at the communicating ends is authenticated only once—at the beginning of the communication. However, as you might expect, the per-packet authentication strategy is slower than the per-user authentication strategy and incurs comparatively large overheads. Regardless, IPSec has been recommended as the security protocol for all VPN tunneling protocols, be it PPTP, L2F, or L2TP.

 NOTE

Refer to Chapter 6, "An Introduction to IPSec," for in-depth information about IPSec.

L2F Data Authentication

L2F authentication is accomplished at two levels. The first level of L2F-based authentication occurs when a remote user dials in to the ISP's POP. Here, a further tunnel establishment process commences only after the user has been authenticated. The second level of authentication is done by the host network's gateway, which does not establish a tunnel between the two ends (NAS and itself) until it authenticates the remote user.

Like PPTP, L2F also uses security services supported by PPP for authentication purposes. As a result, L2F uses PAP to authenticate a remote client when an L2F gateway receives a connection request. L2F also uses the following authentication schemes for enhanced data security:

◆ **CHAP (Challenge Handshake Authentication Protocol).** CHAP was developed to address the problem of sending passwords in cleartext while using PAP. In CHAP, when a client is challenged for identification, it responds with a secret hashed value derived from the MD5 hashing algorithm. If the same hash value is calculated at the server-end using the same procedure followed by the client, the client is authenticated successfully. Consequently, no cleartext passwords are exchanged during the process. Another problem commonly associated with PAP is that communicating ends are authenticated only once during the entire communication process. CHAP, however, can force multiple authentication challenges during a session, which makes it difficult for a hacker to break into the communication.

◆ **EAP (Extensible Authentication Protocol).** Unlike PAP and CHAP methods that are performed at the time of LCP configuration, during PPP connection setup, EAP is performed after the LCP phase, when PPP authentication is performed. Therefore, EAP allows extensive authentication because the increased number of connection parameters can be optionally used as authentication information.

 NOTE

L2F also uses the *Shiva Password Authentication Protocol* (*SPAP*) for authentication. SPAP is a proprietary protocol that uses encrypted passwords and can support enhanced functionality, such as changing passwords and support to callback mechanisms.

In addition to the aforementioned authentication mechanisms, L2F also employs *Remote Access Dial-In User Service* (*RADIUS*) and *Terminal Access Controller Access Control Service* (*TACACS*) as additional authentication services. Both services authenticate users that access the local remote access server, if the remote access server does not authenticate these users. RADIUS- and TACACS-based remote authentication is generally implemented by ISPs and large-scale organizations.

 NOTE

RASs generally are capable of processing a remote connection request and granting access. However, if the number of remote users is very large, they can forward the request to a RADIUS or TACACS server or a connected database that can authenticate the user and subsequently grant (or deny) access.

Refer to Chapter 11, "VPN Security Technologies," for detailed information on RADIUS and TACACS.

L2F Pros and Cons

Although L2F requires extensions to deal with different LCP and authentication options, it is more extensive than PPTP because it is a low level frame forwarding solution. It also provides a better VPN solution platform for enterprise networks than PPTP.

The main advantages of implementing an L2F-based solution include the following:

◆ Enhanced security of transactions

◆ Platform-independence

◆ No need of special arrangements with the ISP

◆ Support to a wide range of networking technologies, such as ATM, FDDI, IPX, NetBEUI, and Frame Relay

Despite the advantages mentioned above, there are a few disadvantages associated with L2F.

◆ L2F-based solutions require extensive configuration and support.

◆ Implementation of an L2F-based solution is highly dependent on the ISP. If the ISP does not support L2F, implementation of the solution is not possible.

◆ L2F does not provide flow control. As a result, if the tunnel is crowded data packets can be dropped arbitrarily. This causes the retransmission of data, which in turn further slows the transaction speed.

◆ Due to the large overheads associated with L2F authentication and encryption, transactions carried out across L2F-based tunnels are slow when compared to PPTP.

 NOTE

You might want to refer to RFC 2341 for further information on L2F. This RFC is available at http://www.armware.dk/RFC/rfc/rfc2341.html.

With the development of L2F, there were two tunneling technologies—PPTP and L2F—vying for the control of VPN market. These two protocols were incompatible. As a result, organizations were wary of either since the requirements of each were different. IETF decided to end the confusion by mandating that the features of the two technologies be combined to produce a protocol that would be used as a standard in VPN solutions. Layer 2 Tunneling Protocol (L2TP) was the outcome of this mandate.

Layer 2 Tunneling Protocol (L2TP)

Developed by IETF and endorsed by industry giants, such as Cisco Systems, Microsoft, 3COM, and Ascend, L2TP is a combination of earlier VPN protocols, PPTP and L2F. In fact, it merges the best features of PPTP and L2F. L2TP provides the flexible, scalable, and cost-effective remote access solution of L2F and the fast point-to-point connectivity of PPTP.

The key benefits offered by L2TP, therefore, are a mix of PPTP and L2F attributes. A benefit listing follows:

◆ L2TP supports multiple protocols and networking technologies, such as IP, ATM, FR, and PPP. As a result, it can support separate technologies with a common access infrastructure.

◆ L2TP allows various technologies to fully leverage the intermediate access infrastructure of the Internet and other public networks, such as PSTNs.

◆ L2TP does not require implementation of any extra software, such as additional drivers or operating system support. Consequently, neither the remote user nor the private intranet needs to implement special software.

◆ L2TP allows remote users with unregistered (or private) IP addresses to access a remote network across a public network.

◆ L2TP authentication and authorization is performed by the host network gateways. Therefore, ISPs do not need to maintain a user authentication database or access rights for remote users. In addition, private intranets can also define their own access and security policies. This makes the process of tunnel establishment much faster than earlier tunneling protocols.

The main feature of L2TP tunnels is that L2TP establishes PPP tunnels that, unlike PPTP, are not terminated at the nearest ISP site. Instead, these tunnels extend to the gateway of the host (or destination) network, as shown in Figure 5-15. L2TP tunnel requests can be initiated either by the remote user or the ISP's gateway.

 NOTE

L2TP Access Concentrator (LAC) is an L2TP component and is discussed in the following section.

When the PPP frames are sent through the L2TP tunnel, they are encapsulated as User Datagram Protocol (UDP) messages. L2TP uses these UDP messages both for tunneling data as well as maintaining the tunnel. Also, the L2TP tunneled data and tunnel maintenance packets, unlike the earlier tunneling protocols, have the same packet structure.

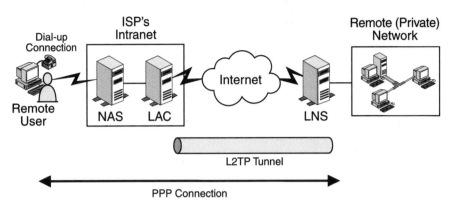

FIGURE 5-15 *The L2TP tunnel.*

L2TP Components

L2TP-based transactions basically employ three components, a *Network Access Server* (*NAS*), an *L2TP Access Concentrator* (*LAC*), and an *L2TP Network Server* (*LNS*).

Network Access Server (NAS)

L2TP NASs are point-to-point access devices that provide on-demand Internet connectivity to remote users who dial in (across a PSTN or ISDN line) using PPP connections. NASs are responsible for authenticating remote users at the ISP end and determining if a virtual dial-up connection is really required. Like PPTP NASs, L2TP NASs are located at the ISP site and act as the client in the L2TP tunnel establishment process. NASs can respond to and support multiple connection requests simultaneously and can support a wide range of clients (Microsoft networking products, Unix, Linux, VAX-VMS, and so on).

L2TP Access Concentrators

The role of LACs in L2TP tunneling technology is to establish a tunnel across public networks (such as PSTN, ISDN, or the Internet) to the LNS at the host network end. In this manner, LACs serve as the termination point of the physical media between the client-end and the LNS of the host network.

The most important thing that you should remember about LACs is that they are generally located at the ISP site. However, as you will learn a little later in this chapter, the remote user can also act as the LAC in the case of L2TP voluntary tunneling.

L2TP Network Server

LNSs, as mentioned earlier, are located at the host-network end. Therefore, they are used to terminate the L2TP connection at the host-network end in the same manner as LACs terminate the tunnel from the client end. When an LNS receives a request for a virtual connection from an LAC, it establishes the tunnel and authenticates the user who initiated the connection request. If the LNS accepts the connection request, it creates the virtual interface.

L2TP Processes

When a remote user needs to establish an L2TP tunnel across the Internet or other such public network, the following sequence of steps occurs:

1. The remote user sends the connection request to its nearest ISP's NAS and in doing initiates a PPP connection with the ISP end.

2. The NAS accepts the connection request after authenticating the end user. NAS uses PPP-based authentication methods, such as PAP, CHAP, SPAP, and EAP for the purpose.

3. NAS then triggers the LAC, which obtains the information with the LNS of the destination network.

4. Next, the LAC establishes an LAC-LNS tunnel over the intermediate internetwork between the two ends. The tunnel media can also be ATM, Frame Relay, or IP/UDP.

5. After the tunnel is established successfully, LAC allocates a Call ID (CID) to the connection and sends a notification message to the LNS. This notification message contains information that can be used to authenticate the remote user (original tunnel requestor). The message also carries LCP options that have been negotiated between the user and the LAC.

6. The LNS uses the information received within the notification message to authenticate the end user. If the user is authenticated successfully and the LNS accepts the tunnel request, a virtual PPP interface (L2TP tunnel) is established with the help of the LCP options received in the notification message.

7. The remote user and the LNS then begin exchanging data across the tunnel.

Figure 5-16 depicts the process of L2TP tunnel establishment.

L2TP, like PPTP and L2F, supports two L2TP operation modes, which include the following:

◆ **Incoming call mode.** In this operation mode, the connection request is initiated by the remote user.

◆ **Outgoing call mode.** In this operation mode, the connection request is initiated by the LNS. Therefore, the LNS instructs the LAC to place a call to the remote user. After the LAC establishes the call, the remote user and the LNS can exchange tunneled data packets.

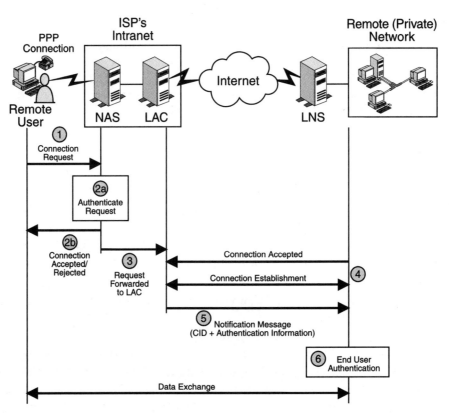

FIGURE 5-16 *Establishing the L2TP tunnel.*

L2TP Data Tunneling

Similar to PPTP tunneled packets, L2TP data packets undergo multiple levels of encapsulation. The various stages of L2TP data tunneling that are shown in Figure 5-17 include:

◆ **PPP Encapsulation of data.** Unlike PPTP-based encapsulation, the data is not encrypted before encapsulation. Only a PPP header is added to the original data payload.

◆ **L2TP Encapsulation of PPP frames.** After the original payload is encapsulated within a PPP packet an L2TP header is added to it.

◆ **UDP Encapsulation of L2TP frames.** Next, the L2TP-encapsulated packet is further encapsulated within a UDP frame. In other words, a UDP header is added to the L2TP encapsulated frame. The source and destination ports within this UDP header are set to 1701 per L2TP specifications.

◆ **IPSec Encapsulation of UDP datagrams.** After the L2TP frame is UDP encapsulated, this UDP frame is encrypted and an IPSec ESP header is added to it. An IPSec AH trailer is also appended to the encrypted and encapsulated datagram.

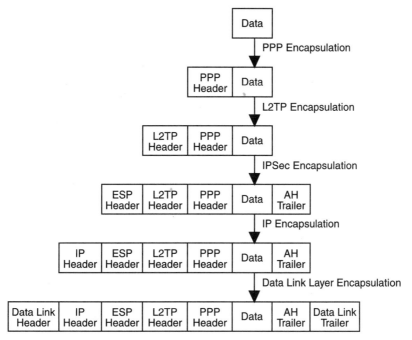

FIGURE 5-17 *The complete process of L2TP data tunneling.*

◆ **IP Encapsulation of IPSec-encapsulated datagrams.** Next, a final IP header is
   added to the IPSec encapsulated packet. This IP header contains the IP addresses of
   the L2TP server (LNS) and the remote user.

◆ **Data Link layer encapsulation**. A final Data Link layer header and trailer are added
   to the IP datagram derived from the final IP encapsulation. This Data Link layer
   header and trailer help the datagram reach the destination node. If the destination
   node is local, the Data Link layer header and trailer are LAN technology-based (for
   example, they could be Ethernet-based). On the other hand, if the datagram is
   meant for a remote destination, a PPP header and trailer are added to the L2TP
   tunneled data packet.

The process of de-tunneling L2TP tunneled data packets is the reverse of the tunneling procedure. When an L2TP component (LNS or end user) receives the L2TP tunneled packet, it
first processes the packet and removes the Data Link layer header and trailer. Next, the packet
is processed further and the IP header is removed. The data packet is then authenticated using
the information carried within the IPSec ESP header and AH trailer. The IPSec ESP header
is also used to decrypt the encrypted information. Next, the UDP header is processed and then
eliminated. The Tunnel ID and the Call ID in the L2TP header serve to identify the L2TP
tunnel and session. Finally, the PPP header is processed and removed and the PPP payload is
forwarded to the appropriate protocol driver for processing.

Figure 5-18 depicts the process of de-tunneling L2TP data packets.

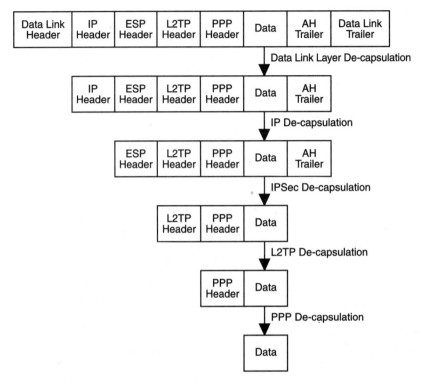

FIGURE 5-18 *De-tunneling L2TP data packets.*

L2TP Tunnel Modes

L2TP supports two tunnel modes—the *compulsory tunnel mode* and the *voluntary tunnel mode*. These tunnels play an important role in the secure transmission of data from one end to another. The following sections discuss these tunnels in further detail.

L2TP Compulsory Tunnel Mode

An L2TP compulsory tunnel, as shown in Figure 5-19, is established between the LAC at the ISP end and the LNS at the host network end. It is important for the successful establishment of a compulsory tunnel that the ISP be able to support L2TP technology. In addition, the ISP also has to play a key role in establishing L2TP tunnels because whether a compulsory tunnel is actually required for the given session is decided at the ISP end.

In the case of L2TP compulsory tunneling, the end user (or the client) is only a passive entity. Other than issuing the original connection request, the end user has no role to play in the process of tunnel establishment. Consequently, no major changes are required at the L2TP client-end.

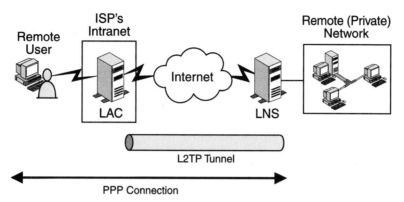

FIGURE 5-19 *L2TP compulsory tunneling.*

L2TP tunneling is considered a better option from the point of view of security because the dial-up connection at the client-end is used to establish the PPP connection with the ISP. As a result, the end user cannot access the Internet except through the gateway in the corporate intranet, which allows network administrators to implement stringent security mechanisms, access control, and accounting strategies.

The steps for establishing L2TP compulsory tunnels are depicted in Figure 15-20 and are as follows:

1. The remote user requests a PPP connection from the NAS located at the ISP site.
2. The NAS authenticates the user. This authentication process also helps the NAS learn about the identity of the user requesting the connection. If the user's identity maps to an entry in the ISP-maintained database, services that are allowed to the remote user are mapped. The NAS also determines LNS tunnel endpoints.
3. If the NAS is free to accept the connection request, a PPP link is established between the ISP and the remote user.
4. The LAC initiates an L2TP tunnel to the LNS at the host-network end.
5. If the connection is accepted by the LNS, the PPP frames undergo L2TP tunneling. These L2TP-tunneled frames are then forwarded to the LNS across the L2TP tunnel.
6. The LNS accepts the frames and retrieves the original PPP frame.
7. Finally, the LNS authenticates the user and the received data packets. If the user is validated successfully, the appropriate IP address is mapped to the frame and the frame is then forwarded to the destination node within the intranet.

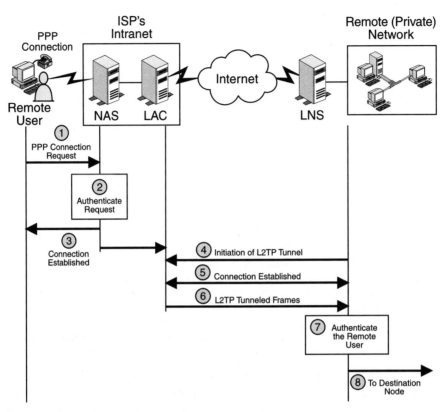

FIGURE 5-20 *Establishing an L2TP compulsory tunnel.*

L2TP Voluntary Tunnel Mode

An L2TP voluntary tunnel, as shown in Figure 5-21, is established between the remote user and the LNS located at the host network end. In this case, the remote user itself acts as the LAC. Because the ISP's role in the establishment of L2TP voluntary tunnels is minimal, the ISP's infrastructure is transparent to the communicating ends. This fact might remind you of PPTP-based tunnels in which the ISP intranet is transparent.

The biggest advantage of L2TP voluntary tunneling is that it allows remote users to connect to the Internet and establish multiple VPN sessions simultaneously. However, in order to make use of this benefit, the remote user must be assigned multiple IP addresses. One of these multiple IP addresses is used for PPP connection to the ISP and one is used to support each separate L2TP tunnel. But this benefit is also a disadvantage as the remote client and, consequently, the host network can be vulnerable to malicious attacks.

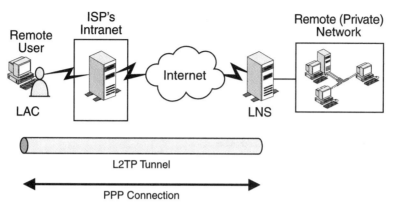

FIGURE 5-21 *L2TP voluntary tunneling.*

Establishing a voluntary L2TP tunnel is simpler than establishing a compulsory tunnel because the remote user employs a pre-established PPP connection to the ISP end. The steps involved in establishing L2TP voluntary tunnels include:

1. The LAC (in this case, the remote user) issues a request for an L2TP voluntary tunnel to the LNS.

2. If the tunnel request is accepted by the LNS, the LAC tunnels the PPP frames per L2TP specifications and forwards these frames through the tunnel.

3. The LNS accepts the tunneled frames, strips the tunneling information, and processes the frames.

4. Finally, the LNS authenticates the user identity and if the user is authenticated successfully, forwards the frames to the destination node within the intranet.

The process of L2TP voluntary tunnel establishment is illustrated in Figure 5-22.

L2TP Connection Control

As you might recall, PPTP uses separate TCP connections for tunnel maintenance. On the other hand, L2TP connection control and management frames are based on UDP. The format of a typical L2TP control message is depicted in Figure 5-23.

UDP datagrams, on which L2TP control messages are based, are connectionless in nature. This implies that they might be delivered out of sequence and are not acknowledged by the recipient upon receipt. For this reason, L2TP employs the technique of *message sequencing*. This technique ensures that messages are delivered to the other end in sequence. Two special fields—Next-Received and Next-Sent—are used in the L2TP control messages to ensure that packets are delivered to the other end in order.

Table 5-2 lists some of the commonly used L2TP control and maintenance messages.

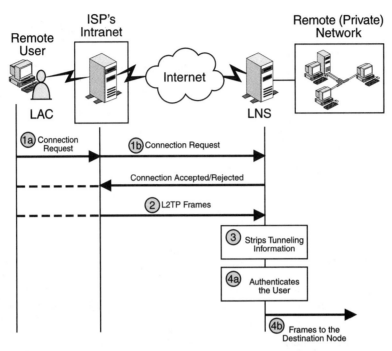

FIGURE 5-22 *Establishing L2TP voluntary tunnels.*

Data Link Header	IP Header	IPSec ESP Header	UDP Header	L2TP Message	IPSec ESP Trailer	IPSec ESP Authentication Trailer	Data Link Trailer

FIGURE 5-23 *Format of the L2TP control message.*

Table 5-2. Common L2TP Control and Maintenance Messages

Name	Description
Start-Control-Connection-Request	Request from the L2TP client to establish the control connection.
Start-Control-Connection-Reply	Response from the L2TP server (LNS) to the client's Start-Control-Connection-Request message. This message is also sent as a reply to the Outgoing-Call-Reply message.
Start-Control-Connection-Connected	Reply from the L2TP client to the LNS's Start-Control-Connection-Reply message.

Name	Description
Outgoing-Call-Request	Request from the L2TP client to the LNS to create the L2TP tunnel. This request contains the Call ID that identifies a call within the tunnel.
Outgoing-Call-Reply	Response from the L2TP LNS to the client's Outgoing-Call-Request message.
Hello	Keep-alive message sent either by the LNS or the client. If this message is not acknowledged by the other end the tunnel is terminated.
Set-Link-Info	Message from either side to set the PPP-negotiated options.
Call-Disconnect-Notify	Response from the L2TP server to indicate that the specified call within the L2TP tunnel is to be terminated.
WAN-Error-Notify	Message from the L2TP server (LNS) to all the connected L2TP clients to notify it of errors in the server's PPP interface.
Stop-Control-Connection-Request	Message from the L2TP client or server to notify the other end about the termination of the control connection.
Stop-Control-Connection-Reply	Response from the opposite end to the Stop-Control-Connection-Request message.
Stop-Control-Connection-Notification	Response from the opposite end to indicate that the tunnel is to be terminated.

L2TP Security

L2TP uses PPP authentication methods to authenticate users. The commonly implemented L2TP authentication schemes include:

- ◆ PAP and SPAP
- ◆ EAP
- ◆ CHAP

In addition to the aforementioned authentication mechanisms, L2TP also uses IPSec to authenticate individual data packets. Although this reduces the speed of transactions considerably, using IPSec for per-packet authentication ensures that hackers and crackers cannot take chances with your tunnels and data.

L2TP over IPSec Authentication

IPSec plays a key role in securing L2TP-based packet authentication. IPSec authenticates individual packets even after the remote user has been authenticated successfully. Additionally, IPSec takes care of the following:

◆ Encrypting cleartext PPP payloads

◆ Automatically generating encryption keys and securing key exchange over the established tunnel

Figures 5-24 and 5-25 illustrate the role of IPSec in protecting L2TP compulsory and voluntary tunnels.

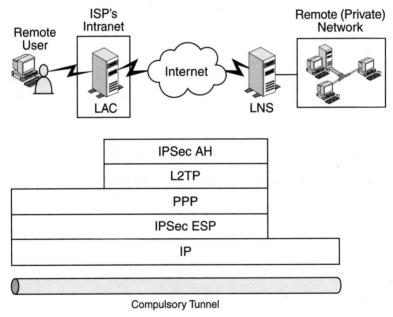

FIGURE 5-24 *Protecting L2TP compulsory tunnels using IPSec.*

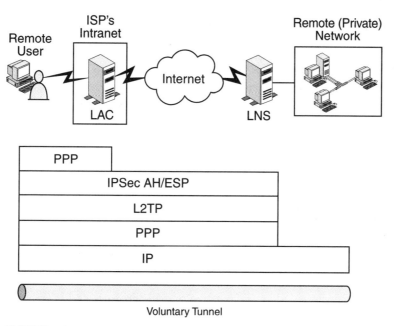

FIGURE 5-25 *Protecting L2TP voluntary tunnels using IPSec.*

L2TP Data Encryption

L2TP often uses *ECP* for encryption purposes. ECP stand for Encryption Control Protocol and is used to negotiate mutually agreeable encryption algorithms, such as DES, after the link has been established. Therefore, ECP offers advanced encryption capabilities in addition to the built-in encryption mechanisms supported by PPP. However, the main disadvantage associated with ECP is that keys, once exchanged between the two ends, are not refreshed periodically. This increases the possibility that a hacker can break into the keys and, subsequently, the transaction during a prolonged data-exchange session.

 NOTE

L2TP also uses MPPE occasionally. However, this is a weak encryption mechanism and is usually avoided.

L2TP Pros and Cons

The main advantages offered by L2TP are as listed below:

◆ L2TP is a generic solution. In other words, it is platform independent. It also supports various networking technologies. In addition, it can support transmissions across non-IP WAN links without the need of an IP.

◆ L2TP tunneling is transparent to the ISP as well as remote users. Therefore, no additional configuration is required at the user or ISP end.

◆ L2TP allows an organization to control the authentication of users instead of the ISP.

◆ L2TP provides flow control and as a result data packets can be dropped arbitrarily if the tunnel is crowded. This makes L2TP-based transactions faster than L2F-based transactions.

◆ L2TP allows remote users with unregistered (or private) IP addresses to access a remote network across a public network.

◆ L2TP offers enhanced security due to the use of IPSec-based payload encryption during tunneling, and implementation of the IPSec's per-packet authentication capability.

The implementation of L2TP also has its disadvantages. Major disadvantages of L2TP-based implementations follow:

◆ L2TP is slower than either PPTP or L2F because it uses IPSec to authenticate each packet received.

◆ Although PPTP is shipped as a built-in VPN solution, a Routing and Remote Access Server (RRAS) needs extensive configuration.

 NOTE

You might refer to RFC 2661 for detailed information on L2TP. This RFC is available at http://www.armware.dk/RFC/rfc/rfc2661.html.

Table 5-3 summarizes all three VPN protocols associated with Layer 2.

Table 5-3. Layer 2 Protocol Summary

Feature	PPTP	L2F	L2TP
Support to multiple protocols	Yes	Yes	Yes
Support to multiple PPP links	No	Yes	Yes
Support to multiple connections per tunnel	No	Yes	Yes
Operation modes supported	Incoming & Outgoing	Incoming	Incoming
Tunnel modes supported	Voluntary	Voluntary & Compulsory	Voluntary & Compulsory
Carrier protocol	IP/GRE	IP/UDP, IP/FR, IP/ATM	IP/UDP, IP/FR, IP/ATM
Control Protocol	TCP, Port: 1723	UDP, Port: 1701	UDP, Port: 1701
Authentication mechanisms	MS-CHAP, PAP	CHAP, PAP, SPAP, EAP, IPSec, RADIUS & TACACS	CHAP, PAP, SPAP, EAP, IPSec, RADIUS & TACACS
Encryption mechanisms	MPPE	MPPE, IPSec	MPPE, IPSec, ECP

Summary

In this chapter you learned about the tunneling protocols associated with Layer 2 of the OSI model. These protocols are PPTP, L2F, and L2TP. You learned about the working of each protocol in detail, including the components that are involved in each protocol tunneling, the processes involved, and the connection control maintenance employed by each protocol. You explored the process of establishing a tunnel for each protocol and the process of data tunneling and its role in data security. You also explored the security aspects of each protocol, including the various authentication and encryption mechanisms used by each protocol to ensure that data is secure while being tunneled. Finally, you looked into the advantages and disadvantages associated with each protocol.

Check Your Understanding

Multiple Choice Questions

1. Which of the following are tunneling protocols associated with Layer 2 of the OSI model?

   a. PPTP

   b. L2F

   c. IPSec

   d. L2TP

2. The network port used by L2F for connection establishment and control is
   _____.

   a. TCP: 1701

   b. UDP: 1723

   c. UDP: 1701

   d. TCP: 1723

3. The network port used by PPTP for tunneling data to the other end is
   _____.

   a. IP: 47

   b. TCP: 47

   c. UDP: 47

   d. TCP: 1723

4. Which of the following are valid frames used for connection control?

   a. Link Control Protocol

   b. Link termination

   c. Network Control Protocol

   d. Link establishment

5. Which of the following tunneling protocols is natively supported by Windows NT 4.0 Server?

   a. PPTP

   b. L2TP

   c. L2F

   d. All of the above

6. Which of the following are public networks?
   a. ISDN
   b. PSTNs
   c. Internet
   d. Intranet

7. Which of the following are components of an L2TP-based tunnel?
   a. LLC
   b. LNS
   c. NAS
   d. LSN

8. Which of the following tunneling protocols first allowed multiple connections (calls) per tunnel?
   a. PPTP
   b. L2TP
   c. L2F
   d. None of the above

9. Which of the following statements about L2F is true?
   a. It is a proprietary tunneling protocol by Cisco.
   b. It offers advanced flow-control services.
   c. It supports voluntary tunnels.
   d. It supports compulsory tunnels.

10. Which of the following tunneling protocols support IKE?
    a. PPTP
    b. L2TP
    c. IPSec
    d. L2F

Short Answer Questions

1. How is L2F-based tunneling different from L2TP-based tunneling?

2. Best Solutions, Inc. is a large firm in the Midwest that is slowly expanding toward the East Coast. Their network administrator, Brian, recently attended a seminar on enterprise network security. He was quite impressed by the L2TP-based VPN technology, as it would allow him to ensure data security without having to invest much cash. As a result, he implemented what he learned during his seminar. However, a minor case of hacking was still reported. What might be wrong and how should Brian deal with it?

Answers

Multiple Choice Answers

1. **a, b,** and **d.** Point-to-Point Tunneling Protocol (PPTP), Layer 2 Forwarding (L2F), and Layer 2 Tunneling Protocol (L2TP) are the tunneling protocols associated with Layer 2 (the Data Link layer) of the OSI model. IPSec is a layer 3 (Network layer) tunneling protocol.

2. **c.** The network port used by L2F for connection control is UDP: 1701. The port TCP: 1723 is used by PPTP for establishment of connection control.

3. **a.** The network port used by PPTP for tunneling data to the other end is IP: 47.

4. **b** and **d.** PPP uses three frames for link control. These include: link termination, link establishment, and link maintenance frames.

5. **a.** PPTP is a proprietary Microsoft protocol. Therefore, it is shipped with all Microsoft networking products, including Windows 9x, Windows NT 4.0 Server and Workstation, and Windows 2000.

6. **b** and **c.** Public Switched Telephone Networks (PSTNs) and the Internet are real public networks. Intranets are private to a corporation or an organization. Integrated Switched Digital Network (ISDN) is a digital switching technology. Public networks can use ISDN-based connectivity.

7. **b** and **c.** L2TP Access Concentrator (LAC), L2TP Network Server (LNS), and Network Access Server (NAS) are the three components of L2TP.

8. **c.** L2F was the first tunneling protocol to incorporate the mechanism of multiplexing multiple connections within a single tunnel.

9. **a** and **d.** L2F is Cisco's proprietary VPN tunneling protocol and supports compulsory tunnels because a direct tunnel between the remote user and the host network's gateway.

10. **c.** Internet Key Exchange (IKE) is a third-party protocol supported by IPSec. It offers secure key exchange and key management during tunneling and other Internet-based transactions.

Short Answers

1. Although the functionality of L2F and L2TP is very similar, a few differences exist between the two:

   1. L2F only supports the incoming operation mode. Therefore, only the end user can initiate a connection to the private network. Conversely, L2TP supports both incoming and outgoing operation mode. As a result, L2TP offers network administrators the capability to trace remote users who have a roaming profile.

    2.   L2F does not support flow control. Therefore, if the tunnel is crowded data packets can be dropped arbitrarily. This necessitates the retransmission of data, which in turn further slows the transaction speed. L2TP, on the other hand, supports flow control mechanism and does not face the problem of crowded tunnels.

2.   Brian has probably implemented L2TP voluntary tunnels, which are directly established between the remote user and the host network gateway. For this, the allocation of multiple IP addresses is required for each remote user. As a result, the end user can connect to the Internet as well as take an active part in tunneling data. However, this approach makes the client vulnerable to hackers as not all transactions involving IP addresses are secure. Consequently, the hacker can also get to the private intranet using the remote client.

Chapter 6

An Introduction to IPSec

Many of us tend to carry a mistaken notion that the main aim of VPNs is to bring down the total cost of ownership (TCO) of a network that spans long distances. This perception is far from the truth. The main aim of VPNs is not to reduce the total cost of implementation of a long-distance network, but to ensure the safety and security of data while it is being transmitted across an unsecured intermediate network. The fact that by the implementation of VPN technology, you can also bring down the total cost of implementation of your intranet is just an added benefit.

In Chapter 5, "Tunneling Protocols at Layer 2," you learned about VPN protocols, such as PPTP, L2F, and L2TP that operate at Layer 2 of the OSI model. This chapter focuses on the VPN protocol that operates at Layer 3 of the same model. Because of its strong authentication, confidentiality, and key management characteristics, IPSec has fast emerged as the de facto VPN standard. In fact, the majority of VPN solutions of today are based on IPSec.

So, what is IPSec? How does it ensure security of data during transmissions? Why has it become so popular? This chapter attempts to answer these questions.

Understanding IPSec

The term IPSec is the short form of the longer term *Internet Protocol SECurity*. It refers to a suite of protocols (AH, ESP, FIP-140-1, and other standards) that were developed by the Internet Engineering Task Force (IETF). The main aim behind the development of IPSec was to provide a security framework at the third layer (Network layer) of the OSI model, as shown in Figure 6-1.

Application Layer
Presentation Layer
Session Layer
Transport Layer
Network Layer
IPSec
Data Link Layer
Physical Layer

FIGURE 6-1 *The position of IPSec in the OSI model.*

Despite the physical implementation of an IP-based network or the transport mechanism used, every communication in an IP-based network is based on the IP protocol. As a result, when a strong security mechanism is integrated with the IP protocol, the entire network is secure because every communication has to pass through the third layer. (This is the reason why IPSec was developed as a Layer 3 protocol instead of Layer 2.) In addition, the developers of IPSec have kept the current version of IP—IPv4—as well as the future version of IP—IPv6—in mind. Consequently, the IPSec protocol suite is not only compatible with the current breed of IP networks, but with those to come.

Also, with IPSec all applications running at the Application layer of the OSI model are dependent on the Network layer to route data from source to destination. Because IPSec is tightly integrated with IP, these applications can use IPSec's inherent security services without the need for major modifications. Also like IP, IPSec is transparent to the end users who do not need to be aware of the extra security framework constantly at work behind the scenes.

IPSec Security Associations

Security Associations (SAs) are a fundamental concept of the IPSec protocol suite. As quoted by the developers of IPSec, an SA is a logical unidirectional connection between two entities that use IPSec services. An IPSec SA defines

◆ The authentication protocols, keys, and algorithms.

◆ The mode and keys for the authentication algorithms used by Authentication Header (AH) or Encapsulation Security Payload (ESP) protocols of the IPSec suite.

◆ The encryption and decryption algorithms and keys.

◆ The key-related information, such as the change interval and the time-to-live interval of the keys.

◆ The information related to the SA itself, which includes the SA source address and the time-to-live interval.

◆ The usage and the size of any cryptographic synchronization used, if any.

Figure 6-2 depicts a generic representation of an IPSec SA.

SPI	Destination IP Address	Security Protocol

FIGURE 6-2 *A generic representation of the three fields of an IPSec SA.*

As shown in Figure 6-2, the IPSec SA is comprised of three fields.

◆ **SPI (Security Parameter Index).** This is a 32-bit field that identifies the security protocol, as defined by the Security protocol field, from the IPSec suite in use. SPI is carried as a part of the header of this security protocol and is normally selected by the destination system during the SA negotiation.

◆ **Destination IP address.** This is the IP address of the destination node. Although it might be a broadcast, unicast, or multicast address, the current SA management mechanism is defined only for unicast systems.

◆ **Security protocol.** This represents the IPSec security protocol, which might be either AH or ESP.

 NOTE

Broadcasts are meant for all the systems that belong to a network or subnet. On the other hand, multicasts are sent to multiple (but not all) nodes of the given network or subnet. Unicast addresses are meant for a single destination node.

Because of the unidirectional nature of an SA, two SAs must be defined between the communicating ends—one in each direction. Also, an SA can provide security services to a VPN session that is being protected by either AH or by ESP. Therefore, if a session needs to be doubly protected by both AH and ESP, two SAs must be defined in each direction. This set of SAs is referred to as the *SA bundle*.

An IPSec SA uses two databases. The *Security Association Database* (*SAD*) maintains the information related to each SA. This information includes the algorithm keys, SA lifespan, and sequence numbers. The second IPSec SA database, the *Security Policy Database* (*SPD*), maintains the information about security services along with an ordered list of inbound and outbound policy entries. Much like firewall rules and packet filters, these entries define what traffic must be processed and what traffic must be ignored per IPSec standards.

As defined by the Security protocol field of the SA, two protocols from the IPSec suite are considered to be the key security protocols.

IPSec Security Protocols

The IPSec suite offers three main capabilities. These include the following:

- **Authentication and data integrity.** IPSec provides a strong mechanism to verify the authenticity of the sender and identify any previously undetected modification of the data packet's content by the recipient. IPSec protocols offer strong protection against spoofing, sniffing, and denial-of-service attacks.

- **Confidentiality.** IPSec protocols encrypt the data using advanced cryptographic techniques, which prevents unauthorized users from accessing the data while it is in transit. IPSec also uses the tunneling mechanism to hide the IP addresses of source (sender) and destination (receiver) nodes from eavesdroppers.

- **Key management.** IPSec uses a third-party protocol, Internet Key Exchange (IKE), to negotiate the security protocols and encryption algorithms before and during a communication session. More importantly, IPSec distributes and tracks encryption keys and updates these keys when required.

The first two capabilities of the IPSec suite—authentication and data integrity, and confidentiality—are provided by two key protocols in the IPSec protocol suite. These protocols include Authentication Header (AH) and Encapsulating Security Payload (ESP).

The third capability, namely key management, falls within the realm of another protocol, which was adopted by the IPSec suite because of its strong key management services. This protocol is IKE. You'll learn more about IKE later in this chapter.

The Authentication Header Protocol

The Authentication Header (AH) protocol adds an additional header to the IP datagram. As the name suggests, this header serves to authenticate the origin of the IP datagram at the receiver end. In addition, this header helps identify any undetected modifications to the content of the datagram by an unauthorized user during transit. However, AH does not provide confidentiality.

In order to generate the AH, a Hashed Authentication Message Code (HMAC) is generated at the sender end. This hashed code is generated on the basis of the specified SA, which in turn determines the transformation sequence that will be applied to the datagram. The resultant code is then attached to the datagram after the original IP header. At the receiver end, the HMAC is decoded and serves to establish the authenticity of the sender as well as the integrity of the message.

 NOTE

Commonly implemented hashing codes (also known as security transformations) used in AH are HMAC-MD5 and HMAC-SHA1. DES-MAC is an optional AH authentication transformation.

AH doesn't offer confidentiality during a transmission. It only adds an additional header to the IP datagram; the rest of the datagram's content is left as is. In addition, AH does not protect any field in the IP header because some of them might change while in transit. Only those fields that do not change during transit are protected by AH. Source IP address and destination IP address are such fields and, hence, are protected by AH.

Figure 6-3 depicts the original IP datagram after the IPSec AH has been added.

IP Header	AH Header	Payload

FIGURE 6-3 *The IP packet after the authentication header has been added to it.*

An authentication header is 24-bytes long and the format of the IPSec Authentication Header is shown in Figure 6-4.

Next Header	Payload Length	Reserved
Security Parameter Index		
Sequence Number		
Authentication Data (variable size)		

FIGURE 6-4 *The format of the IPSec Authentication Header.*

The various fields that make up the AH follow:

◆ **Next Header.** This field identifies the security protocol.

◆ **Payload Length.** This field specifies the length of the message (payload) that follows the AH header.

◆ **Reserved.** As the name suggests, this field is reserved and is not used.

◆ **SPI (Security Parameter Index).** This field specifies the context in which the various security associations (to the destination address and the security protocol used) should be interpreted.

◆ **Sequence Number.** This field identifies the sequence of the datagram in a given session.

◆ **Authentication Data.** This field contains the authentication data along with the Integrity Check Value (ICV), which is used to check the integrity of the message being sent.

The Encapsulating Security Payload (ESP) Protocol

The main aim of ESP is to provide confidentiality in addition to sender authentication and the verification of data integrity during transit. ESP encrypts the content of the datagram using advanced encryption algorithms, as specified by the SA. Some of the encryption algorithms used by ESP include DES-CBG, NULL, CAST-128, IDEA, and 3DES. The authentication algorithms are similar to those used in AH and include HMAC-MD5 and HMAC-SHA.

As compared to AH, which offers authentication and data integrity to the IP datagram, ESP does not protect the entire datagram. Only the payload is protected, as shown in Figure 6-5. However, ESP is strong in terms of encryption. Also, it does not burden the CPU with extra load. As a result, it is much faster than AH. But, the 24 bytes that it tends to add to the datagram can slow down the throughput calculation and fragmentation.

| IP Header | ESP Header | Payload | ESP Trailer | ESP Authentication |

FIGURE 6-5 *The IP packet after the ESP header and trailer are added.*

The format of the ESP-based IP datagram, as shown in Figure 6-6, includes the following fields:

◆ **SPI (Security Parameter Index).** This field specifies the context in which various SAs (with the destination address and the security protocol used) should be interpreted.

◆ **Sequence Number.** This field identifies the sequence of the datagram in a given session.

◆ **Padding.** This field is used to pad the payload, if the payload is not of requisite length.

◆ **Pad length.** This field indicates the length of the padding. It helps the receiver demarcate the original payload from the padded bits.

◆ **Next Header.** This field identifies the security protocol used for encapsulation.

◆ **Authentication Data.** This field contains the authentication data along with the Integrity Check Value (ICV), which is used to check the integrity of the message being sent.

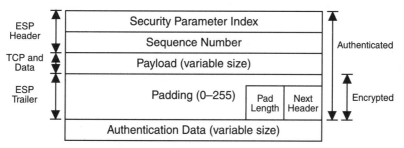

FIGURE 6-6 *The format of ESP header.*

Now that you have a fair idea of key IPSec protocols, you can move on to the various modes IPSec offers to ensure safer transmissions.

IPSec Modes

SAs in IPSec are implemented in two modes concurrently. Depicted in Figure 6-7, these are the *Transport* mode and the *Tunnel* mode. Both AH and ESP can operate in either mode.

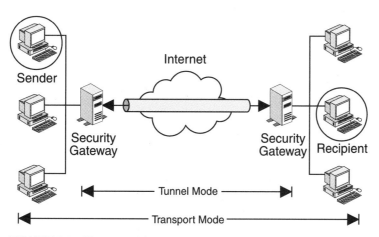

FIGURE 6-7 *The two IPSec modes.*

Transport Mode

Transport mode protects upper-layer protocols and applications. In Transport mode, the IPSec header is inserted between the IP header and the header of the upper-layer protocol, as depicted in Figure 6-8.

Original IP datagram

IP Header	Payload

Datagram with IPSec (AH or ESP) in Transport mode

IP Header	AH or ESP Header	Payload	ESP Trailer	ESP Authentication

Encrypted

Authenticated (ESP)

Authenticated (AH)

FIGURE 6-8 _IPSec Transport mode—a generic representation._

Figure 6-9 shows AH Transport mode. The IPSec header is inserted between the original IP header and the upper-layer protocol header.

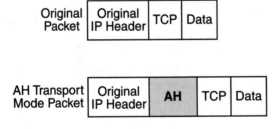

FIGURE 6-9 *AH Transport mode.*

In the case of ESP, the ESP trailer and ESP authentication data are present after the original payload. The new header is inserted before payload, ESP trailer, or ESP authentication data, as shown in Figure 6-10.

Transport mode causes less processing overhead; hence it's faster. However, it is not very effective in the case of ESP as neither authentication nor encryption for the IP header is possible.

FIGURE 6-10 *ESP Transport mode.*

Tunnel Mode

Unlike Transport mode, Tunnel mode protects the entire IP datagram. The entire IP datagram is encapsulated in another IP datagram and an IPSec header is inserted between the original and the new IP header. Figure 6-11 shows a generic representation of IPSec Tunnel mode.

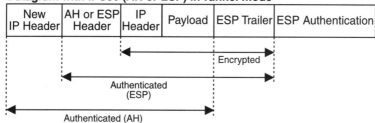

FIGURE 6-11 *IPSec Tunnel mode—a generic representation.*

In AH Tunnel mode, the new (AH) header is inserted between the new IP header and the original header, as shown in Figure 6-12.

In the case of ESP, the original datagram ends up as the payload for the new ESP packet, and, as a result of which, both encryption as well as authentication can be implemented with ease. Figure 6-13 represents the ESP Tunnel mode.

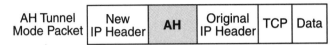

FIGURE 6-12 *AH Tunnel mode.*

Original Packet | Original IP Header | TCP | Data

ESP Tunnel Mode Packet | New IP Header | **ESP Header** | Original IP Header | TCP | Data | **ESP Trailer** | Optional ESP Authentication

FIGURE 6-13 *ESP Tunnel mode.*

As mentioned earlier, the IPSec protocol suite uses a non-IPSec protocol for the purpose of key exchange and management. The following section throws more light on the subject of IKE, its phases, and modes.

Internet Key Exchange

Originally known as ISAKMP/Oakley, where ISAKMP stands for Internet Security Association and Key Management Protocol, IKE helps communicating parties negotiate security parameters and authentication keys before a secure IPSec session is implemented. The security parameters that are negotiated are the ones defined in SA. Besides negotiating and establishing security parameters and cryptographic keys, IKE also modifies these parameters and keys, when required, during a session. IKE is also responsible for deleting these SAs and keys after an IPSec-based communication session is completed.

 NOTE

IKE is a hybrid of ISAKMP, Oakley, and SKEME protocols. It uses ISAKMP as the basic framework and subsets of services of Oakley and SKEME protocols for key exchange.

The main advantages offered by IKE include the following:

◆ IKE is not technology dependent. Therefore, it can be used with any security mechanism.

◆ IKE mechanism, although not fast, is highly efficient because a large number of security associations are negotiated with relatively fewer messages.

As defined by the ISAKMP framework, IKE works in two phases—*Phase I* and *Phase II*.

IKE Phases

Phase I and II are the two phases that make up an IKE-based session. Figure 6-14 depicts a generic representation of these two IKE phases. In an IKE-based session, it is assumed that a secure channel already exists. This secure channel must be established before any negotiation takes place.

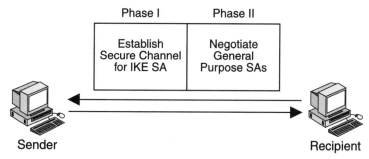

FIGURE 6-14 *The two IKE phases—Phase I and Phase II.*

IKE Phase I

IKE Phase I first authenticates the communicating ends and then establishes a secure IKE channel for establishing the SA. Subsequently, the communicating parties negotiate a mutually agreeable ISAKMP SA, which is comprised of encryption algorithms, hash functions, and authentication methods that serve to protect the encryption keys. The underlying ISAKMP framework uses the security association that is established in this phase.

After the encryption mechanism and hash functions are agreed upon, a shared master secret key is generated. The following information is used to generate this shared secret key:

◆ Diffie-Hellman values

◆ SPI of ISAKMP SA in the form of cookies

◆ Random numbers known as *nonces* (used for signing purposes)

If the two parties agree to use a public key-based authentication, they also need to exchange their IDs. After exchanging the requisite information, both sides generate their own set of keys using this shared secret. In this manner, cryptographic keys are generated without actually exchanging any keys across the network.

IKE Phase II

Whereas Phase I negotiation establishes the SA for ISAKMP, Phase II deals with the establishment of SAs for IPSec. In this phase, SAs used by various services are negotiated. Authentication mechanisms, hash functions, and encryption algorithms that protect the subsequent IPSec packets (using AH and ESP) form a part of this phase's SA.

Phase II negotiations occur more frequently than Phase I negotiation. Typically, a negotiation can be repeated every 4-5 minutes. This frequent modification of encryption keys prevents hackers from breaking these keys and, subsequently, the content of the original packet.

Generally, a Phase II session corresponds to a single Phase I session. However, multiple Phase II exchanges can also be supported by a single Phase I instance. This makes the normally slow IKE transactions comparatively faster.

Oakley is one of the protocols on which IKE is based. Oakley in turn defines four common IKE modes.

IKE Modes

The four commonly implemented IKE modes follow:

◆ Main mode
◆ Aggressive mode
◆ Quick mode
◆ New Group mode

Main Mode

Main mode verifies and protects the identities of the parties that are involved in the transaction. In this mode, six messages are exchanged between the communicating ends. Of these messages:

◆ The first two messages are used to negotiate the security policy for the exchange.
◆ The next two messages serve to exchange Diffie-Hellman keys and nonces. The keys later play an important role in the encryption mechanism. Nonces must be signed by the opposite party for verification purposes.
◆ The final two messages of this mode are used to authenticate the communicating parties with the help of signatures, hashes, and, optionally, with certificates.

Figure 6-15 depicts the transaction in IKE Main mode.

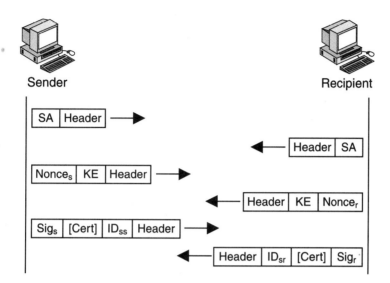

Header: an ISAKMP header corresponding to the used mode
SA: the negotiated Security Association
Nonce: a random number sent for signing
KE: key exchange data for Diffie-Hellman key exchange
Sig: signature payload used for authentication
Cert: a certificate for the public key
ID: identity payload (ss is sender and sr is recipient in Phase I)

FIGURE 6-15 *Message exchange in IKE Main mode.*

Aggressive Mode

Aggressive mode is essentially the same as Main mode. The only difference between the two modes is that instead of the six messages of Main mode, only three messages are exchanged. As a result, Aggressive mode is much faster than Main mode. The messages that are exchanged during Aggressive mode follow:

◆ The first message is used to propose a security policy, pass data for key material, and exchange nonces for signing and subsequent identification.

◆ The next message acts as the response to the first message. It authenticates the recipient and finalizes the security policy along with the keys.

◆ The final message of this mode is used to authenticate the sender (or the initiator of the given session).

Figure 6-16 depicts the transaction in IKE Aggressive mode.

Both Main mode and Aggressive mode belong to IKE Phase I.

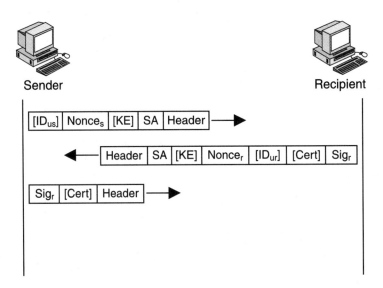

Header: an ISAKMP header corresponding to the used mode
SA: the negotiated Security Association
Nonce: a random number sent for signing
KE: key exchange data for Diffie-Hellman key exchange
Sig: signature payload used for authentication
Cert: a certificate for the public key
ID: identity payload (us is sender and ur is recipient in Phase II)

FIGURE 6-16 *Message exchange in IKE Aggressive mode.*

Quick Mode

The third IKE mode, Quick mode, is a Phase II mode. It is used to negotiate the SA for IPSec security services. In addition, Quick mode may also generate new keying material. If the policy of Perfect Forward Secrecy (PFS) is negotiated in the earlier phase (Phase I), a full Diffie-Hellman key exchange is initiated. Otherwise, new keys are generated using hash values.

Message exchange in Quick mode is depicted in Figure 6-17.

New Group Mode

The New Group mode is used to negotiate a new private group to facilitate Diffie-Hellman key exchange. Figure 6-18 depicts New Group mode. Although this mode occurs after Phase I, it is not a part of Phase II.

In addition to the four commonly implemented IKE modes, there is the Informational mode. This mode is associated with Phase II exchanges and SAs. As the name suggests, this mode provides involved parties with some additional information, generally related to failure(s) in negotiations. For example, if decryption failed at the receiver end or the signature was not verified successfully, Informational mode is used to notify the other party.

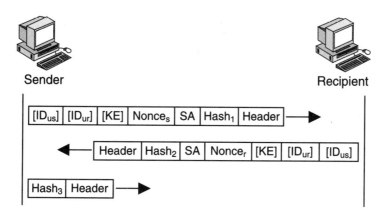

Header: an ISAKMP header corresponding to the used mode
SA: the negotiated Security Association
Nonce: a random number sent for signing
KE: key exchange data for Diffie-Hellman key exchange
Hash: the output of a hash function over specified payload data
ID: identity payload (us is sender and ur is recipient in Phase II)

FIGURE 6-17 *Message exchange in IKE Quick mode, which belongs to Phase II.*

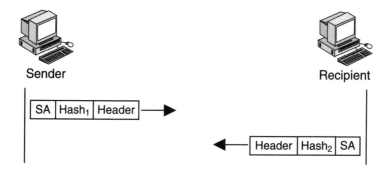

Header: an ISAKMP header corresponding to the used mode
SA: the negotiated Security Association
Hash: the output of a hash function over specified payload data

FIGURE 6-18 *Message exchange in IKE New Group mode.*

Summary

In this chapter, you learned about the most commonly implemented VPN security protocol—IPSec. You learned about the basics of IPSec and how security associations form the base of the IPSec protocol. Authentication Header (AH) and Encapsulating Security Payload (ESP) are the key IPSec protocols. While AH serves to protect the complete original packet, ESP protects only the payload part of the original message. Next, you learned about IPSec modes—the Tunnel mode and the Transport mode—and the role they play in protecting original IP packets (or datagrams) from unauthorized access, sniffing, spoofing, and hijacking.

Finally, you learned about Internet Key Exchange (IKE), which plays a very important role in the management of cryptographic keys. The two IKE phases (Phase I and II) were discussed. The four commonly implemented IKE modes—Main, Aggressive, Quick, and New Group—were also briefly discussed.

Check Your Understanding

Multiple Choice Questions

1. Which of the following fields make up an IPSec SA?

    a. SPI

    b. Payload

    c. Destination IP Address

    d. Security Protocol

2. Which of the following databases contain entries that might resemble a firewall rule?

    a. SPD

    b. SPI

    c. SAP

    d. SAD

3. _____ offers confidentiality and data integrity, but not the capability for key management.

    a. IKE

    b. AH

    c. ESP

    d. None of the above

4. Which of the modes listed below is NOT a valid IPSec mode?

    a. Informational mode

    b. Tunnel mode

    c. Aggressive mode

    d. Quick mode

5. Which of the following statements is true?

    a. Main mode is slower than Quick mode.

    b. ESP in Transport mode offers higher security than ESP in Tunnel mode.

    c. Aggressive mode belongs to IKE Phase II.

    d. All of the above statements are correct.

Short Questions

1. Why do you think IPSec was developed as a Layer 3 protocol instead of Layer 2 protocol?

2. What are nonces and what role do they play IKE-based exchanges?

Answers

Multiple Choice Answers

1. **a, c,** and **d.** Security Parameter Index (SPI), Destination IP address, and Security payload are the three fields that comprise an IPSec security association.

2. **a.** The Security Policy Database maintains the information about security services along with an ordered list of inbound and outbound policy entries. Much like firewall rules and packet filters, these entries define the traffic that must be processed as per the IPSec standards and the traffic that must be ignored.

3. **c.** AH offers authentication and data integrity, but not confidentiality. IKE is only meant for key management and related issues. ESP offers strong confidentiality in addition to authentication and data integrity.

4. **a, c,** and **d.** Tunnel mode and Transport mode are the only IPSec modes. Main, Aggressive, Quick, Informational, and New Group modes are IKE modes.

5. **a.** Quick mode is faster than Main mode because only three messages are exchanged in Quick mode whereas in Main mode six messages are sent back and forth between the communicating ends.

Short Answers

1. IPSec was developed as a Layer 3 protocol instead of Layer 2 protocol because today's long-distance (internetwork) communications are predominantly IP based due to the immense popularity of the Internet, an IP-based network. Therefore, if a strong security mechanism is tightly woven into the IP framework, the entire network can be secured and protected as all the communication must pass through the Network layer in which the IP functions.

2. Nonces are randomly generated numbers that must be signed by the opposite communicating party for verification. Hence, nonces server as another authentication mechanism.

PART III

Building and Implementing VPNs

Chapter 7

The preceding six chapters have given you technical insight as to what pertains to the much-hyped VPN technology. You are now familiar with the requirements of a VPN, the building blocks of a VPN, various VPN architectures, and the security components of a VPN setup. By now, you must also be fairly comfortable with tunneling technology and the various tunneling protocols, such as PPTP, L2F, L2TP, and IPSec. With this knowledge, the next logical step in your VPN education is toward VPN implementation.

In this chapter, you will learn about the various issues and considerations that you must keep in mind when designing a VPN-based solution for your organization. This chapter explores VPN design issues, such as security, addressing and routing, performance, scalability, and interoperability. Issues related to the firewall implementation, NAT, Domain Name Service (DNS), key distribution, and trust relationships between involved entities are also covered. You will also consider each VPN environment—remote access, intranet, and extranet—individually to understand the considerations involved when implementing VPNs in these environments. Finally, you'll learn about the five generic steps of VPN implementation—laying the groundwork, choosing products and service providers, testing the results, VPN design and implementation, and managing and monitoring the setup.

VPN Design Issues

A well-thought and well-planned design is the mainstay of a network. The same holds true for any VPN. If you fail to analyze the requirements of your organization and plan accordingly, you will feel the ripple effect later. For example, you may have a lot of trouble getting things to work correctly and seamlessly— and the end-user will still feel the brunt of your lack of planning.

When you design your network you need to keep every aspect of the setup in mind, omitting nothing. The main issues that you'll need to consider when developing your VPN design include the following:

- ◆ Security
- ◆ Addressing and routing
- ◆ DNS-related issues
- ◆ Router/gateway, firewall, and NAT issues
- ◆ Server and client considerations
- ◆ Performance
- ◆ Scalability and interoperability

Next, you'll explore each of these VPN-design issues individually.

Security

A VPN extends across an "unsafe" public network to safely connect to the far-scattered branches and resources of an organization. However, most network administrators still consider the security quotient of a VPN to be a major consideration when designing a VPN setup because of the use of intermediate public networks, which are open to all types of unethical individuals with malicious intent. This makes VPNs vulnerable to all sorts of threats, including spoofing and sniffing, content modification, brute force attacks, Man-in-the-Middle attacks, dictionary attacks, timing attacks, Denial-of-Service (DoS) attacks, and attacks on VPN protocols, to name a few.

 NOTE

The question of VPN security is so important that an entire chapter is dedicated to various security threats that your VPN might have to face. The attacks mentioned above, as well as other security threats, are discussed in detail in Chapter 10, "VPN Security Issues."

When you consider the typical VPN setup, four components of VPN connectivity stand out as highly vulnerable to external attacks and threats.

◆ **Remote user (end user or remote VPN client).** This entity might be a part of an organization's mobile workforce or an end user who accesses the organization's intranet from home. This entity uses a valid user ID and password to work remotely. As a result, the remote user is most vulnerable to the possibility of his or her user ID or password being stolen. If a hacker, cracker, or other individual with malicious intent gets a hold of this valid user ID and password, he or she can easily gain access to the organization's intranet and the resources located within it.

◆ **Connection segment to the ISP.** A remote user or branch requires an access option to connect to the ISP's POP, which would in turn establish the connection to the destination network. This connection segment can either be a leased line or a more cost-effective dial-up connection. Leased-line connectivity exists between a remote branch and the ISP intranet and provides the subscriber direct connectivity to the ISP site. Although a secure connectivity option, leased lines can be tapped and an attacker can eavesdrop on transmissions. Dial-up connections are relatively cheaper than leased lines and are generally used to connect an individual remote user (such as a telecommuter) to the organization's network. Dial-up connections are accessible to all and, consequently, are easy to tap. This vulnerability makes them highly susceptible to eavesdropping. Because of this, dial-up connections are not as secure as leased lines.

 NOTE

Regardless of connection segment, eavesdropping on a communication might supply an attacker with a valid remote host IP address. The attacker can then use this information to spoof the IP address and breach the organization's safety barrier without problem. Another major problem associated with connection segment, whether leased or dial-up, is that if the ISP itself is malicious, the service provider can easily read all the communications and thus gain access to the confidential data transacted between an end-user and an organization's intranet.

◆ **Public network.** A public network, especially the Internet, does not fall within the realm of a single authority that can control all operations and transactions occurring across it. Moreover, intermediate points, such as routers, that make up the Internet and support VPN tunnels might not be used exclusively for the tunnels of a single organization. An intermediate router might simultaneously support multiple tunnels that may have originated at the intranets of various organizations. As a result, the traffic from one organization may not be completely isolated from the traffic of other organizations. In addition, the public network, being public in nature, is accessible to everyone who wants to use it. A mal-intentioned individual or organization can easily, with right equipment and expertise, tap into a communication and use it to personal advantage. In other cases, an attacker might spoof the packets or modify data content causing much harm to an organization.

◆ **Destination network access point.** A router, gateway, firewall, or a NAT device is generally located at the periphery of a network and serves as an organization's intranet access point. These devices not only have to face security threats and invasion attempts from external entities, but also from dissatisfied internal entities as well. In addition, if the organization supports an extranet, these devices are also vulnerable to harmful traffic from external business partners.

Figure 7-1 illustrates these threat-susceptible components.

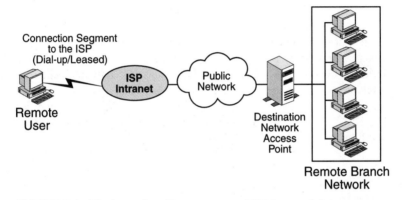

FIGURE 7-1 *The four vulnerable components of VPN connectivity.*

The above discussion pinpoints the security loopholes within a complete VPN setup. Therefore, you cannot afford to ignore these security considerations. You need to take steps well in advance of implementation to ensure that your VPN solution is resistant to all sorts of attacks, yet still allows you to harness the Internet and public network infrastructure to reduce the cost of implementation while increasing the security level of transactions, thus protecting the most valuable asset of your organization—the data.

IPSec, which was discussed in detail in Chapter 6, "An Introduction to IPSec," is considered to be the answer to most of the security concerns related to the four vulnerable VPN elements. It ensures the security of data while in transit, no matter which segment is used. IPSec secures data by encrypting each data packet using strong encryption algorithms. As a result, an eavesdropper or even the intermediate ISP cannot read the data. In addition, IPSec authenticates each packet individually despite the one-time authentication of the end-user. This considerably reduces the possibility of spoofing.

Two more aspects tightly woven into the security of any VPN-based transaction are the trust relationship and key exchange between the involved parties. If either of these aspects is compromised, the security of the entire VPN setup might be compromised.

Trust-related Considerations

Trust is an integral part of the security of any system, including your VPN setup. However, this trust can be exploited to gain access into your carefully-constructed secure setup. Therefore, you need to keep following facts in mind when deciding upon the trust level within your setup and with external entities:

◆ Applications such as Telnet and File Transfer Protocol (FTP) are highly vulnerable to attackers. Consider using more secure applications, such as SSH instead.

 NOTE

Because of the elaborate security mechanism that SSH uses, the performance of SSH over VPN will be slow.

◆ Do not run extra services on your VPN servers. VPN servers must run only minimal VPN-related applications and services so as to minimize the services an intruder can access in case of successful intrusion.

◆ Although distrusting your authorized VPN clients entirely is not advisable, you should maintain a healthy level of distrust toward them. If you provide access to limited resources and services, but allow users to perform their necessary work-related activities, you can effectively reduce the aftermath of an intrusion in which an attacker targets end-user machines. You can use firewalls to limit said access.

Considerations Related to Key Exchange

Key exchange between the involved parties is another aspect of security that when compromised can lead to severe damage within your network. Therefore, it is crucial to be able to distribute keys securely, especially in the case of symmetric encryption. Symmetric encryption, as you learned in Chapter 3, "Security Components of a VPN," depends upon a single secret key for encryption and decryption of data. Therefore, if this key falls into the hands of an intruder, it will give the intruder complete access to the on-going transaction. It is advisable to use IPSec, secure SSH-, and SSL/TLS-based applications, which avoid the exchange of keys in cleartext.

Asymmetric encryption, unlike symmetric encryption, does not depend upon a single key for encryption or decryption purposes. In contrast to symmetric encryption mechanisms, asymmetric mechanisms exchange public keys between the involved parties and use their respective private keys for decryption purposes. However, these mechanisms are not entirely safe and are highly susceptible to Man-in-the-Middle attacks, as you learned in Chapter 3, "Security Components of a VPN." In the case of a Man-in-the-Middle attack, an intruder can substitute his or her public key with the sender's public key, thus gaining complete access to the communication between the two legitimate ends. Because of this, you might need to confirm the public key with the other communicating end after the key exchange phase is complete, but before the data exchange phase begins. Although it is not possible to do so every time, a random cross-checking of the received public keys is highly recommended.

Another point you should keep in mind, regardless of an asymmetric or symmetric encryption mechanism is that keys should never be stored on a VPN end-point, where they might be easily accessible to an intruder. A workable solution to this is to store the keys in a well-protected, centralized location instead of storing all the keys on each VPN server individually. Although the process of key-access is lengthened, this practice not only reduces the storage burden on VPN servers (if the setup supports a large number of VPN clients and servers) but also enhances the key safety.

In addition to addressing security-related issues of a VPN, you must also have a well-defined security policy and ensure that all users—remote or local—are well-versed about the same. This practice will not only inform the users of do's and don'ts, but also increase the overall awareness level of the average user towards possible illegal activities and violations.

 NOTE

Refer to Chapter 3, "Security Components of a VPN", for detailed information about symmetric and asymmetric encryption technology and Man-in-the-Middle attacks.

VPN Addressing and Routing

Another important milestone in the planning and design of VPNs is ensuring that IP addresses that need to be assigned to VPN devices are well planned and correctly assigned. In addition, you need to ensure that your routing scheme will not only be able to handle public network connectivity based on global IP addressing, but also will be able to adapt to any future changes in your IP addressing scheme. Also, adequate measures must be taken to ensure that external business partners and remote clients can also connect to your VPN without problem.

IP Addressing Issues

In a private network, you do not need to buy unique IP addresses (also known as global IP addresses) from an authorized agency, such as the Internet Network Information Center (Inter-NIC), Internet Assigned Numbers Authority (IANA), or from your ISP. You can use private IP addresses or any other addresses that you like for the purpose because communications within a private network are not routed beyond its premises. As a result, hosts and entities located within a private network cannot communicate with other networks across the Internet or other public networks and, therefore, are isolated from the rest of the world.

NOTE

IP addresses within the ranges of 10.0.0.0 to 10.255.255.255, 172.16.0.0 to 172.31.255.255, and 192.168.0.0 to 192.168.255.255 are referred to as private IP addresses and can be used in a private network or an intranet that does not use a public network to connect to its far-flung branches and remote users.

The private addressing scheme does not completely hold true for VPNs because they also rely on a public network backbone for communication. This implies that only the VPN client and server that are involved in a transaction need a public IP address. The actual communication on the virtual VPN interface will work with private IP addresses. As a result, you will require at least one block of globally unique IP addresses from your ISP. You should consider the following facts when addressing VPN devices:

◆ If you use leased lines to connect to your ISP, VPN devices should be allocated static IP addresses. On the other hand, if you use dial-up connections to connect to the ISP POP, VPN clients, especially those used by mobile clients and telecommuters, must be allocated dynamic IP addresses, even though VPN servers will still require a static IP address to be accessible. However, there is an inherent problem associated with VPN clients using dynamic IP addresses. You cannot restrict access to VPN servers strictly on the basis of IP addresses as the ISP might allocate VPN clients different IP addresses each time. In this situation, VPN servers are highly vulnerable to security threats in which an attacker might behave as a trusted user.

◆ No matter if you use a single VPN server or multiple VPN servers, all VPN servers must be allocated a static IP address. If your VPN servers use dynamic IP addresses, VPN clients will not be able to locate the desired servers, even locally.

◆ IP address conflicts might crop up if you need to merge two private networks, as in case of the merger of two organizations. In this scenario, if both merging networks use private IP addressing it is highly possible that some IP addresses might clash. Changing the clashing IP addresses is easy, if only a small number of IP addresses clash. However, if a large number of IP addresses clash (considering the size of the merging networks), you might need to change the addressing scheme of at least one network or, at worst, the entire resulting network. Changing addressing schemes is very time-consuming. You might consider using the facility of automatic configuration of IP addresses, as provided by the Dynamic Host Configuration Protocol (DHCP). This protocol allows a network device to obtain the configuration information, including a dynamic IP address, when that device boots.

◆ If you do not have sufficient globally unique IP addresses, the best approach would be to use private IP addresses within your network and a NAT at the network periphery to realize global connectivity. This NAT would allocate a unique IP address whenever an internal host needs to connect to the Internet or establish a VPN session. This approach will help you ensure that no IP address conflicts occur when you establish Internet connectivity or a VPN session. An important point here is that NAT and the VPN might conflict because of header rewriting, as discussed in Chapter 11, "VPN Security Technologies." As a result, NAT is preferably implemented on the VPN server itself.

 NOTE

A static IP address, once allocated, stays with a device for a long time (until the device is reassigned another IP address). A host that uses dynamic IP addressing allocates a new IP address each time it connects to the network. Static addresses, though expensive, are very easy to manage. On the other hand, the management of dynamic IP addresses can be considerably difficult, though they are comparatively less expensive than static addresses.

Routing Issues

As in the case of traditional networks, routing in VPNs involves dealing with routes to a specified destination. In traditional routing, any currently available route to the destination router works. However, in the case of VPNs, routing also means ensuring the availability of routes only through secure VPN tunnels and connections instead of intermediate public networks.

You should keep the following facts in mind when deciding on the routing scheme for your VPN:

◆ The VPN server that remote VPN clients connect to allocates a default route to these remote VPN clients. Any further interaction between the two ends in the given VPN session is routed through this pre-defined route. Similarly, in case of a dial-up client, where the tunnel is established between the ISP site and the destination network, the VPN client uses the route to the ISP's intranet as the default route.

◆ If the VPN server is located behind a firewall, all default routes should point to that firewall.

◆ If you explicitly assign a route (or a set of routes) to each client for a VPN session, you can have complete control over the transaction paths. However, doing so entails manually configuring routes on each VPN client. This might be an extremely tedious task if the number of VPN clients is large. In addition, there is a high possibility of network congestion if the number of explicitly assigned routes is limited.

◆ You might want to use static routes when setting up a VPN solution for the first time. These routes are pre-defined and pre-configured on both VPN servers as well as VPN clients. As a result, these static routes can play an important role in testing a new VPN setup. Similarly, static routes can also help you debug route-related problems.

◆ Despite the usefulness of testing new VPN setups and troubleshooting problems, you should use static routes sparingly because they can cause a lot of management and reconfiguration overhead, especially if there is a change in addressing scheme or arrangement of VPN devices.

◆ Generally, in a VPN session that uses voluntary tunnels and extends across the Internet, you can either access the Internet hosts or the intranet hosts, but if a default gateway is used for the VPN, not both simultaneously. Therefore, you'll need to configure a default route between the VPN client and the ISP's NAS. This will allow the VPN client to access Internet-based as well as intranet-based hosts concurrently.

TIP

The easiest and the most secure method of assigning routes for VPN sessions is to configure the default VPN router, firewall, or the default VPN gateway with all possible VPN-related routes. This practice will save you a lot of time and effort because you would then only need to configure a default route on all client machines. The situation can be still further simplified if the VPN router, gateway, or firewall can share this routing information with other routing devices. As a result, you will be spared from configuring each of these devices individually.

CAUTION

Dial-up VPN clients are typically allocated two IP addresses—first, when establishing a PPP connection with the ISP site and the second, while establishing the VPN session. Therefore, you must be extremely careful while assigning routes to VPN sessions because if you add a PPP route instead of VPN route, all your traffic will be routed through the unsecured PPP route (or the plain Internet route) in unencrypted format. In addition, if the packets have private IP addresses they will be dropped at the ISP router.

VPNs also require that you choose the correct routing protocol. You will need to choose the routing protocol according to the conditions and requirements of your organization. Some factors that might help you in deciding the protocol include the following:

◆ **Bandwidth used by the protocol.** For example, you might want to use BGP as it uses a small amount of bandwidth.

◆ **Overhead generated.** Some routing protocols generate very high communication overhead as compared to the others. RIP is a classic example of this. Though IPSec is not a routing protocol, it's important to know that it, too, generates high overhead.)

◆ **Direction of communication.** Some routing protocols, such as RIP, only support broadcast addresses. Other protocols like Border Gateway Protocol (BGP) support only unicast addresses. On the other hand, RIP version 2 (RIPv2) and Open Shortest Path First (OSPF) support broadcast and multicast addresses.

◆ **Security provided.** Some routing protocols offer higher security as compared to other protocols. For example, IPSec offers the maximum security, though it generates larger overhead.

DNS-related Considerations

Domain Name System (DNS) is a distributed global directory that is used for the conversion of name-based addresses, such as www.yahoo.com, into corresponding numeric IP addresses, such as 64.58.76.223. You'll need DNS in VPNs for the same purpose—to map name-based addresses of hosts to their corresponding numeric IP addresses.

In the case of Intranet VPNs, which allow access only to resources located within an organization's intranet, you will need to create a separate domain for the main (corporate or central) network and multiple individual domains for each remote branch or network. For example, you might create a domain called "MyIntranet.com" and create internal domains, such as "RemoteBranch1.MyIntranet.com," "RemoteBranch2.MyIntranet.com," and so on. You can now configure the DNS server to support this domain hierarchy. In addition, you'll also need to set at least one internal domain server as a secondary domain server for each internal domain that you create. This will facilitate the sharing of updates and other DNS-related information between the multiple internal domains.

The previous configuration takes care of intranet-based VPN access. However, internal hosts will still not be able to access the Internet. If you want internal hosts to be able to access the Internet or resources located within the Internet, you'll need to set up an additional external DNS server, which will receive all queries for external hosts from internal DNSs and map the external name-addresses to the corresponding numeric addresses.

In the case of telecommuters and mobile users who use a VPN to access your intranet, there is an inherent problem with DNS settings. If these remote users are dependent on a dial-up connection (which is generally the case), the VPN clients connect to your intranet using a new IP address each time Therefore, you cannot hardcode your DNS to accommodate these clients.

To solve this problem, you'll need to set up the individual client machines to use internal DNS servers. If the remote users require a simultaneous Internet-connectivity, you'll need to configure these remote ends to search for external DNS servers in addition to the internal DNS servers.

 NOTE

When connecting to the Internet, you might face huge delays or even application timeouts during name/address resolution if you set VPN hosts to first look for an internal DNS server and then look for an external DNS server (in both intranet or remote access scenarios). This is because hosts will search for an external DNS server only after searching through all internal DNS servers to which they are registered. Therefore, the VPN host should look for an internal DNS server, which in turn should be set up to forward the request to the ISP's DNS. The search, as a result, is much faster because it allows you to cache the names looked up.

In addition to the considerations just mentioned, you'll also need to be alert for the following DNS server vulnerabilities:

◆ If you fail to secure your DNS servers well, an intruder can take over your servers and gain absolute control over the domains registered with them. This type of attack is referred to as domain hijacking.

◆ An intruder can use Denial-of-Service (DoS) attacks on your DNS servers. In this case, affected domains will not be able to locate hosts in other domains and the Internet. Because all Internet-based DNS servers communicate with each other, this type of attack can lead to a widespread global slowdown in the name/numeric address mapping process.

◆ If an intruder gains access to your DNS server and modifies the information stored in the server to redirect any traffic intended for the legitimate addresses to a rogue location, the affected domains will not receive any data traffic meant for them. This is referred to as cache poisoning.

In order to avoid these issues, you'll need to secure your DNS servers—internal and external—well.

Router, Firewall, and NAT-related Considerations

As you already know, routers (or gateways), firewalls and NAT devices are peripheral devices. You need to consider a few issues for their security and seamless integration in a VPN environment.

Router-related Considerations

Routers (and gateways) play a significant role in routing traffic across an IP-based internetwork. Because these are peripheral devices, the main concern related to them is about their security. If your routers are poorly secured, they can be easily targeted by intruders who generate rogue traffic causing DoS attacks. They can also be used by intruders to attack other routers.

Other considerations related to routers and gateways in a VPN setup include the following:

◆ Routers and gateways within the Internet environment are mainly configured to pass routed traffic to the next router toward the destination network. This implies that they can "shunt" large amounts of data. However, most routers are incapable of handling the large amounts of data targeted at them. As a result, most routers are highly susceptible to DoS attacks. By gaining complete control over a router, an intruder can gain easy access to the network attached to the given router and cause severe damage to the intranet.

◆ Routers periodically share routing information with their peers to be able to identify where to further direct the traffic they receive. As a result, routers must share a trust relationship with their peers. This feature of routers is often exploited by intruders who then modify or delete existing routes or introduce rogue routes into the routing tables maintained by one or more of the routers. As a result of this modification, routers whose routing tables have been altered might start acting as rogue routers and forward traffic to wrong "untrustworthy" routers.

◆ If you are planning to implement multiple routers and gateways in your intranet, ensure that all support the same level of security. This will prevent an intruder from exploiting a single less-secure point to gain access to the network.

Because of the issues specified, you should be careful when choosing correct routers for your VPN setup. Besides good routing performance, you should also look for strong authentication and encryption capabilities in the routers you select. These capabilities will not only protect your routers, but also prevent the unauthorized reading and scanning of information that is being passed by them.

 NOTE

Refer to Chapter 10, "VPN Security Issues," for detailed information about DoS and other attacks that threaten the security of your VPN-based setup.

Firewall-related Considerations

Although firewalls can help you as primary protection mechanisms against external attacks and intruders, you need to consider a few issues before you implement a firewall-based VPN setup. Some of these issues follow:

◆ If you are planning to implement firewalls that operate on the basis of source and destination IP addresses, source and destination ports, and protocol used, but not on the basis of the content of the data packet, an intruder can hide "harmful" data of another protocol in the packet payloads. As a result, this harmful data will not be detected by the firewall. Another problem associated with these firewalls, also known as packet filter firewalls, is that they cannot handle transactions based on multiple dynamic connections, such as FTP transactions. Therefore, you'll need to explicitly set packet filters to allow traffic related to these transactions.

◆ Other firewalls, such as application proxy firewalls and stateful packet inspection firewalls, largely base their operations on the content of the data packet in addition to IP addresses, port addresses, and protocols used. However, you'll have to remember that application proxy firewalls do not know how to deal with SSH- and HTTPS-based traffic. As a result, this feature of an application proxy firewall can be exploited by an outsider to penetrate the firewall. The functionality of stateful packet inspection firewalls is very similar to application proxy firewalls. However, performance-wise they are much better. Therefore, though you might have to invest more in stateful packet inspection firewalls, you'll significantly increase the overall performance of your VPN setup.

◆ To overcome most of the firewall-related issues, you must define a security policy, which in turn defines how a firewall should behave in your setup. In the security policy, you'll also have to decide what type of traffic should be allowed through the firewall(s). One way to deal with all traffic comprehensively when configuring the firewall operating system is to disallow all traffic and services and then proceed to allow only the required services and traffic until you build the complete rulebase.

◆ If you are planning to create a demilitarized zone (DMZ), you will need to first decide which servers should be part of this zone. A rule of thumb is that servers offering only the essential VPN services should be a part of this zone.

◆ Although a little more expensive, an effective way of securing your intranet and the VPN setup is to build a hierarchical firewall-based security structure using various types of firewalls, as shown in Figure 7-2. For example, the firewall between the Internet and the DMZ can be of one type and the firewall between DMZ and the intranet could be of another type. This will reduce the possibility of exploiting the same weaknesses in the peripheral firewall system to gain access to intranet resources.

◆ By configuring your firewalls to log each and every connection request and activity that takes place through them, and by regularly analyzing this data, you can pinpoint the vulnerabilities in you firewall system and take steps accordingly.

 NOTE

You'll learn more about the three types of firewalls mentioned above in Chapter 11, "VPN Security Technologies."

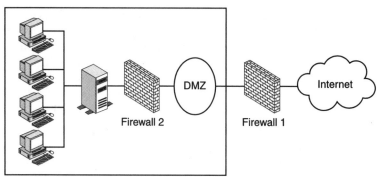

FIGURE 7-2 *A hierarchical firewall system.*

NAT-related Considerations

There are always two main considerations when implementing NAT-based solution in a VPN environment. These include:

◆ Although NAT can operate freely upon PPTP, the most important NATS consideration arises in the case of IPSec-based transactions. For the success of NAT technology, the Layer 3 (IP) addresses must be changed. In contrast, IPSec encapsulates and/or encrypts the Layer 3 IP address of a packet with another Layer 3 network address. As a result, the UDP port number is encrypted and its value is protected with a cryptographic FCS. This makes IPSec traffic non-translatable by NATs because NAT isn't able to work on the packet after the packet goes through the IPSec or IPSec-based L2TP VPN tunneling process. Moreover, in the case of end-to-end IPSec authentication, a packet whose address is changed will always fail the integrity check provided by AH. Consequently, NATs can break an IPSec-based tunnel; consequently, the VPN server will always drop the packets. Therefore, you should avoid the use of NAT if you are planning to implement IPSec encryption and authentication.

◆ NAT does not handle the translation of IP addresses into corresponding Application-layer protocols, as is required by some applications. Therefore, you cannot implement a standard NAT-based solution. You'll have to look for an advanced NAT to handle these situations.

VPN Server and Client Considerations

VPN servers and clients are the endpoints of an entire VPN setup. While VPN servers provide VPN-related services, clients utilize these services. As a result, considerable thought must go into the selection of VPN servers and clients.

Major considerations related to VPN servers include the following:

♦ The VPN server must be high-performance.

♦ The server must host only the most essential VPN services.

♦ The server must be resolvable and reachable to authorized VPN clients. You must use static IP addresses for that purpose. If the server is allocated a private address, network address translation is required so that the server can be accessed by external hosts, especially if your intranet also supports extranets.

♦ If NAT is being used, it must be implemented at the VPN server to avoid conflicts between the NAT and the VPN.

♦ If the VPN server is directly attached to the Internet and the firewall is "behind" the VPN server (between the VPN server and the intranet), you must configure the server to accept only VPN traffic and drop non-VPN data packets. However, if the VPN server lies "behind" the firewall, both the server as well as the firewall must be configured to accept only VPN-related data packets.

 NOTE

To ensure that your VPN server is reachable by VPN clients from outside the intranet, set the ping time of VPN servers to a 5-second timeout. This will help VPN clients determine if the specified VPN server is currently reachable or not.

The facts that you should keep in mind when selecting and implementing VPN clients include the following:

♦ You should opt for manual configuration of VPN clients only if the number of clients is limited. However, if your VPN setup supports a large number of clients, you'll have to look for tools that can help you to configure these client machines. For example, if the number of VPN clients is large, you can consider using Microsoft Connection Manager in a Microsoft-based VPN environment.

♦ You should select VPN clients after analyzing and understanding the organization's requirements. This is important because, though you might have a high-performance overall setup, a low-performance client can become a major performance bottleneck as it may not be able to keep up with the fast rate of transactions.

Performance

Performance of a VPN largely depends upon VPN servers and the underlying network infrastructure. With this in mind, it is important to know some of the regular responsibilities that optimizing performance entails:

◆ You should review the performance of VPN servers regularly, preferably weekly or even more frequently, if possible. This will help you to identify any drop in the performance-level of your servers.

◆ It is advisable to maintain detailed system logs of each and every VPN-related activity. In addition, you should periodically transfer these logs to a separate machine so that when an intruder gains access to any of the VPN servers, he or she cannot alter the logs to evade early detection.

◆ You should also monitor overall network performance on a regular basis. This will help you identify potential bottlenecks and will help you determine how many users your VPN setup can support before users start feeling any performance degradation.

◆ Encryption, algorithms, and authentication schemes can generate considerable overhead, thus slowing down normal network operations along with VPN operations. You can increase the overall performance of your network by carefully analyzing the pros and cons of the algorithms you can implement, balancing security and performance.

◆ VPN clients are another neglected aspect of VPN performance. You need to control VPN clients located within the intranet and advise the remote clients with roaming profiles—telecommuters and mobile users—on which client software and operating system to use so that the transactions between the end-user and the VPN server(s) is not hampered by the low performance of the VPN client.

Scalability and Interoperability

Like any network setup, a VPN should be able to accommodate any future changes in the requirements and growth of the organization. This holds true specifically in the case of enterprise VPNs that are scattered across multiple sites. The design of your setup will define the scope of future growth as well as the number of connections that can be supported by your VPN currently and the total cost of implementation of the setup. Therefore, you should choose your VPN design carefully before you graduate to the VPN implementation phase.

In most cases, the enterprise setup is comprised of a centralized configuration, where the main corporate network acts as the "hub" of all remote branches. In this configuration, each remote branch is connected to the main branch through a VPN connection, as shown in Figure 7-3.

The configuration depicted in Figure 7-3 is highly scalable and can easily accommodate VPN connections from any new remote branch network without much problem and without affecting other branches. The only modifications required are at the central network. The biggest problem associated with this configuration model is that if the central site goes down, no further communication is possible between any of the sites. Also, all communications are routed through the central site, increasing the traffic overhead at the central location. In addition, a drop in the performance of the central site can negatively affect the performance of all other sites, reducing overall network performance.

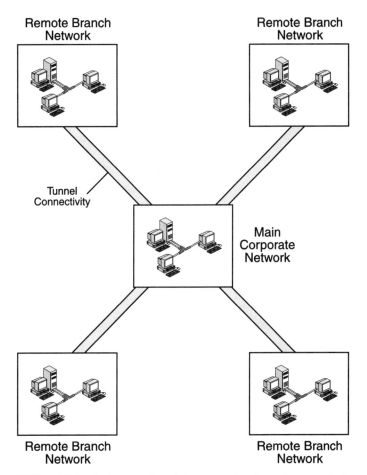

FIGURE 7-3 *Each remote branch is connected to the main network through a VPN.*

Another possible configuration is a ring-like configuration, where each remote site is connected to its immediately adjacent neighbors. This configuration is depicted in Figure 7-4. This configuration is scalable only to an extent because if the number of sites connected to the ring is too large, the performance of the entire intranet degrades considerably.

An alternative to the centralized VPN configuration is a mesh-like configuration, where each site is connected to all other remote networks in the enterprise network. Figure 7-5 depicts this configuration model. This setup, though expensive and difficult to set up and maintain, effectively avoids the single point of failure (SPOF) and ensures that one network cannot affect the performance of other connected networks. In addition, despite being highly scalable, practical implementation of scalability is quite difficult and time-consuming.

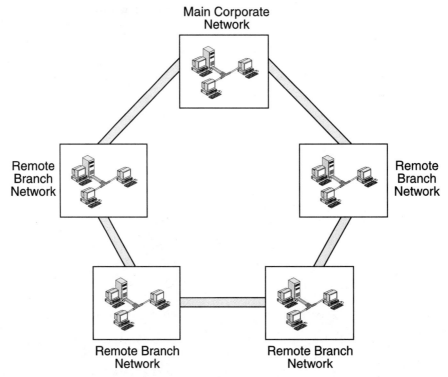

FIGURE 7-4 *Each remote branch is connected to its neighboring intranet site in the through a VPN.*

Interoperability is another important issue to bear in mind when choosing the elements of your VPN, especially considering that administrations tend to mix and match products offered by various vendors to reduce the total cost of implementation. Products offered by different vendors might not be as interoperable as the vendors claim, so you should test the interoperability and compatibility of all the VPN products before you actually implement them in your VPN.

Another point that you should remember with regard to interoperability is that the VPN product you select must work seamlessly with various platforms. Though this might seem to be a waste of money at the moment, especially if your intranet uses only a few platforms, this strategy will stand you in good steed when your VPN grows.

Now that you have a general idea of the considerations you should keep in mind when designing your VPN setup, you can consider the three most-commonly implemented VPN environments and their attributes.

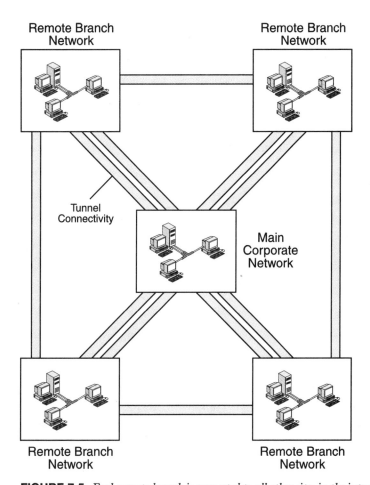

FIGURE 7-5 *Each remote branch is connected to all other sites in the intranet through a VPN.*

Individual VPN Environments

As you learned in Chapter 1, "Introduction to VPN's," depending on the access strategy, VPNs can be categorized as Remote Access VPNs, Intranet VPNs, and Extranet VPNs (the most popular category of present-day VPNs). It is good to consider each VPN access environment individually to understand the specific problems you might face in each environment.

Remote Access VPNs

The Remote Access VPN environment allows remote clients, such as telecommuters and mobile clients, to access an organization's intranet securely across the Internet without having to rely on end-to-end dial up connections, as shown in Figure 7-6.

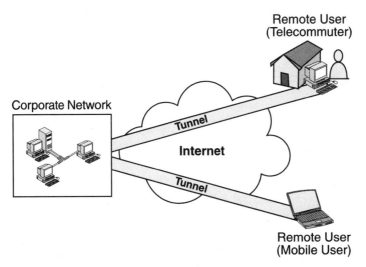

FIGURE 7-6 *The Remote Access VPN setup.*

The issues that might arise with this environment follow:

◆ **Security.** Preferably set up your router "behind" the firewall and configure your routers to redirect all tunneled data to the firewall.

◆ **Addressing scheme.** The ISP dynamically allocates IP addresses to these remote clients because they use a dial-up connection to the ISP POP (and not the intranet). As a result, the VPN server located in the intranet must support the ability to identify these clients. In addition to implementing the DNS server settings discussed in the previous section "DNS-related Considerations," you can resolve this issue using IPSec. IKE, which is a third-party protocol supported by IPSec, supports the capability to identify remote clients by their name-based IP addresses rather than numeric IP addresses.

◆ **Key distribution.** Key distribution should never take place as cleartext. A self-regulated key distribution mechanism, such as IKE, should be used if the number of remote clients is large. In the case of a limited number of remote clients, manual key management is also a possibility. However, this practice of manual key management is not recommended because the probability of key-loss is quite high.

◆ **Data authentication and encryption.** It is highly important that data that is exchanged between the server and the client is encrypted as well as authenticated. In addition, you should set packet filters and stringent security policies to ensure that the peripheral device, such as a router, gateway, or firewall, should reject data that is neither authenticated nor encrypted. Even the routing information exchanged between the peripheral routers and gateways should be encrypted and authenticated.

◆ **Tunneling.** It is advisable to establish direct tunnels between remote hosts and the VPN server. Though this practice offers enhanced security, especially if the trust level in the intranet is not very high, it generates large overheads and is relatively difficult to manage. You'll have to analyze the trust level in your intranet and then decide between the two options (end-user to peripheral-device tunnels, or end-user to VPN server tunnels) so as to maintain a high level of security.

◆ **Tunneling protocols.** If your remote clients use non-IP tunneling protocols, peripheral VPN devices, such as firewalls and routers, must support appropriate tunneling protocols.

Intranet VPNs

The intranet-based VPN environment allows remote branch networks to access other parts of an organization's intranet securely across the Internet without having to rely on end-to-end leased lines and end-to-end dial-up connections, as shown in Figure 7-7.

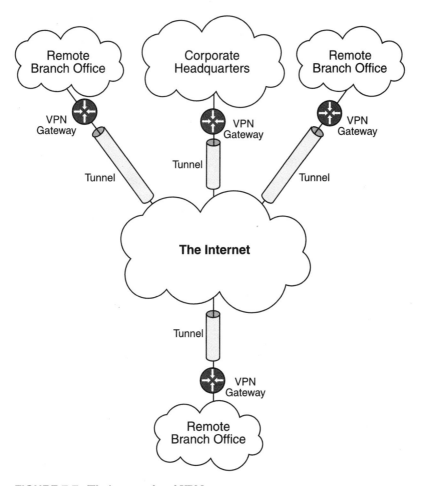

FIGURE 7-7 *The intranet-based VPN setup.*

The facts that you should keep in mind while designing a VPN solution for an intranet-based VPN environment follow:

◆ **Security.** Although no security protocols need to be implemented on the internal routers and gateways, peripheral devices should support a security mechanism, such as IPSec. In addition, preferably, these peripheral devices should be hidden "behind" the firewall with clearly defined security policies.

◆ **Addressing scheme.** Due to the fact that the entire intranet belongs to one organization, addressing is not an issue because remote-branch networks largely follow the addressing scheme used in other parts of the intranet. Therefore, the addressing scheme used in the rest of intranet can be used as-is, as long as all the IP addresses in the intranet are unique Because of this, addressing-based issues are rare in this VPN environment.

◆ **Key distribution.** Because an intranet is largely trusted, host-to-host key distribution is not a primary requirement. However, keys should be exchanged between the vulnerable points of this setup, namely the peripheral devices—routers and gateways. For this purpose, an automated and secure key distribution and management mechanism, such as IKE is recommended.

◆ **Data authentication and encryption.** Any data that is exchanged between the server and the client must be encrypted as well as authenticated—despite the fact that they belong to the same intranet—because data that is routed across the Internet or other such public network is susceptible to security threats and corruption. Quite like the security policies used in a remote access environment, you should set packet filters and enact stringent measures to ensure that data that is neither authenticated nor encrypted should be dropped at the periphery of the network by the peripheral device, such as a router, gateway, or firewall. Even the routing information exchanged between the routers should be encrypted and authenticated.

◆ **Tunneling.** It is advisable to establish direct tunnels between the peripheral devices located at each network end. Though this practice offers enhanced security, especially if the trust level in the intranet is not very high, it generates large overheads and is relatively difficult to manage. You'll have to analyze the trust level in your intranet and then decide between the two options (end-user to peripheral-device tunnels or end-user to VPN server tunnels) so as to maintain a high level of security.

◆ **Tunneling protocols.** If your remote clients use non-IP tunneling protocols, peripheral VPN devices, such as firewalls and routers must support appropriate tunneling protocols.

Extranet VPNs

The Extranet VPN environment allows external entities, such as business partners and suppliers, to access an organization's intranet securely using the Internet without relying on end-to-end leased line and end-to-end dial-up connections, as shown in Figure 7-8.

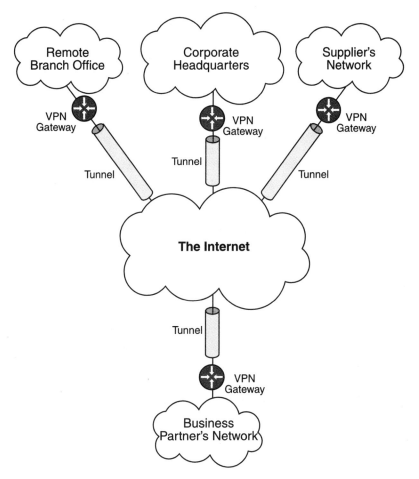

FIGURE 7-8 *The extranet-based VPN setup.*

The design considerations that you should keep in mind when designing a VPN solution for an extranet-based environment follow:

◆ **Security.** Stringent security protocols and measures need to be implemented at the peripheral routers, gateways, and firewalls. In addition, these peripheral devices should be hidden "behind" the firewall with clearly defined security policies.

◆ **Addressing and routing schemes.** In this environment, you cannot expect to accommodate external networks without initial hiccups. If two networks use a private addressing scheme, there is a high possibility that the private addresses used might coincide. This can cause routing issues as routers and gateways will not be able to resolve these ambiguous addresses. As a result, you'll need to ensure that this discrepancy is resolved before the two ends can start exchanging information securely over the VPN.

◆ **Key distribution.** Because an extranet-based setup is quite complex and involves non-trusted external entities in addition to a large number of VPN clients and communications, an automated and secure key distribution and management mechanism, such as IKE and/or ISAKMP/Oakley, is a must for all involved parties—servers, clients, routers, gateways, firewalls, and so on.

◆ **Data authentication and encryption.** Any data that is exchanged between the server and the client must be encrypted end-to-end as well as authenticated thoroughly. This is necessary because the data might be from a non-trusted environment and has been routed across the Internet or another such public network and, therefore, is highly susceptible to security threats and corruption. Like the security policies used in remote access and intranet environments, you should set packet filters and adopt stringent measures to ensure that data that is neither authenticated nor encrypted should be dropped at the periphery of the network by the peripheral device. Even the routing information exchanged between the routers should be encrypted and authenticated.

◆ **Tunneling.** It is advisable to establish direct tunnels between the peripheral devices located at each network end. Though this practice offers enhanced security, especially if the trust level in the intranet is not very high, it generates large overheads and is relatively difficult to manage. You'll have to analyze the trust level in your intranet and then decide between the two options (end-user to peripheral-device tunnels or end-user to VPN server tunnels) so as to maintain a high level of security.

◆ **Tunneling protocols.** If your remote clients use non-IP tunneling protocols, peripheral VPN devices, such as firewalls and routers, must support the appropriate tunneling protocols, in addition to tunneling protocols with strong security mechanisms.

In the next section, you'll learn about the generic steps of VPN implementation.

Generic Steps to Building VPNs

As you might have noticed with any technology, once you implement and start using it, it becomes a part of your work. The same holds true for VPNs. Once implemented, and before you even realize, VPNs become an integral part of your everyday business operations. Therefore, if you made any mistakes during the implementation phase or planned any less rigorously than necessary, your organization and users will suffer. And undoing the wrong might be a complicated, tedious, and time-consuming task.

This is why you should understand the requirements and future plans of your organization really well before you even start planning. Only after your plan and, subsequently, design are in place, should you graduate to the actual implementation phase.

The complete implementation of a VPN-based solution can be broken down into the following five steps:

- Laying the groundwork
- Choosing products and a service provider
- Testing the results
- Designing and implementing the solution
- Managing and monitoring

Following sections discuss these steps in detail.

Laying the Groundwork

Implementation of a VPN-based solution can slightly reduce the performance of your intranet. Therefore, it is very important that you do enough research to be able to choose optimal products and services. In addition, the more detailed the groundwork you do, the more optimal your return on investment (ROI).

You need to determine the following information as a part of this research and analysis phase:

- **A rough estimate of the number of users.** You need to have a rough estimate of the expected number of users to determine the scope of your VPN solution and services. This number will also help you to determine the optimal number of VPN ports that your setup should have.

- **Categories of users depending on their requirements.** You'll then need to study the profiles of users exhaustively in order to determine their requirements and categorize them into various groups that include branch office user group, mobile user group, telecommuter group, and home worker group. The users who belong to the branch office group are stationary and require on-demand unlimited access to the corporate office network and other branch office sites within the intranet. The mobile user group is the set of personnel with roaming profiles who generally use a laptop or a notebook to access the corporate intranet. They typically use VPN connectivity to access email and a few necessary, limited resources. The telecommuter group works from home and requires access to limited resources and services. Quite like the telecommuter group, the home worker group accesses the organization's intranet for short periods and limited resources.

- **Connectivity and access requirements.** The next logical step is to determine the network access and connectivity requirements of each category of VPN users. You'll need to determine the type of WAN connectivity that can be accommodated within your allocated budget and its performance constraints. You'll also need to determine the required average data rates for different users and connection types.

- **Security requirements.** Security in a VPN-based setup entails authentication, integrity, and confidentiality. To ensure all of these in your VPN transactions, you'll need to implement various security measures, such as encryption mechanisms, authentication mechanisms, and hardware-based security solutions that include RADIUS, AAA, TACACS, firewalls, NAT, and so on. You cannot choose any of these security implementations arbitrarily. You'll need to analyze the requirements of your organization to understand the solution that should be implemented. The selection of an appropriate security solution also depends upon the level of security and integrity demanded by the network traffic. For example, if your organization deals with sensitive data in e-commerce transactions, you'll need to implement one or more security solutions to ensure proper authentication, integrity, and confidentiality of data.

Choosing Products and Service Providers

After you have analyzed and understand the requirements of your organization and the expectations of the users, it is now time to choose products to implement your VPN. This is not an easy decision because there are a wealth of VPN hardware and software products now available. Keeping budgetary constraints in mind, the best method is to choose products that satisfy your requirements and are affordable.

Some parameters that will help you choose appropriate hardware as well as software products for your VPN include the following:

◆ Performance-related parameters, such as highest sustained throughput and lowest response time

◆ Security-related parameters, such as authentication and encryption mechanisms supported

◆ Session-related parameters, such as highest data transfer rate

◆ Number of simultaneous connections supported

 NOTE

You must be careful while choosing encryption and authentication mechanisms. Though they offer enhanced security, they are highly CPU-intensive and therefore can reduce the overall performance of the network. As a result, you'll need to find a workable trade-off between security and performance.

Because you still haven't graduated to the implementation phase, this is the point where you can decide to outsource the solution based on your groundwork and product analysis. The service provider will have the required expertise and technical know-how to design and implement a VPN solution tailored to your organization's requirements. In addition, outsourcing the solution will also take the burden of monitoring and management off your (and, therefore, your organization's) shoulders. However, the risk here is that you're handing over the security of your organization to an outsider. This is not acceptable to many administrators and organizations. Therefore, you should analyze to the minutest detail the SLA that the service provider offers you. An in-depth understanding of each point in the SLA will also help you verify that the service provider is providing you the level of services promised in the SLA.

Testing the Results

If you have decided to go for an in-house implementation of the VPN setup, you'll now need to test and evaluate each VPN product that you have chosen. This will help you ensure right at the beginning that the selected hardware and software products are interoperable and compatible with each other.

Generally, the testing is conducted as a small-scale pilot that incorporates a group of select remote users, telecommuters, various branch office users, and a few home users. Each aspect of the VPN should be tested and you should see how each product will behave in the real environment. This pilot also ensures that the products are correctly configured and are implemented per specifications.

If you have decided to use the services of a service provider, again a small pilot to test and verify the solution offered by the service provider in the real-time environment is recommended.

TIP

The best way to test the experimental setup is to first see how the VPN solution behaves in ideal conditions with no traffic load or bandwidth constraints. You should then add stress to the solution to see how the performance changes. You'll want to continue adding stress to determine functionality under the worst conditions. This will help you proactively identify any problematic situations that might occur later, when your VPN is up and running.

If the pilot (in-house or outsourced) fails, you'll need to either replace products that do not fulfill your requirements or reconfigure them, as indicated by the pilot. In case of outsourced implementation, you'll need to renegotiate the SLA offered.

Designing and Implementing the Solution

You graduate to the design and implementation phase only after you have successfully completed the pilot, or testing, phase. In the design and implementation phase, you will implement your organization's planned, full-scale VPN solution.

TIP

It is recommended that you have the VPN vendor or the solution provider present when you implement your VPN. The presence of an experienced professional will help you implement and troubleshoot the solution quickly and efficiently.

After the solution has been implemented successfully, you'll need to re-test the complete setup. After successful testing, you might also need to fine-tune the solution to optimize its performance and security.

Managing and Monitoring

Maintenance and management of any network setup is an ongoing process. The bigger the scope of your VPN setup the more complex it is to monitor .With this in mind, you'll need to plan a strategy that will constantly manage and monitor your network.

The following practices will help you ensure that your VPN setup is always optimized:

◆ Gather usage and performance statistics on a regular basis.
◆ Maintain detailed logs of each and every activity related to the VPN, regardless of the activity's success.

An in-depth knowledge and understanding of the way your service provider implements your VPN solution also plays an important role in enabling you to monitor and evaluate the performance, effectiveness, and integrity of the solution provided.

Networking technologies are advancing at a very fast pace. So is the case with VPN technology. Therefore, you might need to upgrade your existing VPN setup from time to time. You might also need to migrate to different platforms and environments to accommodate any future growth of your organization and its requirements.

As most network designers and administrators will tell you, your task (as the organization's administrator or IS manager) does not end with the mere implementation of a solution. You'll need to manage and monitor the solution so that it provides the promised performance. From time to time, you'll also need to don your working gloves to identify, troubleshoot, and resolve any problems that might arise.

Summary

In this chapter, you learned about the various issues and considerations that you must keep in mind when designing a VPN-based solution for your organization. This chapter explored VPN design issues, such as security, addressing and routing, performance, scalability, and interoperability.

Other issues related to the implementation of firewalls and NAT, DNS, trust level in the intranet, and key distribution were covered.

You also explored each VPN environment—remote access, intranet, and extranet—individually to understand the possible difficulties and considerations that you may have to plan for when implementing VPNs in these environments.

Finally, you learned about the five generic steps in implementing a VPN-based security solution for your intranet. These include a research phase to determine the needs of the organization and the end users of the system, a selection phase to choose products and a service provider, a testing phase to test the selected products and service provider, a design and implementation phase, and a monitoring and management phase to regularly evaluate the performance and other aspects of the VPN.

Check Your Understanding

Multiple Choice Questions

1. Which of the following statements are true?

    a. FTP and SSH are secure applications.

    b. IPSec is vulnerable to Man-in-the-Middle attacks.

    c. Dial-up connections are not as secure as leased line connections.

    d. Asymmetric encryption is based on a single key.

2. IPSec supports _____ communications.

    a. Broadcast

    b. Unicast

    c. Bi-directional

    d. Multicast

3. Which of the following threats is a DNS vulnerable to?

    a. Cache poisoning

    b. Domain hijacking

    c. Denial-of-Service

    d. Man-in-the-Middle

4. According to the expert recommendations, the optimal timeout period for a VPN server is _____.

    a. 5 seconds

    b. 4 seconds

    c. 2 seconds

    d. 1 second

5. Which of the following is a category of VPN users?

    a. Home users

    b. Administrators

    c. Telecommuters

    d. Branch office users

6. DHCP stands for _____.

    a. Domain Host Configuration Protocol

    b. Dial-up Host Configuration Protocol

    c. Dedicated Host Configuration Protocol

    d. Dynamic Host Configuration Protocol

Short Questions

1. Bob has added a new VPN server at the main corporate network of his organization. He has also set up another server at the branch office network. However, he has been receiving complaints that both servers are inaccessible. What might be the problem? How can he solve it?

2. Until recently, XYZ Inc. hosted a private intranet. Internal computers within the intranet were provided with Internet connectivity and the mobile workforce of the organization, which amounts to about 47 people, were allowed to connect to the intranet using VPN connectivity. Remote branch offices also use VPN connectivity to connect to each other. In addition, the organization uses a public IP addressing scheme across the intranet as the intranet is not very large. Now, they have decided to allow their business partners to access a few resources within their intranet. What are the issues that the IS manager of XYZ Inc. should keep in mind when planning for this new requirement?

3. How can static routes help you in the process of setting up a new VPN solution?

Answers

Multiple Choice Answers

1. **c**. Dial-up connections are relatively cheaper than leased lines and are generally used to connect an individual remote user (such as a telecommuter) to the organization's network. Dial-up connections are accessible to all and consequently are easy to tap. Because of this, they are not as secure as leased lines. This vulnerability makes them highly susceptible to eavesdropping.

2. **b**. IPSec is a unicast protocol and, hence, supports communication with a single host at a time.

3. **a, b** and **c**. DNS is vulnerable to cache poisoning, domain hijacking, and DoS attacks. When an intruder takes over your DNS server and gains absolute control over the domains registered with the given server, the category of DNS attacks is referred to as domain hijacking. If an intruder succeeds in modifying the domain-related information stored in the DNS server so that all the traffic for a legitimate domain is rerouted to a rogue domain, the attack is referred to as cache poisoning. DoS attacks include a broad category of attacks, all of which illegitimately and harmfully flood a host with data. When the resources of the host are occupied by the onslaught of this harmful traffic, legitimate requests may be denied. In the worst cases, if the rate and volume of data reach a certain level, the host may crash.

4. **a**. According to expert recommendations, the optimal timeout period for a VPN server is 5 seconds.

5. **a, c**, and **d**. The categories of VPN clients include branch office users, mobile users, telecommuters, and home workers. The users that belong to the branch office group are stationary and require on-demand unlimited access to the corporate office network and other branch office sites within the intranet. The mobile user group is the set of personnel with roaming profiles who generally use a laptop or a notebook to access the corporate intranet. They typically use VPN connectivity to access email and a few necessary limited resources. The telecommuter group works from home and requires access to limited resources and services. Quite like the telecommuter group, the home worker group accesses an organization's intranet for short periods and limited resources.

6. **d**. DHCP stands for Dynamic Host Configuration Protocol. This protocol allows a network device to obtain configuration information, including a dynamic IP address, when the device boots.

Short Answers

1. The problem in this case is that Bob must not have allocated a static address to the two servers in question. As a result, the VPN servers must use dynamic IP addresses. Because of this, VPN clients have not been able to locate the desired servers, even locally. To solve the problem, Bob must allocate static IP addresses to both servers.

2. In the given scenario, stringent security protocols and measures need to be implemented at the peripheral routers, gateways, and firewalls. In addition, these peripheral devices should be hidden "behind" the firewall with clearly defined security policies. Because the extranet-based setup is quite complex, and involves non-trusted external entities, an automated and secure key distribution and management mechanism, such as IKE and/or ISAKMP/Oakley is a must for all involved parties—servers, clients, routers, gateways, firewalls, and so on. Any data that is exchanged between the server and the client must be encrypted end-to-end and must be authenticated thoroughly because the data may be from a non-trusted environment and may have been routed across the Internet or other such public network and, therefore, is highly susceptible to security threats and corruption. Quite like the security policies used in remote access and intranet environments, you should set packet filters and stringent measures to ensure that data that is neither authenticated nor encrypted is dropped at the periphery of the network by the peripheral device. Even the routing information exchanged between the routers should be encrypted and authenticated. It is advisable to establish direct tunnels between the peripheral devices located at each network end. Peripheral VPN devices, such as firewalls and routers must support tunneling protocols that offer strong security mechanisms, in addition to appropriate tunneling protocols if your remote clients use non-IP tunneling protocols.

3. You might want to use static routes when setting up a VPN solution for the first time. These routes are pre-defined and pre-configured on both VPN servers as well as VPN clients. As a result, these static routes can play an important role in testing a new VPN setup. Static routes can also help you debug route-related problems.

Chapter 8

Implementing a VPN on Windows 2000

Of all the platforms that are used in networked environments today, two are becoming increasingly popular: Microsoft's Windows 2000 and Linux. These platforms are marked by their ubiquitous presence around the globe. Therefore, you'll be considering the implementation of VPNs on them both. This chapter covers VPN configuration on Windows 2000. The next Chapter, "Implementing VPNs on Linux," deals with the implementation of VPN solutions on a Linux platform.

In this chapter, you'll learn to configure a VPN solution on Windows 2000. You'll learn to set up a Remote Access VPN server, which is a must in a Windows 2000-based VPN environment for accepting incoming requests from VPN clients. Next, you'll learn to set up and configure a VPN client. You'll also implement Microsoft's RADIUS-based authentication server, which is known as Internet Authentication Server (IAS). PPTP and L2TP are supported natively by Windows 2000 and need not be configured separately. However, IPSec requires comprehensive configuration. Therefore, you'll learn to configure IPSec security policy in Windows 2000. Finally, you'll learn to implement PPTP and L2TP filters in the Windows 2000 environment.

Implementing a Basic VPN Solution

The basic implementation of a VPN solution on Windows 2000 involves the configuration of the following components:

◆ VPN servers
◆ VPN clients
◆ IAS server

You'll learn to set up and configure each of these components in the following sections.

Setting Up and Configuring a VPN Server

The first step in the implementation of a VPN solution on Windows 2000 is to set up a server to allow clients to access your intranet. However, you cannot just configure any machine as a VPN server. Per Microsoft's recommendations, your VPN server must have the following:

◆ A Pentium 133MHz (or higher) processor
◆ At least 128MB of RAM
◆ At least a 4GB hard disk
◆ Microsoft Windows 2000 Server or Windows 2000 Advanced Server installed on the machine

 NOTE

Although the minimum required RAM for a Windows-based VPN server is 128MB, 256MB or higher is recommended for better server performance. Similarly, although 4GB might be sufficient for a small-scale VPN setup, 10GB or higher is recommended. Another point to note here is that a 133MHz processor might prove to be inadequate. At least a 400MHz-processor is recommended. The server should also have dual processors if large-scale VPNs are involved.

As was emphasized in Chapter 7, "Building a VPN," the VPN server must support only the most essential services. This will limit the services available to an intruder, in case your VPN is successfully attacked. Therefore, while keeping the requirements of your organization and users in mind, Microsoft recommends that the following services be disabled:

◆ Fax services
◆ Distributed File Systems
◆ File Replication
◆ Indexing Services
◆ Internet Connection Sharing

- ◆ Messaging Services
- ◆ Task Scheduler
- ◆ Telnet
- ◆ Print Spooler
- ◆ Windows Installer
- ◆ Distributed Transaction Coordinator
- ◆ License Logging Services
- ◆ Kerberos Key Distribution Center

 CAUTION

Do not disable the Remote Registry Service. If you do so, your VPN server will not operate as required—or it might not operate at all.

Setting Up the VPN Server

After you have disabled the unnecessary services on the VPN server, you can start configuring your VPN server. The steps for VPN server configuration are as follows:

1. Choose Start, Programs, Administrative tools, Routing and Remote Access to open the Microsoft Management Consol (MMC) window, as shown in Figure 8-1. Your server will be listed in the left pane of the window.

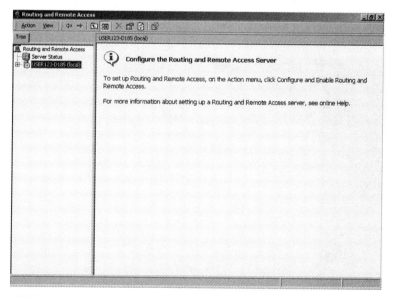

FIGURE 8-1 *The MMC window.*

2. In the left pane, right-click the server name. A shortcut menu will appear, as shown in Figure 8-2. Choose Configure and Enable Routing and Remote Access to initiate the installation of the Routing and Remote Access Server (RRAS).

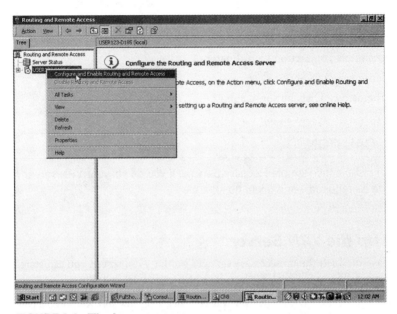

FIGURE 8-2 *The shortcut menu.*

3. The RRAS Setup Wizard appears, as shown in Figure 8-3. This wizard will help you configure the required services that allow your VPN clients to access the VPN server. Click Next to proceed.

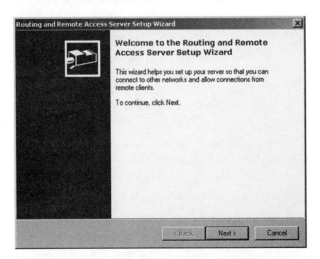

FIGURE 8-3 *The RRAS Setup Wizard.*

4. The Common Configurations window appears, as shown in Figure 8-4. Choose the Manually configured server option and click Next.

CAUTION

Do not choose the Virtual private network (VPN) server option. There might be a bug in the wizard that configures routing improperly.

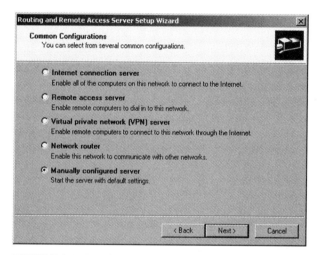

FIGURE 8-4 *The RRAS Setup Wizard—choosing a common configuration.*

5. Click Finish to complete the RRAS setup. A message box might appear, as shown in Figure 8-5. Do not feel anxious about this message. Click OK to close the message box. Another message box will appear, as shown in Figure 8-6.

FIGURE 8-5 *Finishing the Routing and Remote Access Server (RRAS) Setup Wizard.*

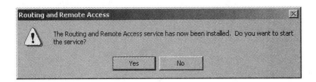

FIGURE 8-6 *Starting the Routing and Remote Access Server (RRAS) service.*

6. Click Yes when prompted to start the RRAS you just configured. RRAS is initialized and its MMC interface is displayed, as shown in Figure 8-7. Make sure that your VPN server is selected in the left pane of the window. Here, you'll also see that the properties that you have just configured for your VPN server with the help of RRAS Setup Wizard are displayed.

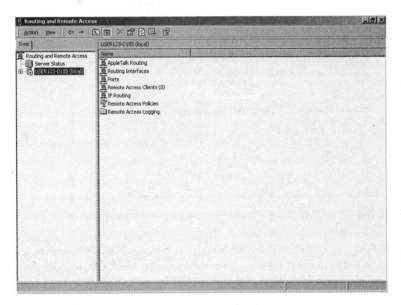

FIGURE 8-7 *The RRAS MMC.*

7. Right-click the server name and select Properties from the shortcut menu that appears. If you are not already there, select the General tab. As Figure 8-8 shows, here you can enable your VPN server to also act as a router by selecting the Router option. However, this practice is recommended only if your RRAS supports a very limited number of VPN clients. If the number of VPN clients is large, do not set up the server as a router as the performance of your RRAS will degrade considerably.

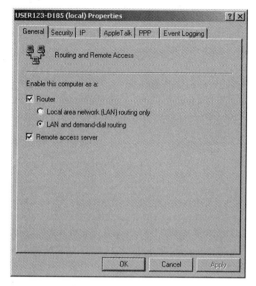

FIGURE 8-8 *Configuring the RRAS server as a router.*

8. Select the IP tab and make sure that the Enable IP Routing option is selected, as shown in Figure 8-9. This option allows you to control the resources your VPN clients can access. If this option is selected, VPN clients will be able to access all resources within the network. If this option is not selected, VPN clients can only

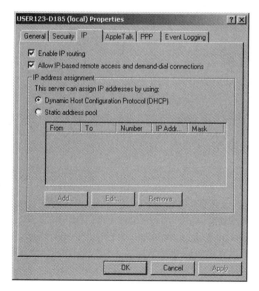

FIGURE 8-9 *Configuring the resources that VPN clients can access.*

access the resources and services located on the VPN server. The second option, Allow IP-based remote access and demand-dial connection, allows VPN clients to obtain IP addressing information from the VPN server.

9. In the IP address assignment pane, select the Static address pool option and click Add. The New Address Range dialog box will appear. As shown in Figure 8-10, enter a range of IP addresses that your VPN (RRAS) server can allocate to remote clients. The number of addresses in the range appears automatically in the Number of addresses field. Click OK to proceed.

TIP

If you use a static address pool, it is recommended that you make the pool part of the same network ID as the VPN server's internal interface. If you don't, you'll either need to deal with routing protocols or create static routes to accommodate VPN clients. Neither of these practices is recommended as both unnecessarily complicate VPN management.

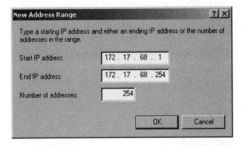

FIGURE 8-10 *Configuring the static address pool.*

10. Next, select the Event Logging tab and choose Log the maximum amount of information, as shown in Figure 8-11. This selection will help you troubleshoot connection-related problems.

11. Click OK to finish configuring the properties of the VPN server and return to the MMC console.

12. When you install RRAS in Windows 2000, five PPTP and five L2TP connections are created by default. You now need to configure these PPTP and L2TP ports. To do so, select Ports in the left pane. (You might need to expand the server by clicking "+.") A list of tunnel ports appears in the RRAS MMC, as depicted in Figure 8-12.

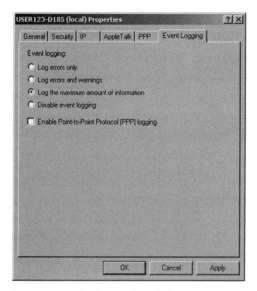

FIGURE 8-11 *Configuring the logging capability on the RRAS server.*

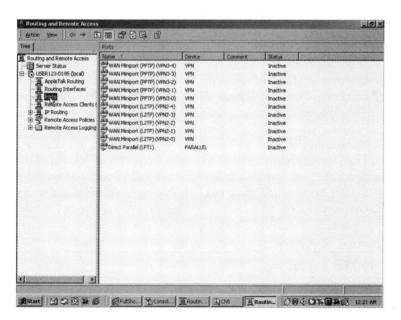

FIGURE 8-12 *The status of PPTP/L2TP ports in the RRAS MMC window.*

13. In the left pane, right-click Ports to display the shortcut menu. Select Properties to open the Ports Properties dialog box, as shown in Figure 8-13.

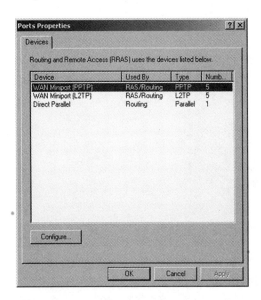

FIGURE 8-13 *The Ports Properties window.*

14. To configure the PPTP ports, select the WAN Miniport (PPTP) option. Then click Configure. In the Configure Device–WAN Miniport (PPTP) dialog box, deselect Demand-dial routing connections (inbound and outbound), as shown in Figure 8-14, because you will not be creating server-to-server tunnels with this server. The Remote access connections (inbound only) option allows VPN clients to access the VPN server. The Phone number for this device: box accepts the IP address of the server you are configuring, if you have already implemented a RAS policy. However, completing this box is not recommended until you have implemented and tested everything. Click OK to continue.

NOTE

The Demand-dial routing connections (inbound and outbound) option in this dialog box allows the VPN server to issue as well as receive a request from the demand-dial router. You must enable this option if you plan to implement router-to-router (or gateway-to-gateway) VPNs. Otherwise, this option must be deselected.

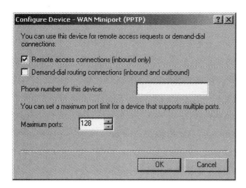

FIGURE 8-14 *Configuring PPTP/L2TP ports on RRAS.*

15. The Configure Device–WAN Miniport (L2TP) dialog box allows you to configure the remote server to accept remote access requests or demand-dial connections. Because you'll be configuring IPSec later, L2TP ports are not required right now. Therefore, select WAN Miniport (L2TP) and click Configure. Set the value of Maximum Ports to 0, as shown in Figure 8-15.

 NOTE

You might receive a warning indicating that currently running VPN connections, if any, may be disconnected. If you receive this warning, click Yes, as there are no current connections right now. This will take you back to the Port Properties window. Click OK to continue.

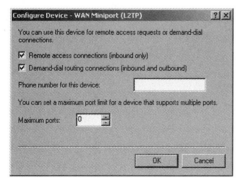

FIGURE 8-15 *Disabling L2TP ports.*

16. Click OK to return to the Ports Properties dialog box. Click OK to return to MMC console. As shown in Figure 8-16, you can now see the new PPTP ports that you just configured.

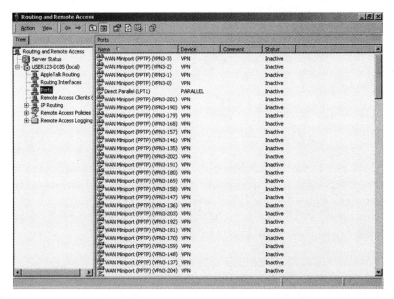

FIGURE 8-16 *The RRAS MMC window displaying the configured PPTP ports.*

17. From the RRAS MMC interface, select Remote Access Logging.

18. Right-click Local File in the right pane of the window. A shortcut menu will appear. Select Properties to open the Local File Properties dialog box. Verify that the Log authentication requests option on the Settings tab is selected, as shown in Figure 8-17. Click OK to finish configuring the RRAS.

Now that you've configured your VPN server, you can configure a remote access policy for it.

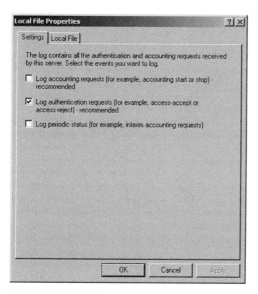

FIGURE 8-17 *The Local File Properties window.*

Configuring a Remote Access Policy

If you already have an existing remote access policy and would like to implement remote access on the basis of this policy, the steps to do so follow.

1. If it is not open, open the MMC window and select Remote Access Policies in the left pane.

2. Double-click Allow access if dial-in permission is enabled. The Allow access if dial-in permission is enabled Properties dialog box appears, as shown in Figure 8-18.

3. In the If a user matches the conditions pane, select the Grant remote access permission option, as shown in Figure 8-19. This will allow all VPN clients to access your VPN server whenever they want to.

4. Click OK to accept the change and close the dialog box. You'll return to the MMC console.

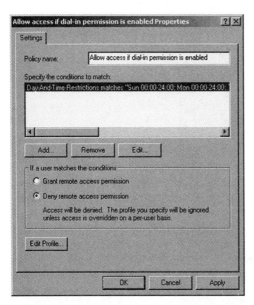

FIGURE 8-18 *The Allow access if dial-in permission is enabled Properties dialog box.*

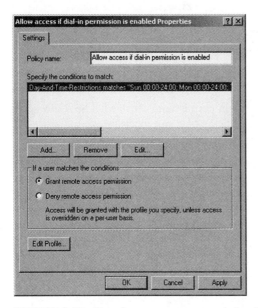

FIGURE 8-19 *Granting remote access permissions in the Allow access if dial-in permission is enabled dialog box.*

Setting Up and Configuring a VPN Client

In the Windows environment, VPN clients can be of the following types:

- ◆ Windows 9x (95/98)
- ◆ Windows NT 4.0 (Server as well as Workstation)
- ◆ Windows 2000 (Professional edition)
- ◆ Windows XP (Home and Professional editions)

 NOTE

Windows 95 and Windows 98 support PPTP connectivity only. L2TP has been incorporated in Windows 98 recently. Similarly, Windows NT Server supports PPTP only. Windows 2000, however, (both Professional and Server) supports PPTP as well as L2TP natively.

In the following sections you'll learn to configure VPN clients on Windows 9x and Windows 2000 machines.

Configuring a VPN Client on Windows 9x

In Windows 95 as well as 98, you can implement a VPN client by configuring the Microsoft Virtual Private Network Adapter. The steps for configuring a VPN client on Windows 9x are listed below:

1. Right-click the Network Neighborhood icon on the desktop. A shortcut menu will appear.
2. Select Properties to open the Network Property sheet shown in Figure 8-20.
3. Click the Add button to open the Select Network Component Type box, as shown in Figure 8-21. Select a network adapter. Click Add to proceed.
4. In the Manufacturers list, scroll down to Microsoft. Corresponding network adapters are displayed in the right pane, as shown in Figure 8-22.
5. Select the Microsoft Virtual Private Networking Adapter and click OK to add the VPN adapter, as shown in Figure 8-23.
6. Click OK and restart your machine to apply the changes. Further changes and actions related to configuring the VPN client will not take place until the machine is rebooted.

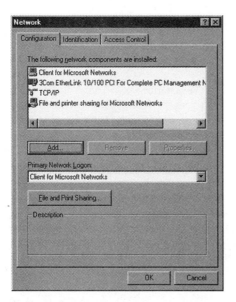

FIGURE 8-20 *The Network Property sheet.*

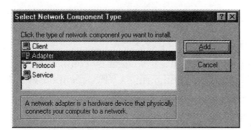

FIGURE 8-21 *Selecting a network adapter.*

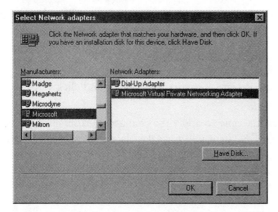

FIGURE 8-22 *Selecting a VPN network adapter.*

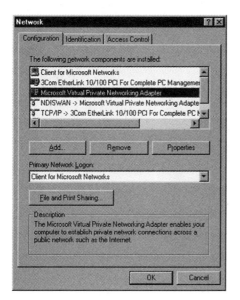

FIGURE 8-23 *Adding the VPN network adapter to configure a VPN client.*

After you have configured the VPN client on the Windows 9x computer, you'll need to configure your VPN connection so that the VPN client can successfully connect to the VPN server. The steps to configure the VPN connection on a Windows 9x platform follow:

1. Select Start, Programs, Accessories, Communications, Dial-Up Networking to open the Dial-Up Networking window, as shown in Figure 8-24.

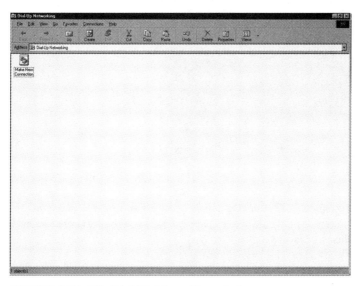

FIGURE 8-24 *The Dial-Up Networking window.*

2. Double-click the Make New Connection icon to create a new connection. As shown in Figure 8-25, a wizard window appears. The wizard will guide you through creating this connection.

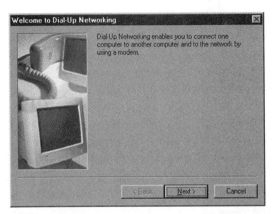

FIGURE 8-25 *The first screen of the Make New Connection Wizard window.*

3. Type a name for the connection in the Type a name for the computer you are dialing: box. Select Microsoft VPN Adapter in the Select a device drop-down list, as shown in Figure 8-26. Click Next to continue.

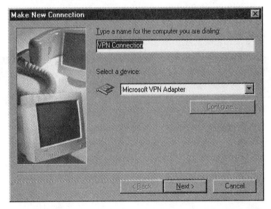

FIGURE 8-26 *Select Microsoft VPN Adapter as the connection device.*

4. As shown in Figure 8-27, the next screen prompts you for the name or the IP address of the VPN server you would like to connect to. Type the server name or IP address and click Next to proceed.

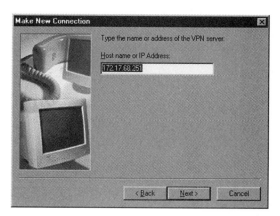

FIGURE 8-27 *Specify the host name or IP address of the target VPN server.*

5. Click Finish. In the Dial-Up Networking window, right-click the new icon and select Properties from the shortcut menu. The connection's property sheet is displayed, as shown in Figure 8-28.

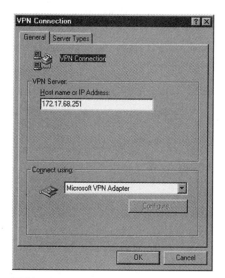

FIGURE 8-28 *The connection's property sheet.*

6. Click the Server Types tab and in the Advanced options pane verify that the Log on to the network option is selected, as shown in Figure 8-29. If you want data to be compressed and the password to be encrypted when the client sends an access request to the target server, you'll should also verify that the Enable software compression and Require encrypted password options are selected.

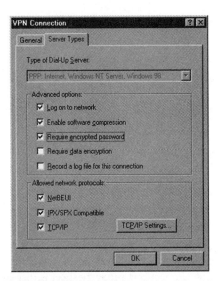

FIGURE 8-29 *Logging on to the network.*

7. In the Allowed network protocols: pane, as shown in Figure 8-30, select the required protocol. Choose NetBEUI if your VPN is local, IPX/SPX if the VPN runs on a Novell platform, and TCP/IP if you use a TCP/IP-based intermediate internetwork for the VPN connection. Click OK to close the dialog box.

You can now double-click the connection icon to initiate and establish the connection.

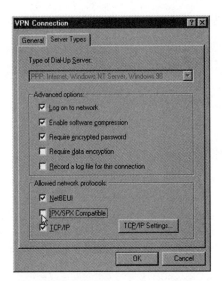

FIGURE 8-30 *Selecting the appropriate transport protocol.*

Creating a VPN Connectoid in Windows 9x

In Windows 9x and Windows NT you can create a script for logging on to the specified network (or host) and distribute that script in the form of an icon to some or all of your VPN clients. This icon is referred to as a connectoid and allows you to configure several VPN clients at once.

NOTE

To create the connectoid you must have the Connection Manager Administration Kit installed. If this kit is not installed, you'll need to install it by selecting Add/Remove Programs, Add/Remove Windows Components in the Control Panel window.

The steps for creating the VPN connectoid are as follows:

1. Choose Start, Programs, Administrative Tools, Connection Manager Administration Kit to start the Connection Manager shown in Figure 8-31. Click Next to proceed.

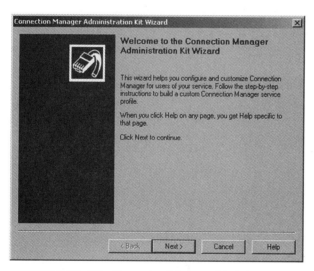

FIGURE 8-31   *The Connection Manager Administration Kit Wizard window.*

2. Select the Create a new service profile option to create a new service profile for client connection. If you already have an existing service profile, select the Edit this existing service profile option and select the required service profile from the list. These options are illustrated in Figure 8-32.

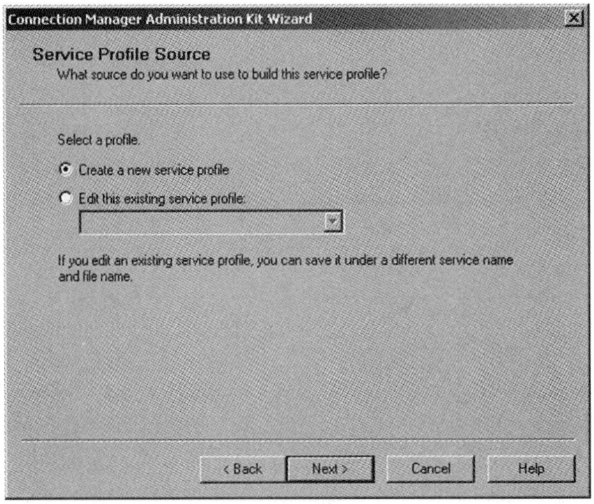

FIGURE 8-32 *Creating a service profile.*

3. The next dialog box of the wizard prompts you to supply a name for the connectoid in form of the Service name, as shown in Figure 8-33. You are also prompted for a File name, which is the name of the executable file that will be created. After supplying the required information, click Next to proceed.

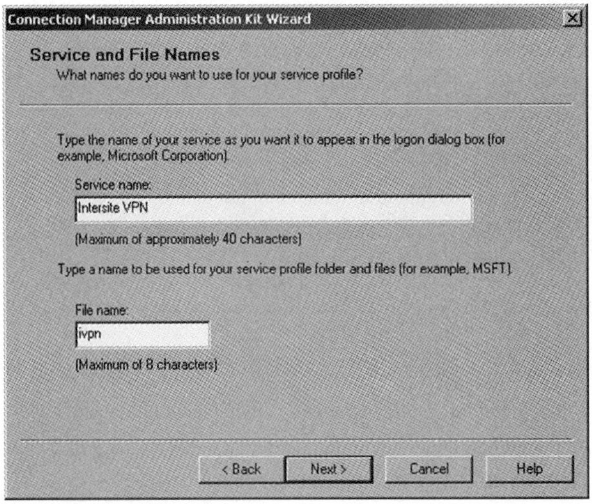

FIGURE 8-33 *Supplying a service name and file name for the connectoid.*

4. If you already have an existing service profile and would like to merge it with the new profile you are creating, you can use the next wizard window, Merged Service Profiles, to do so. However, if you do not have an existing profile, you can click Next to ignore this step. Figure 8-34 depicts the Merged Service Profiles dialog box.

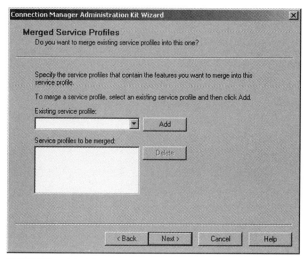

FIGURE 8-34 *The Merged Service Profiles dialog box.*

5. In the next step, depicted in Figure 8-35, you can supply support information to your users so they have a place to turn if they run into problems connecting to the VPN server. Click Next to continue.

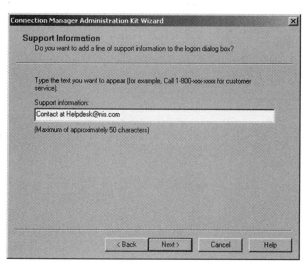

FIGURE 8-35 *Supplying support information (help) to users.*

6. In the next window, shown in Figure 8-36, you'll be prompted for a realm name. If your VPN service does not require a realm name, click Next to continue.

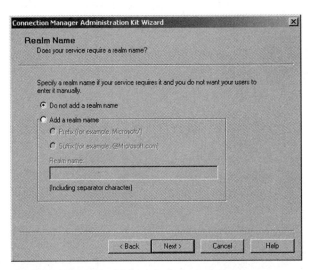

FIGURE 8-36 *Supplying realm information.*

7. The next window, shown in Figure 8-37, prompts you for the dial-up networking numbers that you will need to start the dial-up connection. Because you are not setting custom Dial-up networking entries for your users, you can ignore this step by clicking on Next to proceed further.

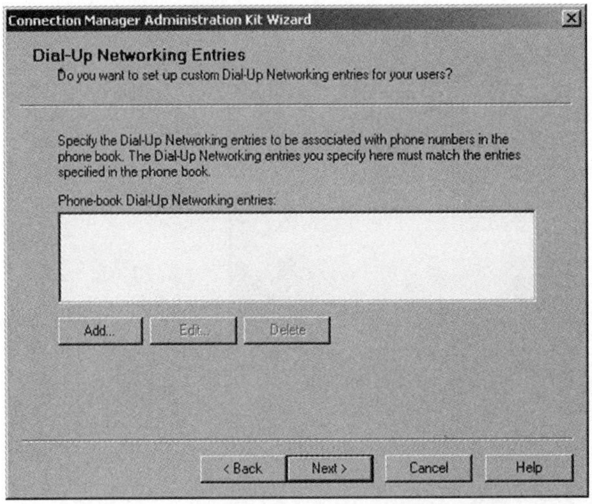

FIGURE 8-37 *Supplying dial-up networking entries for the connection.*

8. The next window, shown in Figure 8-38, prompts you to supply VPN support information. Select the This service profile option if you are not using a merged service profile. Otherwise, select the Merged service profiles option and click Next to continue.

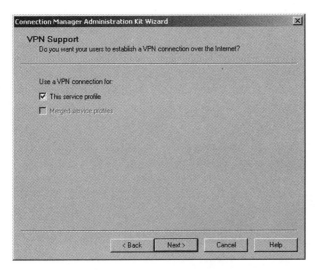

FIGURE 8-38 *Supplying VPN support information.*

9. In the next step, shown in Figure 8-39, you need to supply the name of the target server. You can also supply the IP address of the server. Select the Allow the server to assign an address option if you would like the VPN server to assign the address to the connection. Alternatively, you can assign Primary and Secondary DNS addresses and

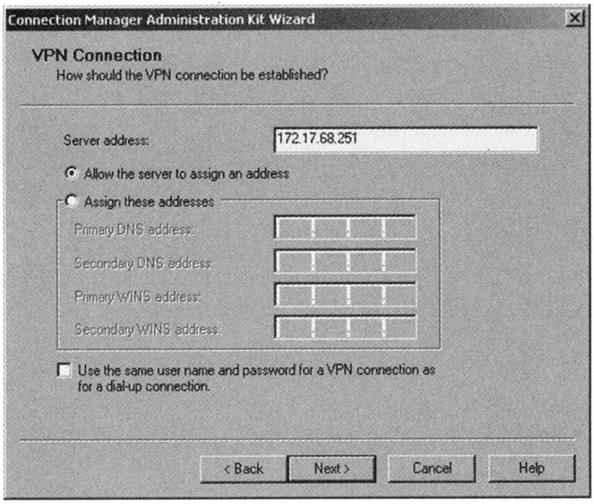

FIGURE 8-39 *Supplying VPN connection information.*

Primary and Secondary WINS addresses to the connection. You can also select the Use the same user name and password for a VPN connection as for a dial-up connection option if you would like to use the same ID and password for the dial-up connection to the target server.

10. The next window, depicted in Figure 8-40, prompts you for any connect actions that would be run before the establishment of the connection or tunnel or after the disconnection of the tunnel or connection. Deselect all checkboxes in the dialog box and proceed by clicking Next.

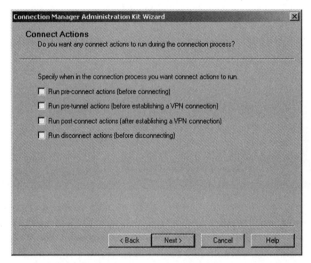

FIGURE 8-40 *Supplying information related to connect actions to be performed before or after the connection is established or terminated.*

11. In the next step, you'll be prompted for any applications you would like to run when a user connects. Figure 8-41 depicts this wizard window. Click Next to continue.

12. The next step, shown in Figure 8-42, prompts you to select a bitmap icon for the logon screen. Here, you can supply any icon of your liking, including the logo of your organization. You can also retain the default icon. Click Next to proceed.

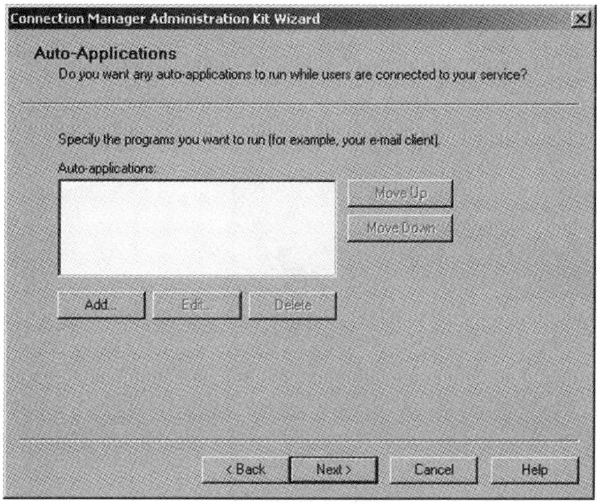

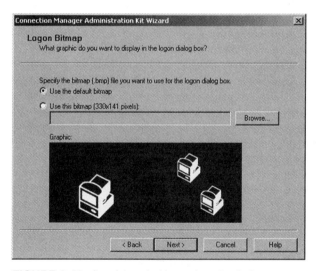

FIGURE 8-41 *Configuring the auto-applications that VPN clients can access.*

FIGURE 8-42 *Supplying the bitmap icon for the logon screen.*

13. The next step, depicted in Figure 8-43, prompts you to select a bitmap icon for the Phone Book dialog box. You can either accept the default icon suggested by the wizard or specify a custom icon. Click Next to continue.

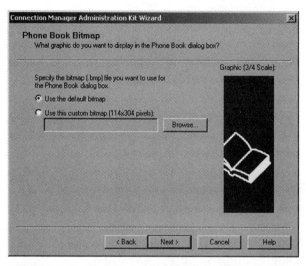

FIGURE 8-43 *Supplying the bitmap icon for the Phone Book dialog box.*

14. Next, you are prompted for a Phone Book file, as shown in Figure 8-44. Click Next to continue configuring the connectoid.

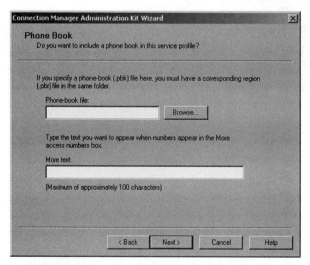

FIGURE 8-44 *Supplying a Phone Book file for the service profile.*

15. The next step, shown in Figure 8-45, prompts you for the icons that will be displayed for the Connection Manager. Click Next to continue.

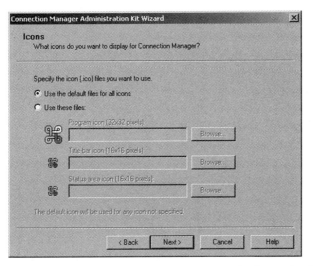

FIGURE 8-45 *Supplying icon information for the Connection Manager.*

16. The next screen prompts you to customize the shortcut menu that appears when users right-click the Status-Area icon. Figure 8-46 depicts this window. You can ignore this step by clicking Next.

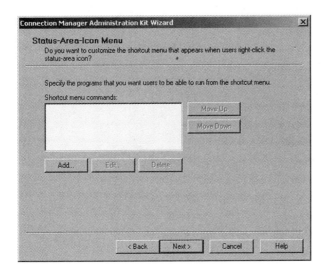

FIGURE 8-46 *Customizing the Status-Area icon.*

17. Next, you are prompted for a customized help file, as shown in Figure 8-47. If you do not have one, you can ignore this step by clicking Next.

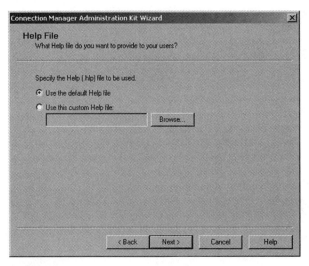

FIGURE 8-47 *Attaching a help file to the connectoid.*

18. As shown in Figure 8-48, you can use the next screen to include Connection Manager 1.2 software in your service profile. Click Next to continue.

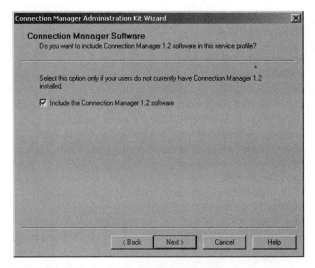

FIGURE 8-48 *Including the Connection Manager software.*

19. The next screen—the License Agreement screen shown in Figure 8-49—helps you specify a license agreement that VPN clients must accept before installing the connectoid. If you do not have a custom license agreement, you can ignore this step by clicking Next.

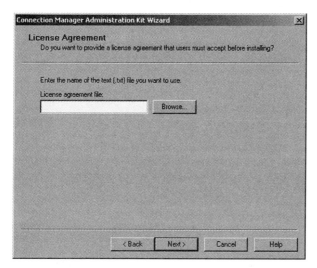

FIGURE 8-49 *Supplying license information to VPN clients.*

20. You can use the next screen, shown in Figure 8-50, to attach any additional files to the service profile. If you do not have any additional files to supply, you can click Next to ignore the step.

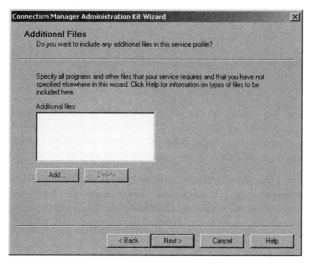

FIGURE 8-50 *Including additional files, if any.*

21. As shown in Figure 8-51, you are now ready to build the service profile. Click OK. The Command Prompt window will appear and will be displayed for few seconds.

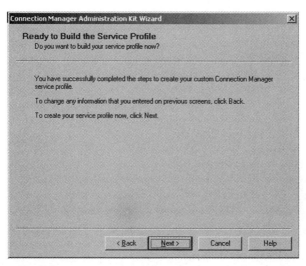

FIGURE 8-51 *Building the service profile.*

22. As shown in Figure, 8-52, the last screen of the Wizard is displayed, which implies that your connectoid is ready. Click Finish to build the connectoid.

FIGURE 8-52 *Building the connectoid.*

Now that your connectoid is created, you'll need to tweek a few post-configuration settings to ensure that your users do not face any problems. The steps for post-configuration settings include the following:

1. As shown in Figure 8-53, locate the executable for the connectoid that you just created under Program Files, CMAK, Profiles, <connectoid name>. The executable of the connectoid has a .cms extension.

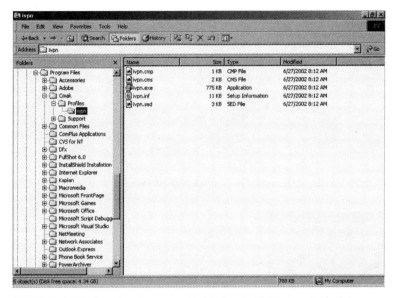

FIGURE 8-53 *Locating the executable file (with .CMS extension) of the connectoid.*

2. Open the file with .cms extension in notepad (or WordPad) for editing, as shown in Figure 8-54. Locate the line with Dialup=1. Change the 1 to a 0. Save the file and exit.

3. Open the Connection Manager Administration Kit application and click Next to proceed.

4. Double-click the connectoid (ivpn.exe) to install it. The installation dialog box appears, as depicted in Figure 8-55. Click OK to install the connectoid.

5. Distribute the .exe file to the VPN clients and ask the clients to run this file. The connectoid will be installed in the clients' Dial-Up Networking window.

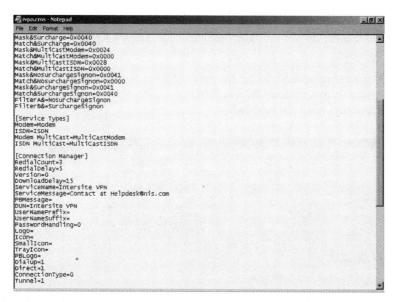

FIGURE 8-54 *Editing the connectoid configuration information.*

FIGURE 8-55 *Specifying the users who can access the connectoid.*

Configuring a VPN Client on Windows 2000

The steps for the configuration of a VPN client on the Windows 2000 platform are as follows:

1. Select Start, Settings, Network and Dial-Up Connections to open the Dial-Up Networking window.

2. Double-click the Make New Connection icon to run the Network Connection Wizard. Click Next to continue.

3. Select the Connect to a private network through the Internet option, as shown in Figure 8-56.

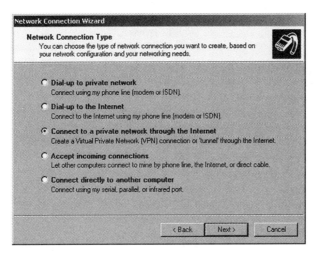

FIGURE 8-56 *Creating a VPN connection.*

4. In the next screen, specify the host name or the IP address of the target VPN server, as shown in Figure 8-57. Click Next to proceed.

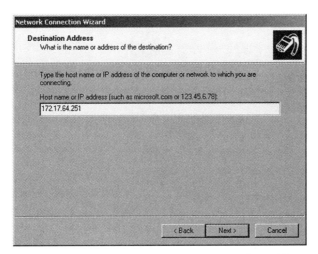

FIGURE 8-57 *Specifying the name or the IP address of the target VPN server.*

5. The next dialog box, shown in Figure 8-58, prompts you to choose which users can make the VPN connection. Verify that the For all users option is selected, if you want all users to connect to the VPN server. You can select the Only for myself option, if you want only the given client (on whose machine the connection is being made) to make use of the connection. Click Next to proceed.

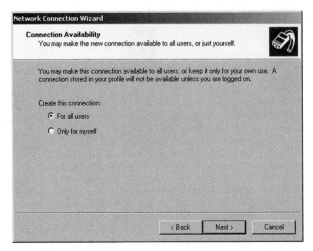

FIGURE 8-58 *Specifying the users that can make use of the given VPN connection.*

6. You can share your Internet connection by selecting the Enable Internet Connection Sharing for this connection option, as shown in Figure 8-59. Click Next to proceed.

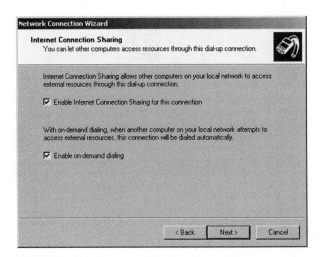

FIGURE 8-59 *Sharing the Internet Connection.*

7. In this final step, shown in Figure 8-60, you're prompted to enter a name for the connection. Click Finish to create the connection and save it in the Network and Dial-Up Connections folder, as shown in Figure 8-61.

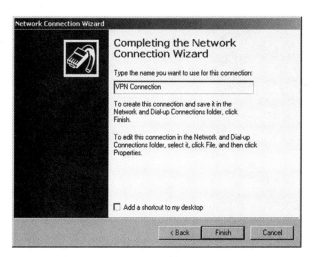

FIGURE 8-60 *Completing the Network Connection Wizard.*

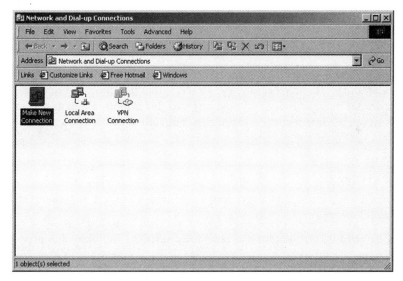

FIGURE 8-61 *Finishing the VPN connection.*

8. After the VPN connection is created, a dial-up window will appear, as shown in Figure 8-62. Enter the User name and corresponding Password to connect to the specified VPN server.

Now that you have implemented a VPN server and a VPN client, the final step of basic configuration is setting up an authentication server.

FIGURE 8-62 *Testing the VPN connection.*

Setting Up and Configuring an Authentication Server

Microsoft uses a proprietary authentication server known as Internet Authentication Service (IAS) for authentication purposes. In addition to its primary task of providing a centralized authentication service, IAS also provides authorization and accounting for remote VPN clients. IAS uses the RADIUS protocol to centrally administer all incoming remote requests regardless of client platform or networking environment.

The main advantage of implementing IAS servers is that they provide a centralized authentication service for multiple remote access servers. In this manner, a remote access server, such as a VPN server, is relieved of the additional task of authenticating users.

Features of IAS

Microsoft IAS offers many features that make the implementation of authentication, authorization, and accounting infrastructure simple and easy. The most important features of IAS include the following:

◆ **Centralized authentication of remote requests.** As you learned in previous chapters, proper authentication of remote requests is an extremely important issue from the perspective of your intranet security. IAS supports various authentication protocols, such as Password Authentication Protocol (PAP), Microsoft-Challenge Handshake Authentication Protocol (MS-CHAP), and Extensible Authentication Protocol (EAP). (Refer to Chapter 5, "Tunneling Protocols at Layer 2," for more information on these authentication protocols.) Another authentication method used by IAS for authentication of remote requests is guest authentication, where the remote users do not need to supply their user IDs and passwords to access the requested resource or service. However, unauthenticated access must be enabled to support guest authentication on IAS.

◆ **Centralized authorization of remote requests.** IAS allows the authorization of remote requests from a single point. For this purpose, it supports Dialed Number Identification Service (DNIS) to authorize users on the basis of the numbers called by the clients to access the Internet. In addition, Automatic Number Identification/Calling Line Identification (ANI/CLI) is also used to authorize users on the basis of the numbers used by the user making the remote request.

◆ **Centralized accounting of resource usage.** Besides centralized authentication and authorization of remote requests, IAS allows the collection of individual account-related information at a central location. IAS logs this usage-related information and detailed request acceptance/rejection information into log files that can be easily imported into databases. This makes the task of analyzing the recorded data extremely simple.

◆ **Integration with Windows 2000 RRAS.** In Windows 2000, IAS and RRAS share the same authorization and account logging services along with common remote access policies. Therefore, RRAS can be configured as a client to an IAS server. Similarly, IAS servers can use RRAS policies and logs. As a result, you can integrate RRAS and IAS as a single physical entity. However, you need to remember that this integration works better in small-scale VPN setups. As the processing load on an integrated IAS and RRAS increases, the performance of both services decreases proportionately—which is typically the case in medium- to large-scale organizations.

◆ **Control of outsourced dialing.** If your remote employees use dial-up services to connect to the ISP, which in turn connects the client to the organization's intranet, implementing an IAS server will allow you to control and monitor the dial-up scenario. All authentication and usage records are forwarded by the NAS at the ISP's POP to the IAS server located on the organization's premises. Therefore, you can track and manage remote users who use a dial-up connection to connect to the ISP site.

◆ **Simpler administration.** IAS, like other Windows products, is a GUI-based administrative tool. GUI is easy to understand and use, even for non-technical end users. In addition, IAS allows you to export the configuration settings of one IAS server to other far-flung IAS servers, making administration much simpler.

◆ **Scalability and extendibility.** IAS servers can be implemented in small-scale intranets and enterprise-wide intranets effectively. In addition, you can use two or more IAS servers to implement a highly fault-tolerant AAA infrastructure. Windows 2000 is shipped with the IAS Software Development Kit (IAS SDK) and the EAP Software Development Kit (EAP SDK), both of which can be used to extend the functionality of IAS servers. By extending the functionality of IAS servers, you can perform additional tasks. These tasks include controlling the number of concurrent remote users, extending remote authorization capabilities, and creating customized EAP authentication methods.

Configuring and Setting up IAS

In order to configure a RADIUS-based authentication and accounting solution in the form of IAS, follow these steps:

1. Choose Start, Programs, Administrative Tools, Routing and Remote Access to open the Microsoft Management Console (MMC) window.

2. In the console tree (left pane), right-click the server for which you want to configure the RADIUS authentication. A shortcut menu appears. Choose Properties to open the server's Property sheet.

3. Activate the Security tab of the Properties sheet. From the Authentication provider drop-down list, select RADIUS Authentication, as shown in Figure 8-63.

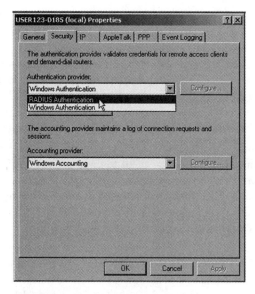

FIGURE 8-63 *Configuring RADIUS authentication on IAS.*

4. Click Configure to open the RADIUS Authentication dialog box, shown in Figure 8-64.

5. Click Add to open the Add RADIUS Server dialog box, shown in Figure 8-65.

6. Specify the name of the RADIUS server in the Server name box. Click Change to specify the shared secret that will be used for securing communication between the VPN server (RAS) and the RADIUS server, as shown in Figure 8-66.

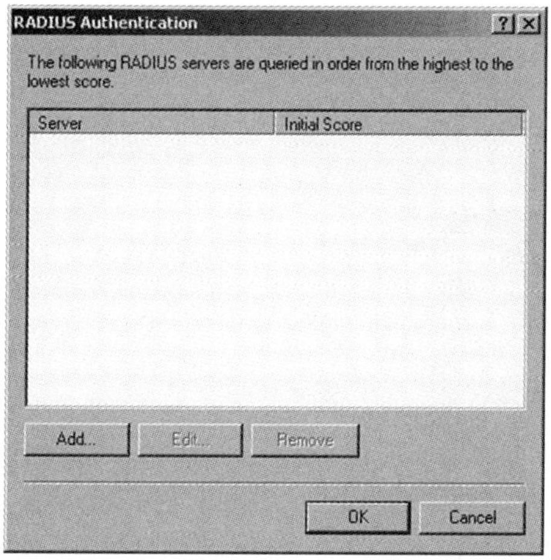

FIGURE 8-64 *The RADIUS Authentication dialog box.*

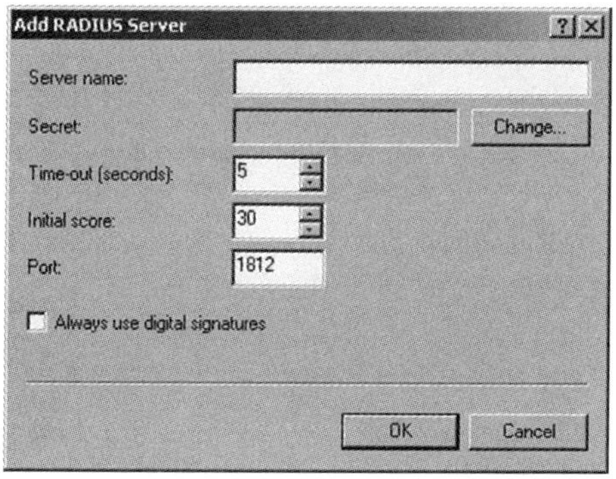

FIGURE 8-65 *The Add RADIUS server dialog box.*

FIGURE 8-66 *Specifying the shared secret information to be used between the RADIUS server and the IAS server.*

7. Click OK to close the Change Secret dialog box. Also, click OK to close the Add RADIUS server dialog box and return to the RADIUS Authentication dialog box. You have now configured RADIUS authentication on the IAS server, as shown in Figure 8-67.

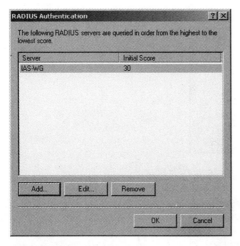

FIGURE 8-67 *The successfully configured RADIUS-based IAS server.*

8. Click OK to close the RADIUS Authentication dialog box. A message box will appear, as shown in Figure 8-68. Click OK to close the message box and return to the Property sheet.

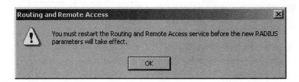

FIGURE 8-68 *The successfully configured RADIUS-based IAS server.*

9. Activate the Security tab of the Property sheet, if necessary. From the Accounting provider drop-down list, select RADIUS Accounting and then click Configure to open the RADIUS Accounting dialog box, shown in Figure 8-69.

10. Click Add… to open the Add RADIUS Server dialog box and configure the settings for your RADIUS Accounting server, shown in Figure 8-70.

11. Click OK to return to RADIUS Accounting dialog box. Again, Click OK. A message box is displayed. Click OK to close the message box and return to the MMC window.

12. You might be prompted for any auto-applications you want to run when a user connects. Click Next to continue. With this, you have successfully configured your IAS server RADIUS for authentication and accounting.

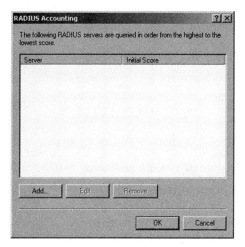

FIGURE 8-69 *The RADIUS Accounting dialog box.*

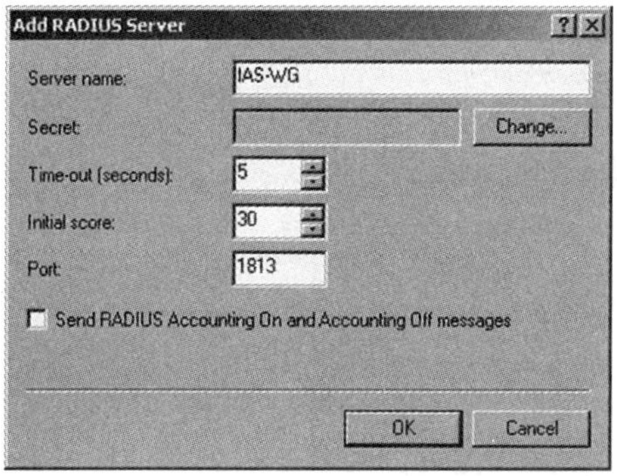

FIGURE 8-70 *Adding the RADIUS server.*

Configuring RADIUS-based IAS Clients

Now that your IAS server is ready, you can register RADIUS clients. The steps for doing so follow:

1. Click Start, Programs, Administrative Tools, Internet Authentication Service to open the Internet Authentication Service window shown in Figure 8-71.

2. In the left pane, right-click Clients. A shortcut menu will appear. Select New Client to open the Add Client dialog box shown in Figure 8-72.

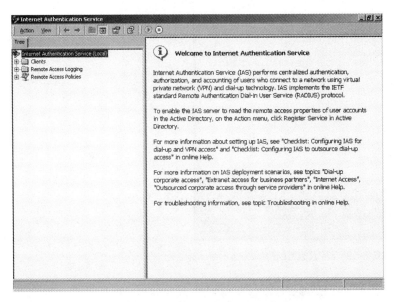

FIGURE 8-71 *The Internet Authentication Service window.*

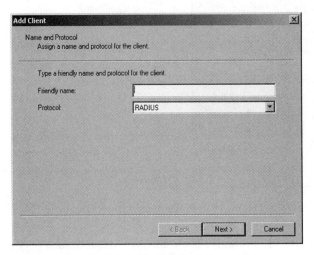

FIGURE 8-72 *The Add Client dialog box.*

3. In the Friendly name box, type a descriptive name of the client you are configuring. In the Protocol drop-down list, ensure that RADIUS is selected. Figure 8-73 depicts an example of this configuration. Click Next to continue.

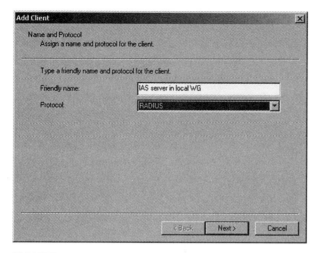

FIGURE 8-73 *Supplying client details.*

4. In the Client address (IP or DNS) box, type the DNS name or the IP address of the client. If you have specified the DNS name, click Verify. The Resolve DNS Name dialog box will appear, as shown in Figure 8-74.

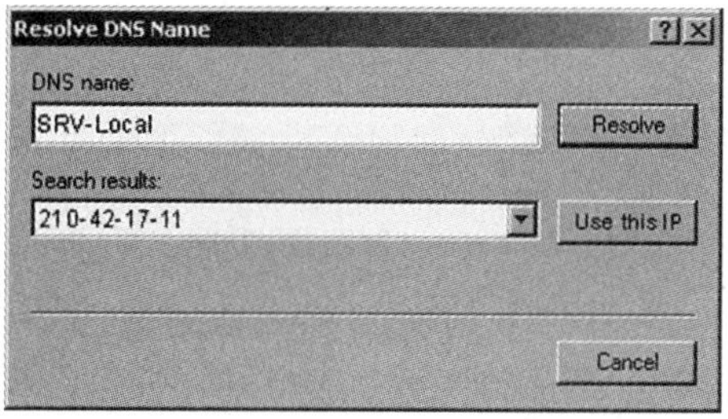

FIGURE 8-74 *The Resolve DNS Name dialog box.*

5. Click Resolve and then select the IP address from the Search results list that you want to associate with that name. Next, click Use this IP to return to the Add RADIUS Client window.

6. If you are registering an NAS client to the IAS server, from the Client Vendor drop-down list select the manufacturer's name. If you do not know the manufacturer's name or the name is not listed, verify that RADIUS Standard is selected, as shown in Figure 8-75.

7. If your NAS supports digital signatures for authentication, select the Client must always send the signature attribute in the request option. However, if the NAS does not support digital signatures, do not select the option. Click OK to proceed.

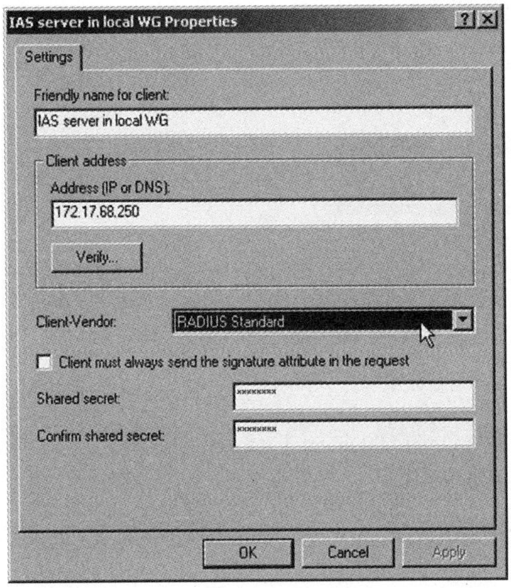

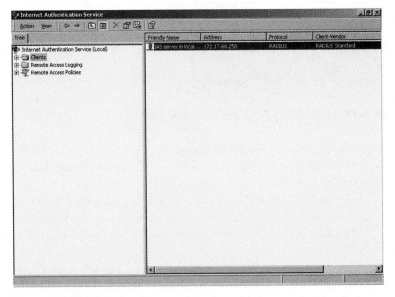

FIGURE 8-75 *Configuring an NAS as a client.*

8. Click Finish to complete the client registration process and return to the Internet Authentication Service window. The registered client should appear in the right pane of the window, as shown in Figure 8-76.

FIGURE 8-76 *The registered client appears in the right pane of the window.*

Copying the Configuration of an IAS to Another Server

In order to copy the configuration of one IAS server to another, you need to take the following steps:

1. Go to the command prompt and type `netsh aaaa show configuration <path of the text file>`. This command is used to store the configuration information in the specified text file (`<path of the text file>`).

2. Copy the text file that you created in Step 1 to the destination machine(s).

3. At the command prompt of the destination machine, type the command `netsh exec <path of the stored text file>`. A message should be displayed indicating the success or failure of the command. If the message indicates success, you have copied the configuration of one IAS server to another.

 NOTE

In the first step, if the `netsh aaaa show configuration` command does not work, you can use the `netsh aaaa dump configuration` command instead. Similarly, use the `netsh ras aaaa` command if the `netsh aaaa` command does not work.

The best aspect of copying the configuration of one IAS server to another server is that you do not need to stop the destination IAS server in order to run the `netsh exec` command. IAS is automatically refreshed and configurations are updated when you run this command.

Advanced VPN Configuration

With the successful configuration of the IAS server and the registration of IAS (RADIUS) clients, the basic implementation of the VPN is complete. You can now implement advanced services, such as IPSec and firewalls. In this section, you'll learn to configure IPSec, PPTP, and L2TP filters.

Configuring IPSec on Windows 2000

As mentioned earlier, IPSec is also supported natively in Windows 2000. However, its implementation might not be as complete as PPTP or L2TP.

The steps to implement IPSec on your VPN devices follow:

1. Choose Start, Run to open the Run box. In the Open box, type mmc to open a new MMC window called Console1 - [Console Root], as shown in Figure 8-77.

2. From the Console menu (first option on the Menu bar), select Add/Remove Snap-in. The Add/Remove Snap-in dialog box, shown in Figure 8-78, appears.

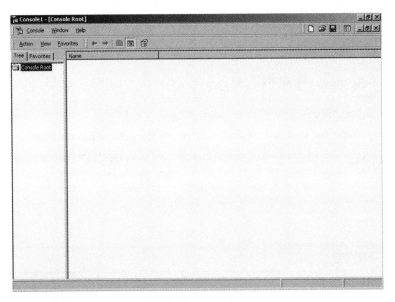

FIGURE 8-77 *The custom MMC window.*

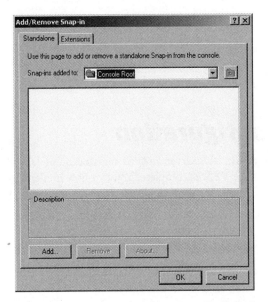

FIGURE 8-78 *The Add/Remove Snap-in dialog box.*

3. Click Add… to open the Add Standalone Snap-in dialog box. From the Available Standalone Snap-ins list, select Computer Management, as shown in Figure 8-79, and then click Add.

FIGURE 8-79 *The Add Standalone Snap-in dialog box.*

4. In the This snap-in will always manage pane of the Computer Management dialog box, make sure that the Local computer option is selected. This is shown in Figure 8-80. Click Finish to return to the Add Standalone Snap-in dialog box.

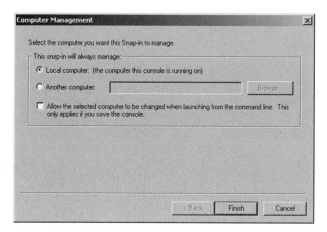

FIGURE 8-80 *The Computer Management dialog box.*

5. Scroll down and select Group Policy in the Available Standalone Snap-ins list. Click Add to open the Select Group Policy Object dialog box. Verify that Local Computer is selected in the Group Policy Object box, as shown in Figure 8-81. Click Finish to return to the Add Standalone Snap-in dialog box.

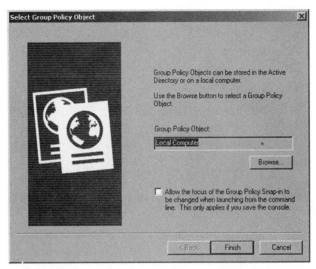

FIGURE 8-81 *The Select Group Policy Object dialog box.*

6. Select Certificates from the Available Standalone Snap-ins list and click Add. The Certificates snap-in dialog box appears, as shown in Figure 8-82. Select the Computer account option from the This snap-in will manage certificates for list and click Next to continue.

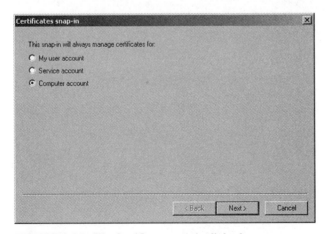

FIGURE 8-82 *The Certificates snap-in dialog box.*

7. Next, verify that the Local computer option is selected, as shown in Figure 8-83, and click Finish to return to the Add/Remove Snap-in dialog box.

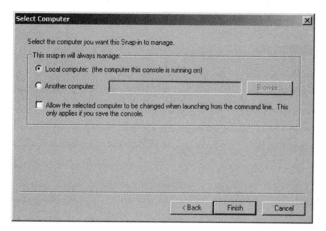

FIGURE 8-83 *Selecting the computer for certificate management.*

8. Click Close to close the Add Standalone Snap-in dialog box. The three snap-ins that you selected should appear in the Standalone tab of the dialog box, as shown in Figure 8-84. Close the Add/Remove Snap-in dialog box by clicking OK. You'll return to the MMC console.

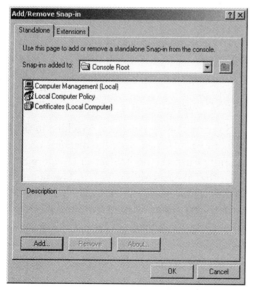

FIGURE 8-84 *Displaying the added snap-ins.*

9. The three snap-ins will also appear in the console window. In the MMC console, select Local Computer Policy in the left pane. Expand the tree by clicking the plus (+) sign. Navigate to Computer Configuration, Windows Settings, Security Settings, Local Policies, and then finally to Audit Policy, as shown in Figure 8-85.

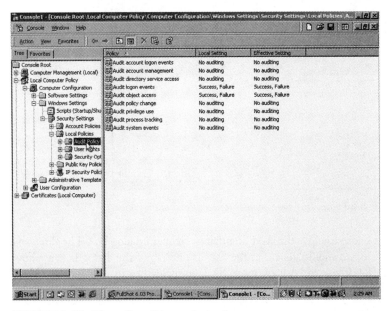

FIGURE 8-85 *The audit policies on the local computer.*

10. In the right pane, double-click the Audit logon events attribute. The Local Security Policy Setting dialog box will appear. Under Audit these attempts, select the Success and Failure checkboxes, as shown in Figure 8-86. Click OK to accept the change and close the dialog box.

11. Repeat Step 10 for the Audit object access attribute.

12. In the MMC console, select IP Security Policies on Local Machine in the left pane. Three entries will appear in the right pane. If you want the machine on which you are currently working to be a server, right-click the Secure Server (Require Security) attribute. From the shortcut menu that appears, select Assign. The status in the Policy Assigned column will change to Yes, as shown in Figure 8-87. Otherwise, right-click the Client attribute in the right pane and choose Assign from the shortcut menu. The status in the Policy Assigned column for the Client attribute will change to Yes, as shown in Figure 8-88.

FIGURE 8-86 *The Local Security Policy Setting dialog box.*

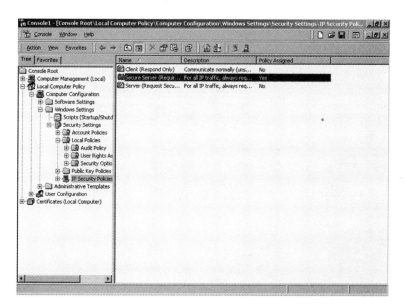

FIGURE 8-87 *Assigning security settings to an IPSec server.*

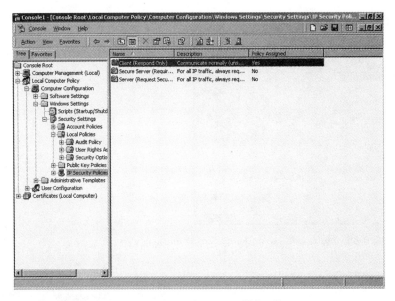

FIGURE 8-88 *Assigning security settings to an IPSec client.*

13. In the left pane, right-click IPSec Policies on Local Machine. A shortcut menu will appear. Select the Create IP Security Policy option, as shown in Figure 8-89, to run the IP Security Policy Wizard. Click Next to continue.

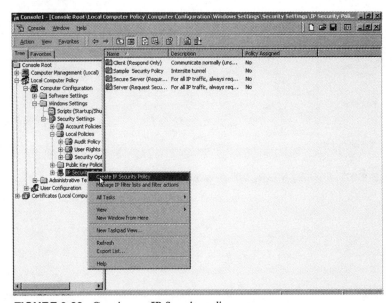

FIGURE 8-89 *Creating an IP Security policy.*

14. In the Name box, type Sample Security Policy. In the Description box, type Intersite tunnel, as shown in Figure 8-90. Click Next to continue.

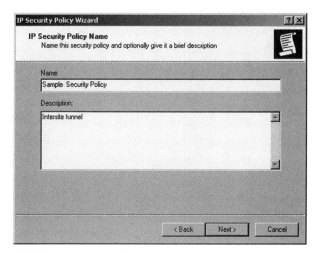

FIGURE 8-90 *Specifying the name of the IP Security policy.*

15. In the next screen, clear the Activate the default response rule checkbox, as shown in Figure 8-91. Click Next to continue.

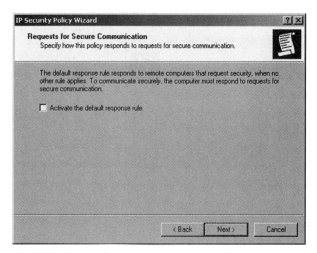

FIGURE 8-91 *Specifying the machine's response to requests for secure communications.*

16. In the next wizard screen, verify that the Edit Properties checkbox is selected and click Finish to close the wizard. The property sheet for the policy that you have created will appear, as shown in Figure 8-92.

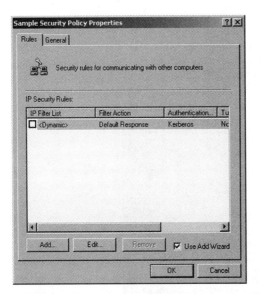

FIGURE 8-92 *The property sheet of the sample policy.*

17. Verify that the Use Add Wizard checkbox is selected. Click Add to run the Security Rule Wizard. Click Next to continue.

18. As shown in Figure 8-93, verify that the This rule does not specify a tunnel option is selected. Click Next to continue.

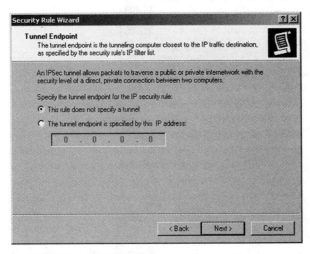

FIGURE 8-93 *Disabling IPSec tunnels.*

19. In the next wizard screen, verify that the All network connections option is selected, as shown in Figure 8-94. Click Next to continue.

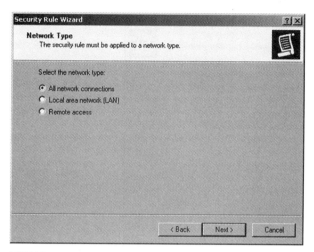

FIGURE 8-94 *Applying the rule to a network.*

20. In the next screen, select the Use this string to protect this key exchange option. Type XNWQ9675 as the protection string. Figure 8-95 shows the screen. Click Next to continue.

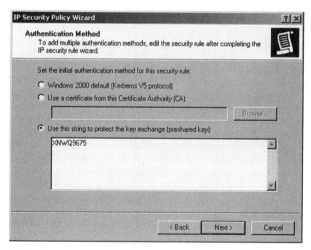

FIGURE 8-95 *Configuring the authentication method for the rule.*

21. In the next screen, default IP filter lists are displayed, as shown in Figure 8-96. You'll now add a custom filter for the rule.

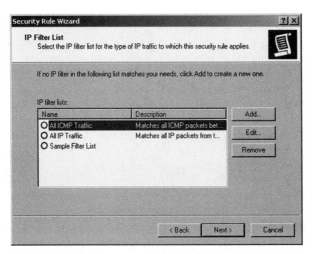

FIGURE 8-96 *Displaying the default IP filter lists.*

22. Click Add... to open the IP Filter List dialog box. In the Name box, type Sample Filter List, as shown in Figure 8-97. Verify that the Use Add Wizard check box is selected and again click Add... to run the IP Filter Wizard. Click Next to continue.

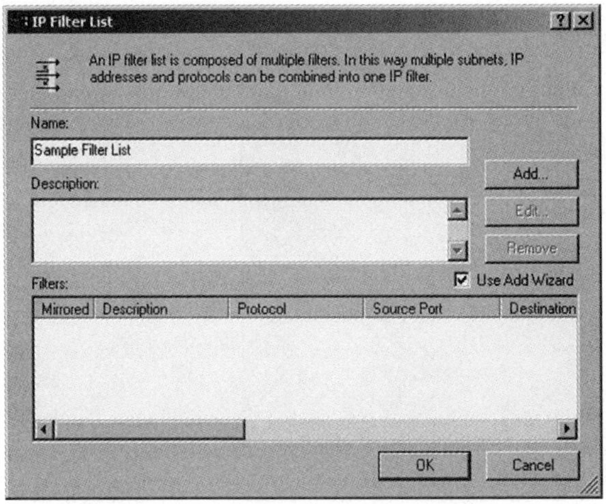

FIGURE 8-97 *Creating a custom IP filter list.*

23. In the next screen, verify that under Source address the My IP Address option is selected, as shown in Figure 8-98. Click Next to continue.

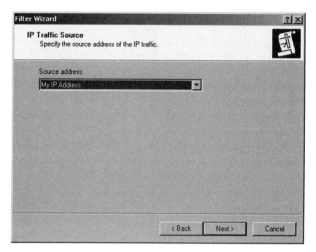

FIGURE 8-98 *Specifying the source address of the IP traffic.*

24. In the next screen, select A specific IP Address from the Destination address drop-down list. Specify the server or the client machine in the IP Address box, as shown in Figure 8-99. Click Next to continue.

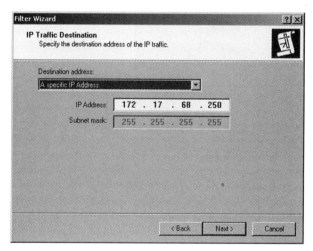

FIGURE 8-99 *Specifying the destination address of the IP traffic.*

25. In the next screen, verify that Any is selected in the Select a protocol type drop-down list, as shown in Figure 8-100. Click Next to continue.

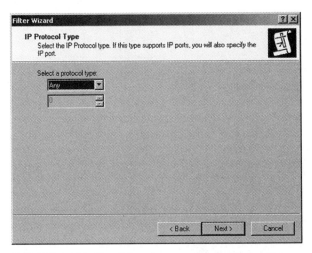

FIGURE 8-100 *Specifying the protocol type of the traffic.*

26. In the next screen, click Finish to create the custom filter. The filter that you created will be displayed in the Filters list, as shown in Figure 8-101.

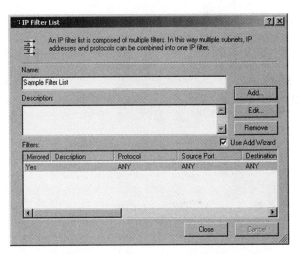

FIGURE 8-101 *The custom filter.*

27. Click Close to close the IP Filter List dialog box and return to the New Rule Wizard.

28. Under IP filter lists, select the radio button next to the Sample Filter List option, as shown in Figure 8-102. Click Next to continue.

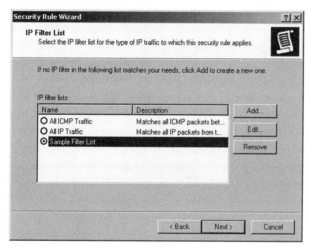

FIGURE 8-102 *Selecting the custom filter.*

29. In the next screen, verify that the Use Add Wizard checkbox is selected, as shown in Figure 8-103, and click Add…. The Filter Action Wizard appears. Click Next to continue.

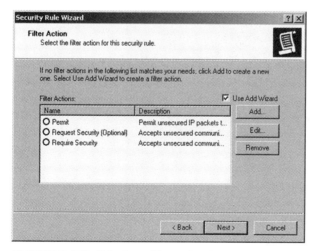

FIGURE 8-103 *Selecting a filter action for the filter rule.*

30. In the next screen, specify the name of the filter action, as shown in Figure 8-104, and click Next to continue.

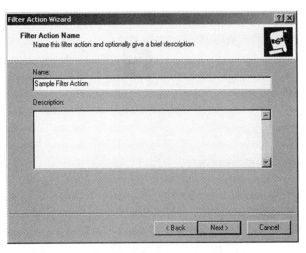

FIGURE 8-104 *Specifying the name of the filter action.*

31. In the next screen, verify that the Negotiate security option is selected, as shown in Figure 8-105. Click Next to continue.

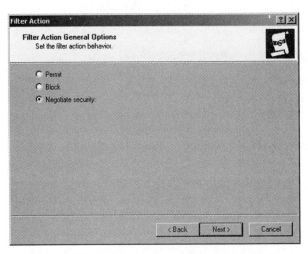

FIGURE 8-105 *Setting the filter action behavior.*

32. In the next wizard screen, verify that the Do not communicate with computers that do not support IPSec option is selected, as shown in Figure 8-106. Click Next to continue.

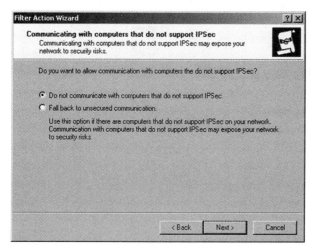

FIGURE 8-106 *Restricting communication with non–IPSec computers.*

33. In the next step, select the Medium option, shown in Figure 8-107, and click Next to continue.

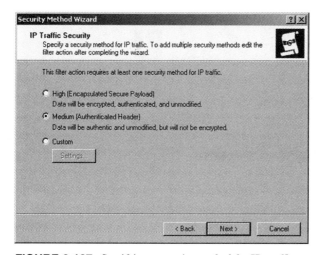

FIGURE 8-107 *Specifying a security method for IP traffic.*

34. Click Finish to close the wizard and return to the Security Rule Wizard dialog box. The filter action that you created should be added to the Filter Actions list, as shown in Figure 8-108. Click Next to continue.

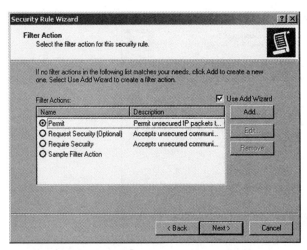

FIGURE 8-108 *The filter action that you created is added to the Filter Actions list.*

35. Click the radio button next to the filter action that you've created, as shown in Figure 8-109. Click Next to continue.

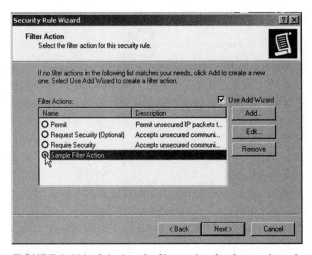

FIGURE 8-109 *Selecting the filter action for the security rule.*

36. Click Finish to close the wizard. The property sheet for the security policy should now be displayed. Click Close to close the property sheet. With this action you have successfully created the IPSec policy for the given computer. You'll now return to the MMC console. The new security policy that you created should be displayed in the right pane of the MMC console, as shown in Figure 8-110.

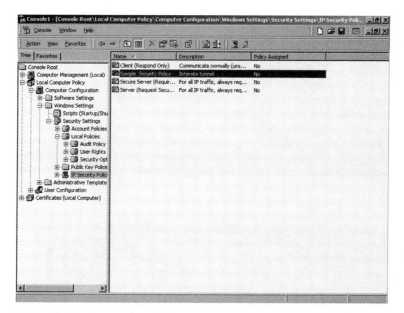

FIGURE 8-110 *The new IP security policy.*

You'll have to repeat this entire procedure on all machines on which you want to configure the custom IPSec policy. And, remember that all servers need to be assigned as servers. (In the MMC console, select IP Security Policies on Local Machine in the left pane. Right-click the Secure Server attribute and choose Assign.) To assign a machine as a client of this IPSec policy, select IP Security Policies on Local Machine in the left pane in the MMC console. Right-click the Client attribute and choose Assign.

Testing the IP Security Policy

Now that you have created the IP Security policy successfully, it is time to test it. The steps to test your custom IPSec policy are as follows:

1. Select Start, Run to open the Open box. Type `ipsecmon` and click OK to open the IP Security Monitor window shown in Figure 8-111. Minimize the window.

2. Run the Command Prompt. To do so, select Start, Run and type `cmd` in the Run box. At the Command prompt, type `ping <IP-address of a machine on which you have implemented the IPSec policy>`. The procedure is successful if four lines indicating the negotiation of IPSec appear in the ping response, as shown in Figure 8-112.

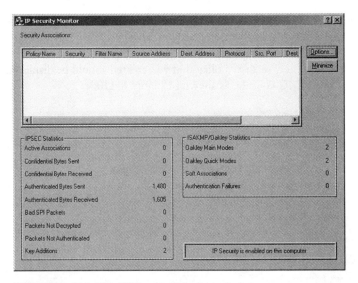

FIGURE 8-111 *The IP Security Monitor window.*

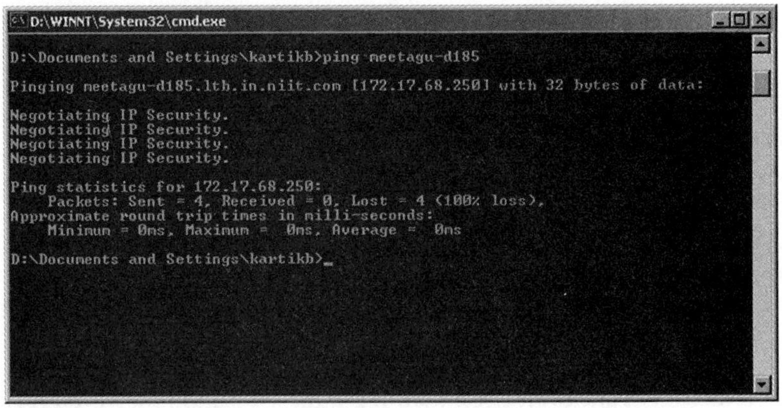

FIGURE 8-112 *The ping response indicates the IPSec negotiation.*

3. Maximize the IP Security Monitor window. The details of the SA in use are displayed, as shown in Figure 8-113.

4. In the MMC console, expand Computer Management to System Tools and further expand System Tools to Event Viewer. Finally, expand Event Viewer and select Security, as shown in Figure 8-114.

5. In the right pane of the MMC, look for event 541 under the Event column. This event records the establishment of an IPSec SA. Double-click the security log. An Event Properties dialog box appears, as shown in Figure 8-115. The first line in the Description pane displays SA-related information. All of this information is shown in Figure 8-116.

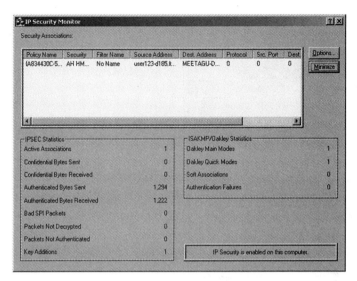

FIGURE 8-113 *Details of the SA in use are displayed in the IP Security monitor.*

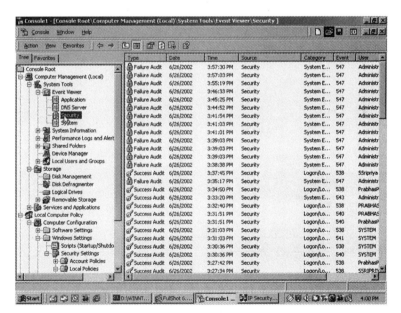

FIGURE 8-114 *Displaying Security logs.*

FIGURE 8-115 *Viewing the SA information.*

```
IKE security association established.
 Mode:
Data Protection Mode (Quick Mode)

 Peer Identity:
Preshared key ID.
Peer IP Address: 172.17.68.250

 Filter:
Source IP Address 172.17.68.137
Source IP Address Mask 255.255.255.255
Destination IP Address 172.17.68.250
Destination IP Address Mask 255.255.255.255
Protocol 0
Source Port 0
Destination Port 0

 Parameters:
ESP Algorithm None
HMAC Algorithm None
AH Algorithm MD5
Encapsulation Transport Mode
Inboundspi -2102127812
OutBoundspi -487824547
Lifetime (sec) 3600
Lifetime (kb) 100000
```

FIGURE 8-116 *The complete SA description.*

Configuring Certificate-based IPSec Policy

In the preceding procedure you created a policy on the basis of IKE. IKE can also be configured to use certificates during the exchange process. IKE specifies which certificate(s) to use during the negotiation and protects these certificates during the exchange.

NOTE

If you do not have a usable certificate, you can download a trial certificate from a site such as VeriSign (www.verisign.com) to learn to implement certificate-based IPSec policy.

The steps to configure certificate-based IPSec policy follow:

1. In the right pane of the MMC window, double-click the policy you created. The policy's Property sheet appears. Verify that the Filter Action that you created is selected. Click Edit. The Edit Rule Properties dialog box appears, as show in Figure 8-117. Click Edit....

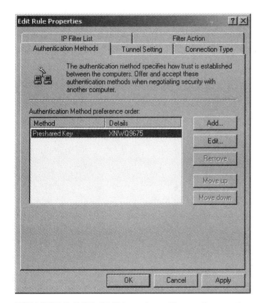

FIGURE 8-117 *Editing the policy to change the authentication method.*

2. The Authentication Method dialog box appears. Select the Use a certificate from this certificate authority (CA) option, as shown in Figure 8-118, and click Browse....

3. In the Select Certificates dialog box, select the certificate that you will use for authentication, as shown in Figure 8-119.

4. Click OK to accept the certificate. Click OK twice and click Close to return to the MMC console.

5. Ping the other machine on which you have configured the certificate-based authentication. If the IPSec negotiation occurs, your configuration is successful.

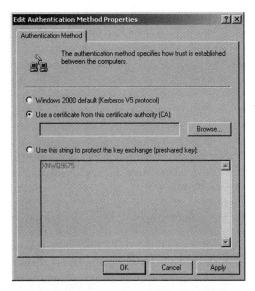

FIGURE 8-118 *Changing the authentication method from IKE to certificates.*

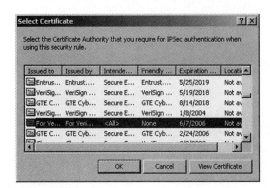

FIGURE 8-119 *Selecting a certificate.*

Configuring PPTP and L2TP Filters

In the previous section you learned about the implementation of IPSec in a Windows 2000 environment. During the process, you also learned about the configuration of IPSec filters. In this section, you'll learn about the configuration of PPTP and L2TP filters on a Windows 2000 device.

Configuring a PPTP Filter

The steps for configuring a PPTP filter on a router, firewall, or server are as follows:

1. In the left pane of RRAS console, expand the server for which you want to configure a PPTP packet filter to IP Routing, General, as shown in Figure 8-120.

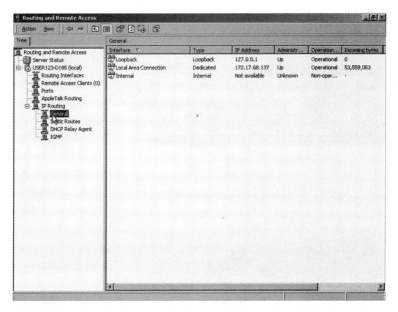

FIGURE 8-120 *The IP routing information displayed in the RRAS window.*

2. In the right pane of the window, right-click the interface that is connected to the Internet. A shortcut menu will appear. Select Properties. The Local Area Connection Properties dialog box for that interface should appear, as in Figure 8-121.

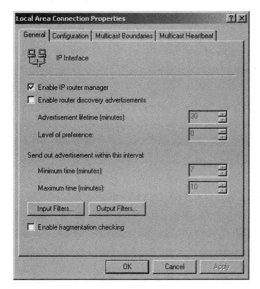

FIGURE 8-121 *The Local Area Connection Properties dialog box.*

3. Verify that the General tab is active. Click Input Filters… to open the Input Filters dialog box shown in Figure 8-122.

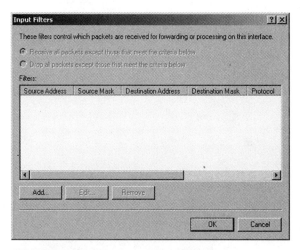

FIGURE 8-122 *The Input Filters dialog box.*

4. Click Add…. The Add IP Filter dialog box appears. Select the Destination network checkbox. In the IP address box, type the IP address of the VPN server, firewall, or router that is connected to the Internet. In the Subnet mask box, type 255.255.255.255. From the Protocol drop-down list, select TCP. In the Destination Port box, type 1723. Figure 8-123 illustrates these settings. Click OK to return to the Input Filters dialog box.

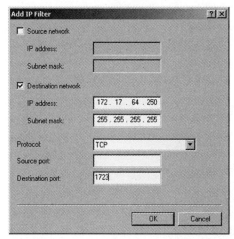

FIGURE 8-123 *Creating an incoming filter that allows TCP packets.*

5. Click Add… to open the Add IP Filter dialog box. Select the Destination
    network checkbox. In the IP address box, type the IP address of the VPN server,
    firewall, or router that is connected to the Internet. In the Subnet mask box, type
    255.255.255.255. From the Protocol drop-down list, select TCP [established]. In the
    Destination Port box, type 1723. Figure 8-124 illustrates these settings. Click OK to
    return to Input Filters dialog box.

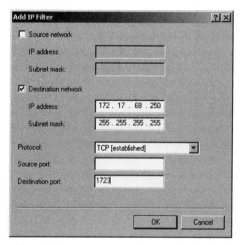

FIGURE 8-124 *Creating an incoming filter that allows TCP [established] packets.*

6. Click Add… to open the Add IP Filter dialog box. Select the Destination
    network checkbox. In the IP address box, type the IP address of the VPN server,
    firewall, or router that is connected to the Internet. In the Subnet mask box, type
    255.255.255.255. From the Protocol drop-down list, select Other. In the Protocol
    number box, type 47. Figure 8-125 illustrates these settings. Click OK to return to
    Input Filters dialog box.

 NOTE

Protocol number 47 is used for Generic Routing Encapsulation (GRE) packets. Here,
GRE packets are added because, as you may remember, PPTP uses a TCP connection known as the PPTP control connection to create, maintain, and terminate the
tunnel, and a modified version of GRE to encapsulate PPP frames as tunneled data.

7. In the Input Filters dialog box, select the Drop all packets except those that meet the
    criteria below option, as shown in Figure 8-126. Click OK to Return to Local Area
    Connection Properties dialog box.

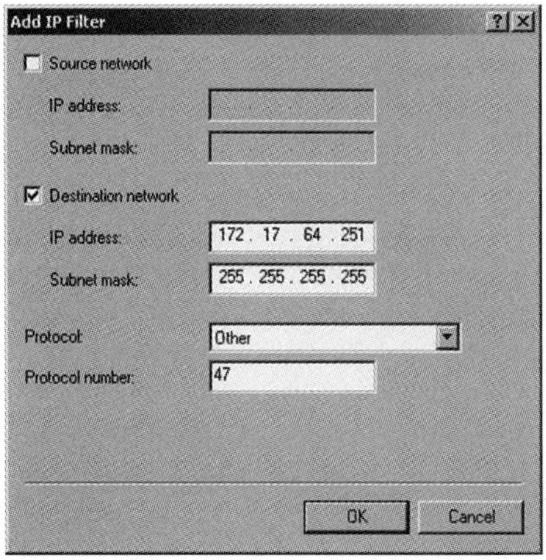

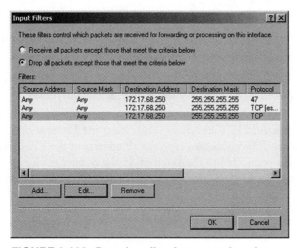

FIGURE 8-125 *Creating an incoming filter allowing UDP packets.*

FIGURE 8-126 *Dropping all packets except those that meet the specified criteria.*

8. In the Local Area Connection Properties dialog box, click Output Filters to open the Output Filters dialog box.

9. Click Add… to open the Add IP Filter dialog box. Select the Source network checkbox. In the IP address box, type the IP address of the VPN server, firewall, or router that is connected to the Internet. In the Subnet mask box, type 255.255.255.255. From the Protocol drop-down list, select TCP. In the Source Port box, type 1723. Click OK to return to Output Filters dialog box.

10. Click Add... to open the Add IP Filter dialog box. Select the Source network check-box. In the IP address box, type the IP address of the VPN server, firewall, or router that is connected to the Internet. In the Subnet mask box, type 255.255.255.255. From the Protocol drop-down list, select TCP [established]. In the Source Port box, type 1723. This is the standard PPTP port, but it also enhances security. Similarly, specify the value of Destination port box as 1723. Click OK to return to Output Filters dialog box.

11. Click Add... to open the Add IP Filter dialog box. Select the Source network check-box. In the IP address box, type the IP address of the VPN server, firewall, or router that is connected to the Internet. In the Subnet mask box, type 255.255.255.255. From the Protocol drop-down list, select Other. In the Protocol number box, type 47. Click OK to return to Output Filters dialog box.

12. In the Input Filters dialog box, select the Drop all packets except those that meet the criteria below option. Click OK to return to the Local Area Connection Properties dialog box.

13. Click OK to save the changes.

Configuring L2TP Packet Filters

The steps for configuring L2TP packet filters on a device are very similar to the steps for configuring PPTP filters. However, there is a small difference. The steps for configuring L2TP filters follow:

1. In the left pane of RRAS console, expand the server for which you want to configure an L2TP packet filter to IP Routing, General.

2. In the right pane of the window, right-click the interface that is connected to the Internet. A shortcut menu will appear. Select Properties. The Local Area Connection Properties dialog box should appear.

3. Verify that the General tab is active. Click the Input Filters button to open the Input Filters dialog box.

4. Click Add.... The Add IP Filter dialog box appears. Select the Destination network checkbox. In the IP address box, type the IP address of the VPN server, firewall, or router that is connected to the Internet. In the Subnet mask box, type 255.255.255.255. From the Protocol drop-down list, select UDP. In the Source port box and the Destination port box, type 500. Click OK to return to the Input Filters dialog box.

5. Click Add.... The Add IP Filter dialog box appears. Select the Destination network checkbox. In the IP address box, type the IP address of the VPN server, firewall, or router that is connected to the Internet. In the Subnet mask box, type 255.255.255.255. From the Protocol drop-down list, select UDP. In the Source port box and the Destination port box, type 1701. Click OK to return to the Input Filters dialog box.

6. In the Input Filters dialog box, select the Drop all packets except those that meet the criteria below option. Click OK to return to the Local Area Connection Properties dialog box.

7. In the Local Area Connection Properties dialog box, click Output Filters to open the Output Filters dialog box.

8. Click Add.... The Add IP Filter dialog box appears. Select the Destination network checkbox. In the IP address box, type the IP address of the VPN server, firewall, or router that is connected to the Internet. In the Subnet mask box, type 255.255.255.255. From the Protocol drop-down list, select UDP. In the Source port box and the Destination port box, type 1701. Click OK to return to Input Filters dialog box.

9. Click Add.... The Add IP Filter dialog box appears. Select the Destination network checkbox. In the IP address box, type the IP address of the VPN server, firewall, or router that is connected to the Internet. In the Subnet mask box, type 255.255.255.255. From the Protocol drop-down list, select UDP. In the Source port box and the Destination port box, type 500. Click OK to return to Input Filters dialog box.

10. In the Input Filters dialog box, select the Drop all packets except those that meet the criteria below option. Click OK to return to the Local Area Connection Properties dialog box.

11. Click OK to save the changes.

With this, you have successfully configured an L2TP filter on a VPN device.

Summary

In this chapter, you learned to configure a VPN a solution on Windows 2000. Specifically, you learned to set up a remote access VPN server, which is a must for accepting incoming requests from VPN clients in a Windows 2000-based VPN environment. Then, you learned to set up and configure a VPN client. You also learned to implement Microsoft's RADIUS-based authentication server, which is known as Internet Authentication Server (IAS). Because PPTP and L2TP are supported natively by Windows 2000 they need not be configured separately. Therefore, you learned to configure IPSec in Windows 2000. Finally, you learned to implement PPTP and L2TP filters in a Windows 2000 environment.

Check Your Understanding

Multiple Choice Questions

1. Which of the following must be disabled before you can configure a VPN server?

    a. Telnet

    b. Print Spooler

    c. Windows Installer

    d. RRAS

2. A Connectoid allows you to _____.

    a. Configure PPTP and L2TP filters

    b. Configure and distribute IPSec policies

    c. Configure and distribute IAS settings

    d. Configure and distribute server login scripts to clients

3. Which of the following steps are correct when copying the configuration of an IAS server? (Please arrange these correct steps chronologically.)

    a. Stop the destination IAS server to run the `netsh .exec` command.

    b. Distribute the settings to the destination machines and implement the settings on the destination machine using the `netsh exec` command.

    c. Store the configuration and settings of the source IAS server in a text file using the `netsh aaaa show config` command.

    d. Stop the source IAS server to copy its settings and configurations to a text file.

4. How do you know that IPSec is configured successfully?

    a. Four lines indicating IPSec negotiation are displayed in the command prompt when you ping an IPSec client or server from another IPSec client or server.

    b. A new IPSec Policy is added to the IP Security Policies on Local Machine.

    c. The IPSec Monitor shows the successful SA negotiation.

    d. Event 541 depicts the successful IKE exchange.

5. Which of the following authentication methods is the default for Windows 2000?

    a. IKE

    b. Certificates

    c. Kerberos v5

    d. IAS

Answers

Multiple Choice Answers

1. **a, b,** and **c.** The services that must be disabled on a device before it can be configured as a VPN server include the Print Spooler, Telnet, and Windows Installer.

2. **d.** A connectoid allows you to configure and distribute VPN server login scripts to various VPN clients simultaneously.

3. **c** and **b.** To copy the configuration of one IAS server to another, you need to store the configuration and settings of the source IAS server in a text file using the `netsh aaaa show config` command. Then, you distribute the file to destination machines. Finally, you need to implement the settings using the `netsh exec` command.

4. **a, c,** and **d.** The indications of successful IPSec configuration include Event 541 depicting the successful IKE exchange, the IPSec Monitor showing the successful SA negotiation, and four lines indicating IPSec negotiation are displayed in the command prompt when you ping an IPSec client or server from another IPSec client or server.

5. **c.** The Kerberos v5 authentication method is the default for the Windows 2000 environment.

Chapter 9

Implementing a VPN on Linux

Microsoft's Windows has made its presence felt worldwide. Its remarkable popularity is mainly attributed to the ease of implementation and use that the Windows platform provides in the form of its GUI. As you learned in the previous chapter, "Implementing VPNs on Windows 2000," Windows 2000 provides a wealth of wizards that help you set up and configure every aspect of your VPN. Comparatively, some find the implementation of VPNs on Linux a bit difficult, especially if you are not well versed with the Linux environment. However, most experts and many administrators vouch for the stability and reliability of Linux-based VPNs, which is the main reason more and more organizations around the globe are ready to consider the Linux platform for their VPN solution.

In this chapter, you'll learn to implement a VPN solution on the Linux platform. In Linux, VPNs over Point-to-Point Protocol (PPP) and Secure SHell (SSH) are considered the popular choices for VPN implementation. However, with the phenomenal emergence of IPSec in the VPN arena, a new IPSec-based solution called FreeS/WAN is taking over. You'll learn to implement VPNs on both PPP over SSH and FreeS/WAN.

Implementing VPNs over PPP with SSH

PPP, as you learned in Chapter 5, "Tunneling Protocols at Layer 2," is a popular protocol for high-speed transmission of data. However, PPP is weak in terms of security. Therefore, it is generally coupled with a secure protocol. This complementary secure protocol in the Linux environment is SSH. SSH offers high security because it does not transmit data in cleartext as other protocols, such as FTP and Telnet, do. SSH uses a public key encryption method to establish secure connections for transmitting encrypted data.

When configuring a VPN using PPP with SSH the most important components are the VPN servers and clients. This type of configuration requires that you have two packages installed on your servers and your clients. These packages include two daemons—pppd (version 2.3 or higher) and sshd (versions 1.2.26 or higher). For seamless interaction between VPN servers and clients, it is preferable that both your servers and clients run the same versions. In addition to these packages, you'll also need pty-redir on your VPN clients.

The following sections discuss the implementation of a PPP/SSH-based VPN solution on Linux-based servers and clients.

Configuring Servers

Before you configure your server to support VPN functionality, there are a few basic requirements that your server must fulfill. Your server must have

- A 486 processor or higher (per recommendations, it is best to use a 133MHz or better Pentium-based machine).
- A minimum of 8MB of RAM (per recommendations, for best results it is best to use 32MB or higher).
- At least 4GB of hard disk space (per recommendations, it is best to use 10GB or higher).
- Linux installed on the machine.

You can divide the process of configuring your VPN server into three distinct phases. These include laying the groundwork, configuration of pppd, and configuration of sshd. What follows is a consideration of what you need to do in each of these phases.

Laying the Groundwork

Before you start configuring your server, you'll need to do some groundwork to ready your VPN server to support the minimum level of performance and security you want from your VPN solution.

First, you'll need to rebuild the kernel of your server machine so that it can support VPN functionality. Here, you'll need to enable PPP-related kernel options, such as CONFIG_FIREWALL, CONFIG_IP_FIREWALL, CONFIG_IP_ROUTER, and CONFIG_PPP. If you are using kernel version 2.0, you'll need to enable the CONFIG_IP_FORWARD parameter. Similarly, you'll need to enable the CONFIG_IP_ADVANCED_ROUTER option if you are using kernel version 2.2.

Next, you'll need to configure the network interface(s) of your server. The command to do so is

```
# /sbin/ifconfig <interface_name> <interface_IP address> netmask <subnet mask> broadcast
<broadcast_IP address>
```

For example, if the server (Ethernet) interface you're currently configuring is eth0 and the address of the interface is 172.17.64.137, then the command will be as follows:

```
# /sbin/ifconfig eth0 172.17.64.137 netmask 255.255.255.0 broadcast 172.17.64.255
```

Next, you'll need to set routes to your organization's remote networks on your server machine. Doing so enables the server and its remote clients to successfully communicate with each other. The command to set routes on your VPN server is

```
# /sbin/route add -net <network address> netmask <subnet mask> dev <interface_name> | gw
<gateway ip address>
```

For example:

```
# /sbin/route add -net 172.17.64.137 netmask 255.255.255.0 dev eth0
```

As you learned in Chapter 7, "Building a VPN," static routes should only be set from the VPN server to a default gateway. Keeping this in mind, the command to direct traffic to a remote client from your server on interface eth0 is

```
# /sbin/route add -net 172.17.0.0 gw 172.17.254.254 netmask 255.255.0.0 dev eth0
```

Similarly, you'll need to configure firewall filters that will allow or deny access to your VPN server. The following example depicts an ipchains-based firewall filter.

```
# /sbin/ipchains -F forward
# /sbin/ipchains -P forward Deny
# /sbin/ipchains -A forward-s 172.17.64.0/26 -d 172.17.68.0/16 -j ACCEPT
# /sbin/ipchains -A forward-b -s 172.17.72.0/8 -d 172.17.68.0/16 -j ACCEPT
```

Based on this filter, the firewall denies all traffic except traffic with a source of 172.17.64.0/26 that is destined toward 172.17.68.0/16. Also, according to the above filter, bi-directional traffic (denoted by -b) exchanged between 172.17.72.0/8 and 172.17.68.0/16 is permitted to pass through the firewall.

Configuring pppd

Now that you have laid the groundwork, you are ready to configure PPP and SSH on the VPN server. Before you can configure SSH, you'll first need to configure pppd. To do so, locate the file named options in the /etc/ppp/ directory. This file contains the global parameters (or options) for pppd. The content of the file should be as follows:

```
ipcp-accept-remote
proxyarp
noauth
```

The first line allows the VPN server to accept the address specified by the client for the given VPN session. This is especially important for remote clients that use a dial-up connection to connect to the server and are allocated IP addresses dynamically.

The next line (`proxyarp`) causes the PPP server to "fool" the rest of its local network into thinking that it is using the IP address(es) of the client(s). Data from the local network to the client would then be sent to the server, which would send it through the PPP link to the client. In this manner, local VPN clients are allowed to tunnel their data to the server, which is not possible if this option is not set.

Finally, the third line allows the client to connect to the server without having to specify the user ID and password. (This should not be alarming because SSH takes care of the authentication part.) You can disable this option, if you want.

NOTE

Options specified in the /etc/ppp/options file cannot be overridden from the command line. This practice enhances the security of the server.

TIP

If you are facing problems with dial-up connections after configuring the /etc/ppp/options file, identify the conflicting options and copy them to a new options file. Save this new options file and use it whenever the corresponding action must take place. You can use a script to automate the task. Also, some scripts allow you to specify the path to an alternative options file.

Configuring sshd

The global sshd configuration information is a part of the ssh_config file, which is located in the /etc directory. You'll need to edit the default configurations according to the security requirements of your organization. It is recommended that you disable all remote applications and other "vulnerable" activities, like checking mail, before configuring sshd.

The following is the sample configuration of the sshd_config file.

```
Port 22
ListenAddress 0.0.0.0
HostKey /etc/ssh_host_key
RandomSeed /etc/ssh_random_seed
ServerKeyBits 768
LoginGraceTime 600
KeyRegenerationInterval 3600
PermitRootLogin yes
IgnoreRhosts yes
StrictModes yes
QuietMode no
FascistLogging yes
CheckMail no
IdleTimeout 3d
X11Forwarding no
PrintMotd no
KeepAlive yes
SyslogFacility DAEMON
RhostsAuthentication no
RhostsRSAAuthentication no
RSAAuthentication yes
PasswordAuthentication yes
PermitEmptyPasswords no
UseLogin no
```

Now that your server is ready to handle VPN clients, you can configure a VPN client on Linux.

Configuring Clients

Quite like the case with servers, the process of configuring VPN clients can also be divided into three phases. These include the groundwork phase, the pppd configuration phase, and the sshd configuration phase.

Laying the Groundwork

As in the case of VPN servers, you'll need to do some groundwork in order to ready your client to support VPN functionality.

You'll first need to rebuild the kernel of your client machine. For this, you'll have to enable kernel options such as CONFIG_PPP, CONFIG_FIREWALL, CONFIG_IP_FIREWALL, CONFIG_IP_ROUTER, CONFIG_IP_MASQUERADE, and CONFIG_IP_MASQUERADE_ICMP. If you are using kernel version 2.0, you'll need to enable the CONFIG_IP_FORWARD parameter. Similarly, you'll need to enable the CONFIG_IP_ADVANCED_ROUTER option if you are using kernel version 2.2.

You'll now need to configure the client's network interface so that your client can communicate with the VPN servers in your intranet. For this, you'll need to add the following command to the /etc/rc.d/rc.inte1 file:

```
# /sbin/ifconfig eth0 172.17.64.137 netmask 255.255.255.0 broadcast 172.17.64.255
```

> **NOTE**
>
> If you are using the RedHat system, the file is located at /etc/sysconfig/network-scripts/ifcfg-eth0.

If you are using kernel 2.0, you'll also need to add the route to the VPN server that the client can access. The command to do this is

```
# /sbin/route add -net 172.17.64.137 netmask 255.255.255.0 dev eth0
```

Configuring pppd

Generally, the file /etc/ppp/options located at the client end does not require any changes if you are using the default options. Using the default options is recommended if you are new to the Linux platform. However, if you have considerable experience working on Linux, you can experiment with advanced options, such as auth.

Configuring sshd

To configure sshd at the client end, move to the root directory and then create the .ssh directory as you did in the case of the server. You'll use the mkdir command to do so. The command should look as follows:

```
# /mkdir /root/.ssh
# chmod 0700 /root/.ssh
```

The second line ensures that /root/.ssh is writeable, readable, and executable only by the users and is inaccessible to others. As an added security measure, all files in this directory (/root/.ssh) should preferably be given a permission value of 0600 so that they cannot be executed by others.

You'll now need to generate keys to be used during the exchange of data over the VPN tunnel. The command to generate keys is

```
# ssh-keygen -f /root/.ssh/identity.vpn -P ""
```

This command creates two files in the .ssh directory. The first file—identity.vpn—contains the private key of the key pair. The second file—identity.vpn.pub—contains the public key of the key pair. As you learned in Chapter 3, "Security Components of a VPN," you should be extremely cautious not to reveal the content of your private key to anyone. Moreover, to ensure the safety of this key, you should never send this key in cleartext. Refer to Chapter 3 for more information on public and private keys.

CAUTION

Before you commence a first-time connection between the VPN client and the server, the client keys (the content of the identity.vpn.pub file) should be copied to the /home/vpn/.ssh/authorized_keys file that is located on the VPN server. When you copy these keys you must ensure that no key is broken into multiple lines. In addition, it is highly recommended that you edit the comment field of the file to identify which key belongs to which client. In addition, make certain that the authorized_keys file has 0600 permission to ensure that the keys cannot be used by unauthorized users.

Now that all configurations are in place, you can proceed to establish the connection between the server and the client that you configured.

Connecting the Server and the Client

After you have configured your server for both pppd and sshd, you can allow clients to access your server. Before a connection can be established between the server and the client, you'll need to ready the server and client for the VPN connection.

To ready the server for the connection, you'll need to set up user accounts on your VPN server. The steps allowing VPN clients to access your VPN server follow:

1. Create a group for the VPN users that can access the given server. To do so, you'll need to run the following command:

    ```
    # /usr/sbin/groupadd <group_name>
    # /usr/sbin/groupadd VPN
    ```

NOTE

After running the command, you can verify that the group was created successfully by locating it in the /etc/group file.

2. After the group is successfully created, you'll need to create a home directory for the group in the /home directory. The command to do so is

```
# /mkdir <location>
# /mkdir /home/VPN
```

3. Next, using the mkdir command, create the .ssh directory in the home directory you created in the previous step.

4. Add VPN clients.

After successfully readying your server for the VPN connection, you'll need to configure the known_hosts file before connecting the server to the client. The format of the command that you'll need to run to configure the known_hosts file is

```
#ssh <host_IP address>
```

For example, to connect to a server with an IP address of 172.17.68.251, the command will look as follows:

```
#ssh 172.17.68.251
```

When the command is run successfully, you'll be prompted for a confirmation to continue. Type yes. Next, you'll receive a message specifying that the permission to access the specified server was denied by the server. Ignore the message and type

```
# /usr/sbin/pty-redir /usr/bin/ssh -t -e none -o 'Batchmode yes' -c blowfish -i
/root/.ssh/identity.vpn -l VPN 172.17.68.251> /tmp/vpn-device
```

NOTE

The parameters in the file might need to be changed according to the environment of your VPN setup.

You'll need to wait for some time while the command is being processed. After the command is processed, type the following:

```
# /usr/sbin/pppd `cat /tmp/vpn-device` 172.17.64.251:172.17.68.137
```

In this command, the first IP address is of the VPN client while the second address belongs to the server interface that receives the client requests.

The final step in the establishment of a connection between the server and the client is to set the route on the client machine, if you haven't done so earlier. The command to do so is

```
# /sbin/route add -net 192.168.0.0 gw 172.17.68.251 netmask 255.255.0.0
```

This command finally allows your VPN server and client to successfully exchange data and other information over the VPN tunnel. If you run into any problems, you can use the `ping` and `traceroute` commands to troubleshoot the problem.

Implementing VPNs over FreeS/WAN

Many people are hesitant to work with Linux because they may feel lost if they are not well versed in it. In addition, implementing solutions and troubleshooting problems in a typical Linux environment is fairly complicated and requires experience as well as a generous dose of patience. FreeS/WAN has been developed as a solution for IS managers and administrators who need to securely connect the far-flung branch offices, telecommuters, home-based users, and mobile users over the Internet at a relatively low implementation cost. In short, FreeS/WAN is an answer for all Linux-based IPSec VPN implementations.

S/WAN in FreeS/WAN is an acronym for Secure Wide Area Network. The prefix "free" denotes that it is a free and open-source implementation. In addition, FreeS/WAN is a highly flexible solution based on IPSec. As a result, transmissions are encrypted end-to-end and each packet is authenticated individually. The best feature of FreeS/WAN is that it is fully compliant with IPSec and imposes minimal overhead. As a result, FreeS/WAN will run even on a low-end PC. The only major requirement is that you must have the Linux operating system on your machines.

 NOTE

FreeS/WAN also works seamlessly with a variety of other IPSec implementations including CISCO PIX and Checkpoint VPN-1.

So what does FreeS/WAN entail? How do you implement it? These are a few of the questions answered in the following sections.

FreeS/WAN—An Overview

As mentioned earlier, FreeS/WAN is an open source IPSec implementation on Linux. It is comprised of two components—*KerneL IP Security (KLIPS)* and a daemon called *Pluto*. The successful operation of FreeS/WAN entails that KLIPS and the Pluto daemon work in tandem, a situation that is realized with the help of constant interactions between the two.

KLIPS is a modification of the standard Linux kernel and is compiled into the kernel itself. Being a part of the standard Linux kernel, KLIPS is responsible for implementing the IPSec functionality. It handles the encapsulation and encryption services provided by the main IPSec protocols—AH and ESP. In addition, KLIPS also handles the data packets.

The other component of FreeS/WAN, Pluto, is the daemon responsible for carrying out the Internet Key Exchange (IKE)-related processes during an IPSec-based secure data exchange. The main responsibility of Pluto, therefore, is to handle IKE authentication requests and key management.

FreeS/WAN ensures data safety and security as it is transmitted across an unsecured medium, such as a public network or the Internet, in the following way: In a communication that involves FreeS/WAN, the two ends authenticate each other and negotiate their own keys. (The keys used by FreeS/WAN are RSA public/private keys pairs. However, the primary authentication in the ipsec.secrets file allows both RSA as well as pre-shared keys.) New keys are generated and exchanged periodically. Therefore, even if a key is compromised during a communication session, the damage is limited to a session or two, thus avoiding long-term trespassing by the intruder.

In addition to the mutual authentication of the communicating parties and regular generation of new keys, FreeS/WAN uses 168-bit 3DES encryption. This encryption algorithm is considered to be one of the strongest and the safest of the current breed of encryption algorithms available today. As a result, even if your tunnel has been successfully intruded upon, the intruder will not be able to discern the content of the data packets as the content appears to be gibberish.

 CAUTION

When you purchase any "secure" DES-based implementation, make sure that it is 3DES. DES, which was earlier version of 3DES is comparatively easier to crack and is highly vulnerable to Brute Force attacks.

Although FreeS/WAN was developed with RedHat Linux in mind, it has no other RedHat affiliations and works on all distributions of Linux and BSD, such as SuSE Linux, OpenBSD, SlackWare, and so on, without any major modifications. A version that will also work on Microsoft Windows 2000 and Sun Solaris is, as of this writing, in development.

In addition, FreeS/WAN is not restricted to Intel-based processors only. It has been proven to work without problems on processors produced by other manufacturers, such as Motorola, DEC, and Sun. FreeS/WAN also exhibits a high degree of interoperability with other VPN products, such as Cisco routers, Raptor and CheckPoint firewalls, and so on. Now that you have the basic idea of FreeS/WAN, you can install and configure it for your VPN environment.

Installing and Configuring FreeS/WAN

According to the requirements specified in the FreeS/WAN documentation, a 500MHz processor with 128MB of RAM is sufficient for the machine on which you plan to implement FreeS/WAN. However, from a more realistic point of view, a 256MB RAM machine is preferable. And, in order to avoid storage-related problems later, at least 10GB of hard disk space is preferable.

You can use the latest available version of the Linux kernel or earlier versions, such as 2.0.x, 2.2.x, and certain versions of 2.4.x. However, per the recommendations, do not use kernel version 2.4.15 because it contains a bug that corrupts the file system.

Installing FreeS/WAN

Before you get down to the actual installation process, make sure you have the following available:

◆ A GNU C compiler (gcc or egcs)

◆ An assembler and linker, such as the bin86 package

◆ Standard compiler libraries, such as glibc

◆ A GNU-Multi-Precision Library (GMP) for Pluto public key calculations

◆ A ncurses library

◆ Miscellaneous tools, such as make(1), patch(1), and Linux source code

NOTE

Do not forget to install the GMP library because the Pluto daemon will not work without it. Similarly, if you forget to install patch(1), you won't be able to apply FreeS/WAN patches to the standard Linux kernel.

With all the prerequisites in place, you can now learn how to install and configure FreeS/WAN. The steps to do this follow:

1. If you don't have a machine with the latest version of Linux installed on it, install RedHat Linux 7.2 or 7.3 on a machine that fulfills the FreeS/WAN requirements of 256MB of RAM and has a 500MHz processor. If you already have the required machine, you can ignore this step.

NOTE

In this case, the FreeS/WAN installation and configuration has been carried out on RedHat 7.3 kernel version 2.4.18-3.

2. Download the FreeS/WAN source code (rpms) and required digital signatures from www.freeswan.org/download.html. The file that you'll download will be in tar.gz form.

3. Move the downloaded file to /usr/local/src/. Change to the same directory using the command:

```
cd /usr/local/src/
```

4. Use the following commands to untar the downloaded file, as shown in Figure 9-1, and set permissions to it:

```
tar xvzf freeswan-x.x.tar.gz
chown -R root:root freeswan-x.x
```

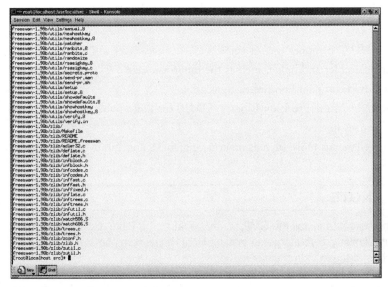

FIGURE 9-1 *The output of the* untar *command.*

5. Test and compile the kernel to ensure that it is functioning properly. The command to do so is

```
cd /usr/src/linux-2.4.18-3
make menuconfig
```

You should see the Custom Configuration menu, as shown in Figure 9-2.

6. Exit the menu (by selecting Exit). When prompted to save the settings, select Yes.

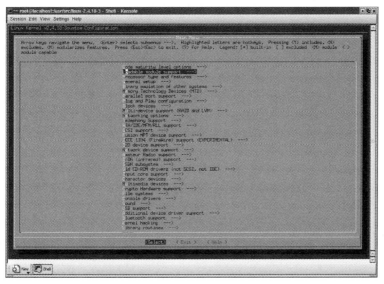

FIGURE 9-2 *The Custom Configuration menu.*

7. Next, ensure that all the dependencies, such as the include files are in place, as displayed in Figure 9-3. The command to do so is

```
make dep
```

TIP

After running the `make dep` command, it is recommended that you run the `make clean` command. This command helps you remove temporary files that were created as a result of the `make dep` command, which helps optimize the kernel.

8. To compile and build all modules that can be added to a running kernel (and update the linux/modules directory), run the following command:

```
make modules
```

The result of the make modules command is displayed in Figure 9-4.

NOTE

This command may take a few minutes to an hour to complete.

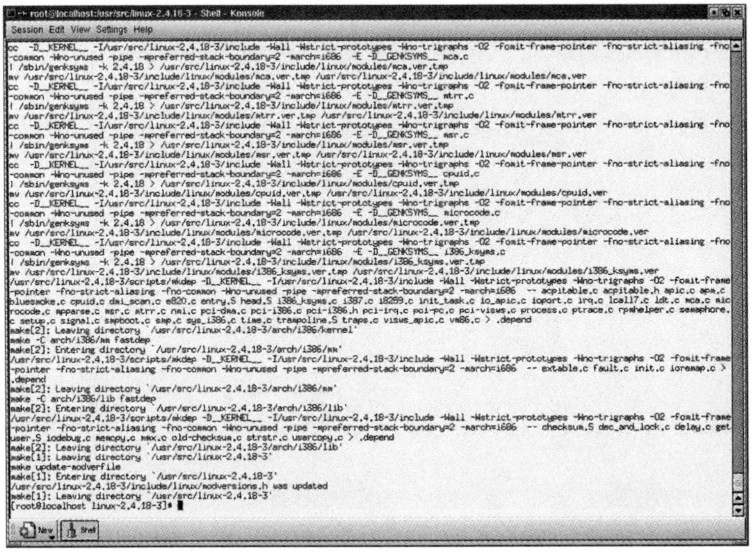

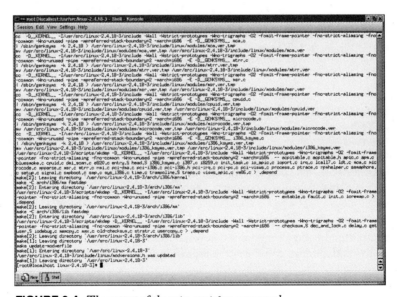

FIGURE 9-3 *The output of the* make dep *command.*

FIGURE 9-4 *The output of the* make modules *command.*

9. Now that you have successfully created the modules, you must now install these modules with the help of the following command:

```
make modules_install
```

10. In order to build a loadable kernel image, run the following command:

```
make bzImage
```

 NOTE

This command may take a few minutes to an hour to complete.

11. To load the kernel image that you created with the help of `make bzImage`, you must run the following command:

```
make install
```

The result of the `make install` command is displayed in Figure 9-5.

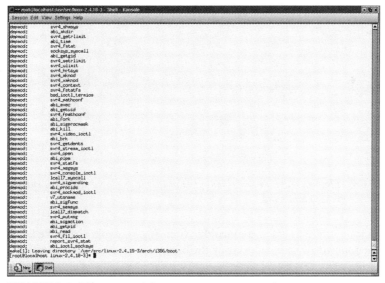

FIGURE 9-5 *The output of the* `make install` *command.*

12. Now, run the `make` utility that sets the kernel compilation option using a menu interface. The `menugo` command will run the menu-driven kernel configurator, which is
based on the ncurses library and is shown in Figure 9-6.

```
cd /usr/local/src/freeswan-x.x
make menugo
```

 NOTE

This command may take a few minutes to an hour to complete.

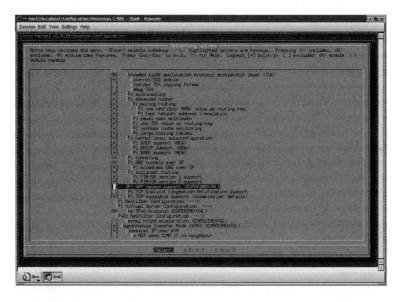

FIGURE 9-6 *The menu-driven kernel configurator that is displayed when you run the* `make`
`menugo` command.

13. When you ran the `bzImage` command in Step 10, you built a loadable kernel image.
Use the following command to copy the boot image to the /boot partition.

```
cp /usr/src/linux/arch/i386/boot/bzImage /boot/vmlinuz-ipsec
```

14. Now, edit the /etc/lilo.conf file, which is the boot loader config file, as shown in
Figure 9-7.

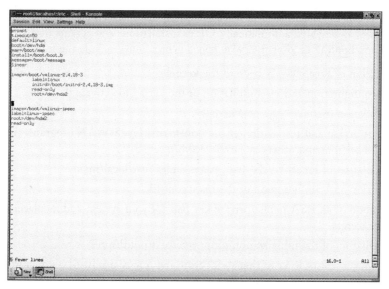

FIGURE 9-7 *Editing the /etc/lilo.conf file.*

15. Run the lilo command as follows:

lilo

You should see the output shown in Figure 9-8.

16. Restart the machine.

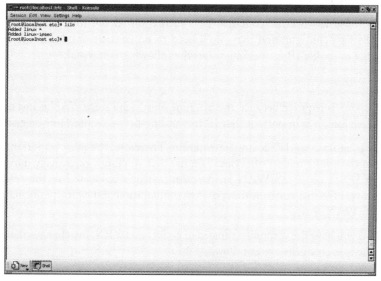

FIGURE 9-8 *The output of the lilo command.*

When you reboot the machine after the installation of FreeS/WAN, the `init` script is executed and IPSec is activated automatically. Other installations and actions that are done automatically (upon booting or after the `make menugo` command) include the following:

◆ Addition of FreeS/WAN code to the kernel

◆ Re-configuration and re-compilation of the kernel to activate that code

◆ Installation (manual) of a new kernel

◆ Construction and installation of the non-kernel FreeS/WAN programs (ipsec in /usr/local/sbin and others in /usr/local/lib/ipsec)

◆ Installation of FreeS/WAN main pages under /usr/local/main

◆ Creation and configuration of the ipsec.conf file

◆ Creation of an RSA public/private key pair for your system and its placement in ipsec.secrets

◆ Installation of the initialization script /etc/rc.d/init.d/ipsec

◆ Establishment of links to that script from the /etc/rc.d/rc[0-6].d directories so that each run level starts or stops IPSec

The signs that tell you that the FreeS/WAN installation was successful include the correct version reported by the kernel, the appearance of a message indicating the initialization of KLIPS, and another message indicating the starting of Pluto. With these signs of successful installation, you can proceed to the configuration of FreeS/WAN. However, note that various KLIPS messages and FreeS/WAN versions are displayed when the kernel is initializing. Also, Pluto messages are only shown if the init scripts are running.

Configuring FreeS/WAN

The /etc/sysconfig/network file contains the information related to IP forwarding between interfaces. The first configuration that you'll need to do consists of editing the /etc/sysconfig/network file to enable IP forwarding using the following command:

```
FORWARD_IPV4 = true
```

This configuration is required because any machine on which FreeS/WAN is installed acts like a gateway. Therefore, it is important that IP forwarding between interfaces be enabled on it.

FreeS/WAN is basically an IPSec implementation. Therefore, the most important configuration relates to the configuration of IPSec. The file that you'll use extensively during the configuration of IPSec on FreeS/WAN is ipsec.conf, which is located in the /etc directory. ipsec.conf is a text file that contains most of the configuration and control information to control the FreeS/WAN setup.

Assuming that you have the common scenario of an intranet VPN, the changes that you'll need to make to the ipsec.conf file are as follows:

◆ You'll need to replace the espenckey and espauthkey parameters specified in the ipsec.conf file with the keys from /usr/local/bin/ranbits. /usr/local/bin/ranbits is the random key generator installed with FreeS/WAN. Type the following command to configure FreeS/WAN for manual keying:

```
/etc/rc.d/init.d/ipsec restart
/usr/local/bin/ipsec manual -up conn_name
```

 NOTE

You can get the value of the conn_name parameter from the value of the connection definition or the connection header in the ipsec.conf file.

◆ To verify that the tunnel has been configured properly, type the following command:

```
usr/local/sbin/ipsec eroute
```

This command displays the extended routes in your VPN setup. If the output of the command displays the end points of the tunnel, your VPN has been configured successfully. You can verify this fact by pinging any of the VPN servers or clients at the other remote network.

The problem inherent with configurations related to the ipsec.conf file is that it is a manually keyed system and doesn't use the autoconnection keyed system. The autoconnection keyed system boasts enhanced security because it uses IKE-based key management and exchange. In order to set the autoconnection keyed system, you'll need to follow these steps:

1. Open the /etc/ipsec.secrets file. This file stores the secret key, as shown in Figure 9-9. Close the file.

2. Open the IPSec.conf file and set the value of the auto parameter to start. This will automatically start the IPSec interface. You can also restart IPSec using the following command:

```
/etc/rc.d/init.d/ipsec restart
```

3. If you have a firewall installed in your VPN setup, allow access through ports 500, 50, and 51. ESP uses port 50 for authentication and encryption, AH uses port 51, and IKE uses UDP port 500 for key-related management activities. The commands to allow access through ports 50, 51, and 500 on the firewall are

```
ipchains -A input -p udp -j ACCEPT -s 0.0.0.0/0 -i eth0 -d $IPSECGW 500
ipchains -A input -j ACCEPT -i eth0 -p 50 -s $IPSECGW
ipchains -A input -j ACCEPT -i eth0 -p 51 -s $IPSECGW
```

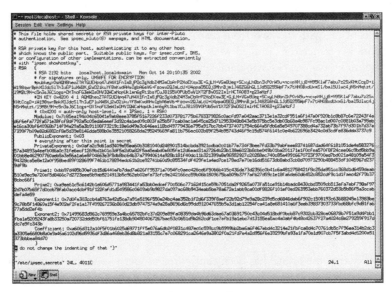

FIGURE 9-9 *The content of the ipsec.secrets file.*

 NOTE

The parameter $IPSECGW takes the IP address of the remote gateway that initiates
the VPN session.

That's it! The implementation of a VPN on FreeS/WAN is that simple.

Summary

In this chapter, you learned to implement a VPN solution on the Linux platform. In Linux,
VPNs over Point-to-Point Protocol and Secure SHell are the popular choices for VPN implementation. However, with the phenomenal emergence of IPSec in the VPN arena, a new
IPSec-based solution called FreeS/WAN is taking over. You learned to implement VPNs on
both PPP over SSH and FreeS/WAN.

Check Your Understanding

Multiple Choice Questions

1. Which of the following statements is true?

   a. FTP and Telnet are secure applications.

   b. PPP offers high-speed transactions.

   c. PPP uses public key encryption to provide security to data transmissions.

   d. Public key encryption is based on a single key.

2. The package that you do not need to install on a VPN client for the PPP over SSH VPN solution is_____.

   a. pty_redir

   b. sbin

   c. pppd

   d. sshd

3. Which of the following ports should be enabled on a firewall to allow ESP authentication and encryption?

   a. 50

   b. 500

   c. 51

   d. 501

4. In the command `ipchains -A input -j ACCEPT -i eth0 -p 51 -s $IPSECGW`, what does $IPSECGW represent?

   a. IP address of the local gateway that received the request for the VPN session

   b. IP address of the remote client that initiated the VPN session

   c. IP address of the remote gateway that initiated the VPN session

   d. IP address of the VPN server that received the request for the VPN session

5. Which of the following files stores the private key?

   a. ipsec.conf

   b. ipsec.etc

   c. ipsec.sbin

   d. ipsec.secrets

Answers

Multiple Choice Answers

1. **b.** PPP offers high-speed transactions.

2. **b.** The package that you do not need to install on a VPN client for the PPP over SSH VPN solution is sbin. It is a standard Linux directory. You'll require sshd, pppd, and pty_redir packages on the VPN client for PPP over SSH VPN implementations.

3. **a.** ESP uses port 50 for authentication and encryption. AH uses port 51, and IKE uses UDP port 500 for key-related management activities.

4. **c.** The parameter $IPSECGW in the ipchains -A input -j ACCEPT -i eth0 -p 51 -s $IPSECGW command represents the IP address of the remote gateway that initiated the VPN session.

5. **d.** The file that stores the private key in a FreeS/WAN-based VPN implementation is ipsec.secrets.

PART IV

Securing VPNs

Chapter 10

VPN Security Issues

A VPN is a high-end network security solution. But, if you assume that the implementation of VPNs will solve all your security-related problems, you are in for a rude awakening. While organizations all over the world have awakened to intranet security threats and have implemented advanced security measures to counter these threats, the fact that attacking technology has also progressed by leaps and bounds is very sobering.

In today's scenario, where a 12-year old kid can take a potshot at your network, you can't just implement a security technology or measure, however advanced, and think of living peacefully for the next few months, until someone comes up with a countermeasure. Today, an attack strategy is ready even before you say the word go! And VPNs have been in the market for quite some time now. Therefore, there is a world of security-related threats that a VPN-based implementation might have to face.

This chapter explores the various security threats that your VPN may encounter. These threats can be broadly categorized into attacks on the VPN implementation (individual elements), attacks against VPN protocols, attacks against the algorithms used in VPN protocols, and Denial-of-Service attacks. However, before proceeding to an understanding of these VPN security threats, you need to understand what a security threat actually is and the motivating factors behind it.

Understanding Security Threats

Gaining unauthorized access to a network and the resources located within it for personal ends is known as intrusion. There are various motivations behind security threats related to intrusions. The most compelling factors that lead to an intrusion and the subsequent security threats faced by the vulnerable organization follow:

◆ **Competition.** Intense competition among organizations motivates some organizations to employ unethical tactics, such as hacking into a rival organization's setup, resulting in the infliction of damage or the theft of sensitive or mission-critical information.

◆ **Greed.** Accessing confidential data for the purpose of later selling it to the highest bidder.

◆ **Revenge**. Avenging a real or imaginary harm perpetrated by an organization against a now-disgruntled employee.

◆ **Thrills.** For the sake of fun, challenge, and curiosity by students, kids and other thrill-seekers.

Security threats faced by a VPN, like any normal network, can be divided into the following broad categories:

◆ Internal security threats
◆ External security threats

External Security Threats

An external security threat is posed by an entity that is external to your organization. These external entities are generally referred to as *hackers*. A hacker can either be a professional hired to break into the targeted system or an amateur hobbyist. Regardless, their ultimate goal is the same—to gain unauthorized access to protected network resources. If their intentions are malicious, hackers can cause a lot of damage to the organization they intrude. Figure 10-1 illustrates an external security threat.

External security threats are the most common form of intrusions. The biggest problem associated with external hacking is that it is extremely difficult, if not impossible, to identify the hacker.

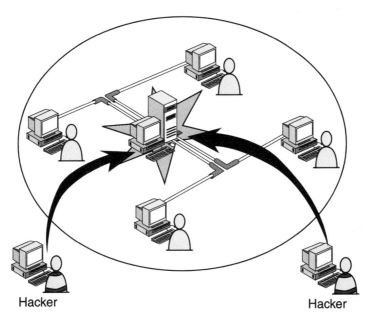

FIGURE 10-1 *A generic representation of external security threats.*

There might be a lot of reasons motivating external security threats. Most of these reasons are quite similar to the ones listed in the previous section and include challenge, fun, curiosity, rivalry, or revenge.

The first two reasons, though harmful, are not as harmful as the last two reasons—revenge and competition. In the cases motivated by challenge and fun, the hacker might not harm internal resources or use them maliciously. These hackers generally lose interest once the system is compromised. On the other hand, intrusions motivated by revenge and competition are more harmful and can cause serious loss to an organization as the intent of the hacker is malicious. In these cases, data can fall into the wrong hands resulting in considerable damage to the organization.

Internal Security Threats

More often than not, organizations focus maximum attention on securing their network setups and data from external entities. However, in doing, they generally tend to forget that they also need to guard their resources and sensitive data from internal entities as well. According to industry estimates, the majority of security threats that an organization faces are internal. In fact, according to a recent survey by the FBI's Computer Security Institute and Ernst and Young, nearly 60 percent of all security threats come from within.

Figure 10-2 illustrates an internal security threat.

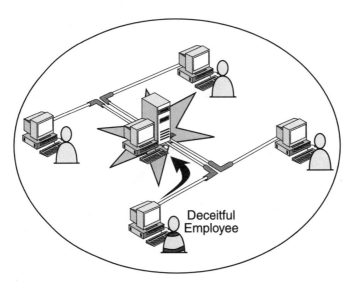

FIGURE 10-2 *A generic representation of internal security threats.*

The motivations behind internal security threats are most often revenge, greed, and boredom. Of these, revenge is the most compelling. For example, if an employee is unhappy with their organization, he or she might try to avenge the unhappiness by causing maximum damage to organization. To do so, he or she may resort to hacking sensitive organization resources. Greed can also motivate an employee to hack the system and sell sensitive information to a competitor. And sometimes, though rarely, an employee might give into boredom, curiosity, or fun and hack the organization setup for one of those reasons.

There are two main types of employees that can pose an internal security threat: employees with in-depth technical know-how who hold positions of responsibility (such as network and group administrators), and employees who do not hold positions of responsibility but who are technically-savvy. It should be noted that non-technical users can also threaten the security of the network setup. This type of user generally falls into a third, less populated, category.

Employees who, in the line of work, are responsible for implementing, maintaining, and managing your IT infrastructure belong to the first category of "potentially dangerous" employees. These employees will have an in-depth understanding of the security solution as well as access to critical company resources. If disgruntled or unhappy, these are the employees who can bring down the entire setup with minimum effort! The after-effects of such intrusions can be severe as these employees have a keen understanding of the technology and can, therefore, harm the setup so badly that it may take days to rectify the situation.

Employees belonging to the second category of potential threats are those unhappy technically-savvy personnel who can use their knowledge and a bit of social engineering to identify vulnerable but valuable resources and gain access (physical or otherwise) to those resources. The after-affects of an intrusion by such personnel may range from the easily-rectified to a total loss.

There is also a third category of employees who have neither the required in-depth knowledge nor in-depth technical know-now to wreck major havoc. These employees usually resort to worms, viruses, and trojans to cause harm.

 NOTE

A worm is a malicious software application that replicates itself endlessly until it brings down the system attacked. It does so by generating excessive network traffic. Like a worm, a virus also replicates itself, but it needs to be attached to a program (generally an executable program) before self-replication can occur. Trojans are the worst of these three. They do not replicate as the other two do. Rather, they execute transparently, behind the scenes, and gather sensitive information, such as user IDs and passwords from the network. This information, when it falls into the hands of a person (internal or external) with malicious intent, can be used to cause serious damage to the organization.

There is no out-of-box solution for the internal security threats. You cannot possibly keep an eye on each and every person in an organization, especially if yours is a large-scale organization. The only viable solution to this problem is proper employee training and education. Employees should be trained in detail about prohibited and threatening activities and should be encouraged to report any suspicious activities. Employees should also be sensitive to the dangerous implications of sharing user IDs and passwords with others, opening suspicious e-mail attachments, and having conventional and predictable passwords.

 NOTE

Passwords should never be short or reflect personal information, such as date of birth, a loved one's name, and so on. Long, difficult-to-remember passwords that use a mix of letters, numbers, and special characters should be encouraged.

Collaborative Security Threats

The most serious attacks result when an internal and an external entity join hands (Figure 10-3 illustrates this combined threat). In this scenario, the internal entity can supply sensitive information, such as user IDs and passwords, to the external entity, who can then use this information to break into the system and cause trouble. As a result, the organization is under fire from within as well as externally. In addition, because the attack is carried out by the external entity, the offender is extremely difficult to trace.

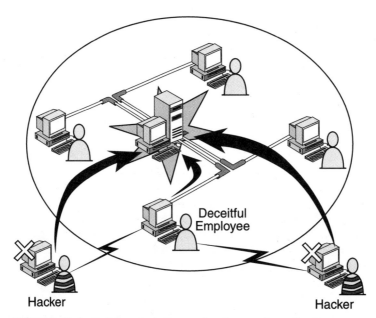

FIGURE 10-3 *Collaboration of internal and external security threats.*

Now that you have a general idea about intrusions, security threats, and the motivations behind these harmful activities, you can consider the potential attacks on present-day VPNs.

VPN Attacks

A VPN-based implementation can be attacked in many ways. The following is a list of the types of possible VPN attacks:

◆ Security threats to VPN elements

◆ Attacks against VPN protocols

◆ Cryptanalysis attacks

◆ Denial-of -Service attacks

Security Threats to VPN Elements

As shown in Figure 10-4, the most important elements of a VPN setup include the following:

◆ The dial-in remote user

◆ The dial-in ISP segments

◆ The Internet

◆ The host network gateway

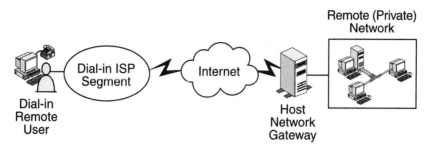

FIGURE 10-4 *Elements of a VPN-based setup.*

The dial-in client (or the end or remote user), such as a notebook or laptop user, is the starting point of a VPN-based transaction. The biggest security threat to the dial-in client is the secrecy of its user ID and password. Therefore, the end user, who initiates the transaction, must protect its user ID and password from falling into the wrong hands. The practice of changing passwords regularly reduces the probability that an unauthorized user will guess the correct password. In addition, the dial-in client must also take steps to physically protect the node when the machine is left unattended, even for short durations. Password-protected screensavers and the practice of locking the workstation are good security measures. In extreme cases, you should consider physically locking the machine or the room housing the machine.

The ISP's dial-in segment is the second vulnerable point in a VPN setup. This segment delivers user data to the ISP's Network Access Server (NAS). If this data is not encrypted, there is a high risk that the data might be read at the ISP end. Also, the possibility that the data will be read during transaction between the end user and the ISP's intranet is quite high. The chances of eavesdropping by the external entity can be eliminated by encrypting the data at the remote user-end before sending it to the ISP end. However if the encryption algorithm is weak, encryption doesn't provide adequate protection against malicious ISPs that can decrypt the data and use it for their profit.

As you already know, Internet connectivity and the subsequent tunneling are dependent upon an ISP. However, if the intentions of the ISP are malicious, it can establish a rogue tunnel and an accompanying rogue gateway. (This type of rogue setup is illustrated in Figure 10-5.) In such a case, the sensitive user data will be tunneled to the imposter gateway, which in turn can retrieve and examine the data for its own use and profit. The rogue gateway could also alter the data and forward to the real destination gateway. The destination gateway will accept the data assuming that it is from the original trusted source. In this manner, unwanted and malicious data can enter the network.

Another point of security threat is the data traveling through the tunnels across the Internet. The data tunnel is rendered across multiple routers and the user datagrams travel through these routers, as depicted in Figure 10-6. As a part of the tunnel, these intermediate routers can examine the data. If any of these routers are malicious, the router could not only examine the data but also modify it, even if the packets are encrypted.

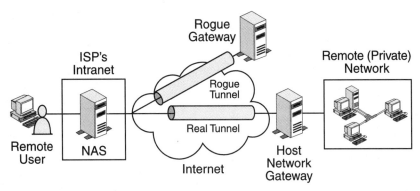

FIGURE 10-5 *The role of a malicious ISP in transmitting harmful data to an organization's intranet.*

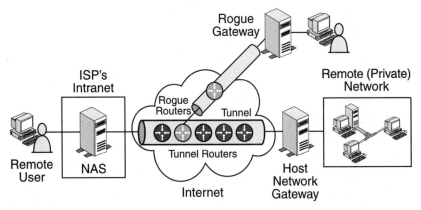

FIGURE 10-6 *Role of a malicious router in transmitting harmful data to an organization's intranet.*

 NOTE

PPTP and even L2TP do not provide robust security mechanisms against rogue ISPs and tunnel routers. However, the advanced and comprehensive encryption capability provided by IPSec does offer a high degree of protection against these rogue elements.

The final destination of a tunneled data packet is the host network gateway. The data packet is vulnerable to hacking if the gateway uses non-cryptographic authentication mechanisms because attacks, such as address spoofing and sniffing, can gain access to the cleartext information that these gateways use. On the other hand, cryptographic authentication mechanisms provide some degree of security, as it takes longer for an attacker or a hacker to break into these algorithms. However, an internal attacker can still access the cleartext information sent into the intranet by the gateway.

Attacks Against VPN Protocols

The main VPN protocols, PPTP, L2TP, and IPSec, are also vulnerable to security threats. The following sections discuss these attacks on VPN protocols.

 NOTE

Refer to Chapter 5, "Tunneling Protocols at Layer 2," for detailed information on PPTP and L2TP. You might also want to refer to Chapter 6, "An Introduction to IPSec," for in-depth information on IPSec.

Attacks on PPTP

PPTP is vulnerable on two fronts. These include:

◆ Generic Routing Encapsulation (GRE)
◆ Passwords exchanged during the authentication process

As you already know, the security of the data passed across the tunnel is the responsibility of the underlying encapsulated data. GRE is a tunneling protocol that simply encapsulates the cleartext data. It is not responsible for providing a secure method of transporting that data. As a result, any attacker or hacker can easily capture GRE-encapsulated packets. Unless the payload encapsulated by the GRE packet has also been encrypted, the attacker can also read the data being transported. This allows the attacker to retrieve information (such as the valid internal IP addresses used within the intranet) that helps him or her attack the data originator and the resources located inside the private networks. In addition, intruders might introduce rogue routes and disrupt traffic. For example, an intruder could actually behave as a GRE endpoint and have full access to not just the data being transmitted, but also the network systems themselves.

 NOTE

GRE tunnels are set up in such a way that the routing is done dynamically, which might defeat the entire purpose of a VPN. To prevent packets from being routed dynamically, it is recommended that you only use static routing across the tunnels and leave the setup and configuration a manual process. Another suggestion to defeat this type of attack is to have the data pass through a firewall after the GRE header is removed. Private network numbers for the tunnel interfaces that are not routed on either side of the network can also help.

Another weak point of GRE is that GRE packets use a sequence # number for the synchronization of the tunnel. However, the GRE specifications do not implement a match for the destination node to respond to duplicate or invalid (or rogue) sequence numbers. As a result, the destination node might ignore the sequence number of the packet and process the rest of the packet. Using this strategy, an intruder can easily introduce invalid packets containing malicious data into the organization's intranet.

In addition to the aforementioned vulnerabilities, PPTP is also open to *Sictionary attacks*. A Dictionary attack refers to an attack that finds passwords in a specific list, such as an English dictionary. PPTP is vulnerable to Dictionary attacks because PPTP uses Microsoft Point-to-Point Encryption (MPPE), which tends to send passwords in the clear. If the intruder obtains a part of sensitive password-related information, such as a hashed-password and/or hashing algorithm and performs a series of computations employing every possible permutation, the correct password can be determined.

Now, passwords are typically small by cryptographic standards. Therefore, the passwords can often be determined by brute-force. Depending on the system, the password, and the skills of the attacker, such an attack can be completed in days, hours, or only a few seconds.

Attacks on IPSec

As you learned in Chapter 6, "An Introduction to IPSec," IPSec is neither a pure encryption algorithm nor an authentication mechanism. In fact, IPSec is a combination of both and helps other algorithms protect data. But, IPSec is vulnerable to the following type of attacks:

- ◆ Attacks against IPSec implementation
- ◆ Attacks against key management
- ◆ Administrative and wildcard attacks

Intruders and attackers exploit two weak points of IPSec implementation—the use of NULL algorithms, and negotiation of a weaker key if one of the communicating ends does not support stronger keys.

As you might recall, IPSec uses DES-CBC for encryption purposes and HMAC-MD5 and HMAC-SHA-1 for authentication purposes. In addition, the use of IPSec protocols ESP and AH is optional. As a result, IPSec also allows the use of NULL algorithms. Usage of NULL algorithms allows an end that does not use DES-CBC to communicate with the other end, which does use DES-CBC. As a result, vendors who implement a NULL algorithm can render the setup more vulnerable to security threats. This problem normally occurs when you are implementing products by different vendors who use different standards.

IPSec also allows the communicating ends to negotiate encryption keys. As a result, if one end supports a weaker key (40-bit), the other end would also have to use the weaker (40-bit) key despite the fact that it supports a stronger key (56-bits and 128-bits). Given the current scenario, 56-bit keys can be broken into within a few months if not a few days; therefore, a 40-bit key is a child's play in comparison and much easier to break.

IPSec uses IKE for the purpose of key management. The *attacks against key management* exploit a weak point of IKE: If one of the communicating sides terminates the current session, there is no way for the other end to learn that the session has been terminated. This opens a security hole that a third party intruder can now use to spoof the identity of the terminated side and continue the data exchange.

The third type of IPSec attack is not yet a reality, but is currently being discussed. IPSec provides for an administrative interface to the SA. This increases the chance that the SA parameters could be attacked using wildcard matching.

 NOTE

L2TP is vulnerable to Dictionary attacks, Brute Force attacks, and Spoofing attacks. However, L2TP is seldom implemented alone. It is usually implemented over IPSec. Therefore, L2TP attacks are not discussed separately.

Cryptanalysis Attacks

Cryptanalysis, as you learned earlier in Chapter 3, "Security Components of a VPN," is the science of deciphering codes and ciphers without the prior knowledge of the cryptographic keys that were used for encryption. Depending on the various cryptographic techniques and algorithms, many cryptanalysis attacks are known to exist. The following sections discuss some well-known cryptanalysis attacks.

Ciphertext-Only Attacks

In Ciphertext-only attacks, the hacker does not have access to the original data packet content, but has access to the ciphertext used. As a result, the intruder can perform reverse engineering to arrive at the plaintext message on the basis of available encrypted message. This attack, though long and tedious and useless against modern ciphers, results in a high-degree of success given the crude method of decryption.

 NOTE

Reverse engineering is the process of intercepting coded information and trying to work out the original message from this encrypted message. This is basically a "hit-and-miss" method, which requires a lot of time and effort.

The success of this type of attack is due to the fact that most messages of similar types use fixed format headers. In addition, frequency analysis of the ciphertext allows the attacker to determine a large number of original characters. As a result, the rest of the message can be guessed easily.

Modern ciphers have been designed and developed with this attack in mind. Because of this, most modern cryptosystems are strong and do not yield to these attacks.

Known Plaintext Attacks

In known plaintext attacks, the intruder already knows a part of the ciphertext and uses this information to guess the rest of the cipher. For example, if the hacker already knows a part of the key and guesses the rest, he or she can easily decrypt the information.

A Linear Cryptanalysis attack is one such popular plaintext attack. In this attack, some of the known plaintext bits are XORed with each other and some of the ciphertext bits are XORed with each other. When the results are once again XORed together, you will end up with bits that are the XOR of some of the key bits. If a significant number of plaintext and ciphertext bits are XORed together, a large part of the key can be determined and the rest can be guessed. The greater the base data for the XORing process, the higher the probability of arriving at the correct key.

Chosen Plaintext Attacks

In chosen plaintext attacks, the hacker has the liberty to randomly choose an encrypted cipher-text. The hacker can then determine the key that was used for encrypting the intercepted ciphertext. When the hacker has been able to determine this key, it can be used to further decode the encoded data.

Differential Cryptanalysis attacks are a well-known example of this category of cryptanalysis attacks. In Differential Cryptanalysis attacks, a pair of ciphertext whose plaintext has known specific differences is chosen. Then, based on the differences of the ciphertext, different probabilities are assigned to determine the key. After a large number of ciphertext pairs have been analyzed, the encryption key begins to emerge.

Cryptanalysis algorithms, such as RSA, are vulnerable to chosen plaintext attacks. Therefore, when such algorithms are used, great care should be taken in developing the application or protocol so that the attacker cannot have the chosen plaintext encrypted.

 NOTE

Refer to Chapter 3, "Security Components of a VPN," for detailed information on RSA.

Man-in-the-Middle Attacks

Man-in-the-Middle attacks are possible when the algorithm used employs cryptographic communication and key exchange, such as Diffie-Hellman. In this type of attack, before the two authorized entities exchange data, a third non-trusted party intercepts the key exchange and forwards its own keys to both the authorized communicating ends. As a result, the original communicating ends do not receive the legitimate key and instead, end up with a different key. The unsuspecting ends assume that the key is sent by the other authorized (and authenticated) end and start using the key for encryption and decryption for the current session. In this manner, the third party has complete access to the entire communication without the original node's knowledge.

 NOTE

Man-in-the-Middle attacks can be prevented with the use of digital signatures. Digital signatures are exchanged after the two ends exchange keys and generate the shared secret. Even though the keys can be forged by the third party, digital signatures are unique and cannot be forged. Therefore, the security of the exchanged is heightened.

Brute Force Attacks

In the case of Brute Force attacks an intruder will randomly generate keys and apply them to the ciphertext until the real key is discovered. The key, thus generated, can then be used for the decryption of data and the eventual retrieval of the original information.

As you might have guessed, the length of the encryption key is a major issue in Brute Force attacks. The longer the key length, the more difficult it is to guess and, consequently, the more secure the information. For example, a 32-bit key requires at least 2^{32} attempts, a 40-bit key requires 2^{40} attempts, and a 56-bit key requires 2^{56} attempts to break the key. With the available technology, a 40-bit key can be broken within a week and 56-bit key can be broken within a few months. Therefore, a 128-bit key is considered the safest bet.

Initially, Brute Force attacks were beyond the scope of everyday hackers because they required a large number of expensive and high-performance computers to break the key. However, with the rapid advancement of computing technology, such PCs are well within the reach of normal users—including hackers.

Timing Attacks

Timing attacks are a relatively new category of cryptanalysis attacks. With this type of attack mechanism the execution interval of the modular exponentiation operation used by the cryptographic algorithm is measured. This interval enables intruders and hackers to make an educated guess about the cryptographic algorithm and encryption keys used.

NOTE

In the past few years, a new category of cryptanalysis attacks has cropped up. Attacks within this category aim at the hardware implementation of the cryptosystem, instead of the cryptographic algorithms themselves. Crypto-parameters such as timing, power consumption, and radiation patterns, if any, related to the cryptosystems are measured accurately. On the basis of this information, encryption keys are generated. Because these attacks are more dependent on hardware now, they are becoming highly independent of the algorithms used. As a result, an intruder can use these attacks to target virtually any cryptosystem, regardless of the cryptographic algorithm it uses.

Denial-of-Service Attacks

Denial-of-Service (DoS) attacks are quite different from other kinds of network attacks. An intruder might use other network attacks, such as impersonation, malware, and viruses to either access resources or damage them. DoS attacks, though, are used to make some services or target computers inaccessible.

DoS attacks are becoming quite common these days because they do not require any special software or access to the targeted network. They are based on the concept of network congestion. Any intruder can cause network congestion by sending loads and loads of junk data into the network. This causes the target computers to be inaccessible for some time as all routes to reach the computers are blocked by the junk congestion. The overload of information can even lead to the crashing of the targeted computers.

Figure 10-7 illustrates how hackers can cause network congestion by introducing spurious data into the network.

DoS attacks enjoy a lot of advantages. First, DoS attacks come in a variety of forms and can target many network services. Second, an intruder can initiate a DoS attack in a number of ways, such as sending a large number of junk mail or sending a large number of IP request packets. And third, the DoS intruder can easily be kept anonymous. Unfortunately, there exists no single measure to consistently determine the identity of the intruder. Intruders employing DoS attacks make use of some innate lapses in communication technologies and the IP protocol. In fact, a successful DoS attack can be instigated by simply tampering with the size of IP packets that are sent to the network.

Some commonly used methods for initiating DoS attacks follow:

- ◆ SYN Floods
- ◆ Broadcast Storm
- ◆ Smurf DoS
- ◆ Ping of Death
- ◆ Mail Bomb
- ◆ Spam Mailing

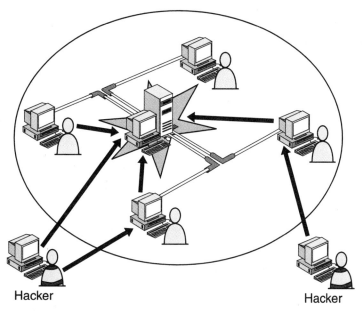

FIGURE 10-7 *Network Congestion by hackers.*

SYN Floods

In an *SYN flood*, all your TCP connections are used, thereby preventing authorized users from accessing resources through those connections. To understand how this works, you need to understand how a TCP connection works.

To initiate a session, TCP uses a three-way handshake mechanism. The steps involved in establishing a TCP connection are as follows:

1. A host sends a data packet to another host on the network. This data packet contains the host ID and is referred to as the *Synchronize Sequence Number* (SYN).
2. The recipient host acknowledges the receipt of the data by sending another data packet known as the Acknowledgement (ACK).
3. The recipient host also sends back the received SYN packet.
4. Upon receiving the data from the recipient host, the first host sends back the third data packet or ACK.

The complete process involves a transfer of only three data packets (thus the term *three-way handshake*).

A TCP connection can lead to network congestion if someone sends a fake ID in the SYN packet. If a fake ID is sent, the receiving host will never receive the acknowledgement. Eventually, the connection times out and the incoming channel becomes free to receive another request. An SYN flood sends so many packets with fake IDs that all incoming channels are tied up waiting for acknowledgements.

In this way, all incoming channels are tied up waiting for acknowledgements and there is no interface available for authorized users. To overcome an SYN flood, there are a number of tools available, such as Cisco IOS software and Cisco PIX Firewall.

Broadcast Storm

A broadcast is a message that is sent to every computer on a network. If there are many broadcasts within a network then there will be a lot of traffic on that network. A condition where there exist a number of broadcast packets on a network is referred to as a *Broadcast Storm*.

A Broadcast Storm can be used maliciously by an intruder if he or she broadcasts a large number of packets containing fake destination addresses into your network. Each computer will try to forward these packets to the specified fake destination addresses. Because the addresses do not exist, the packets remain in the network, moving from one computer to another, until they completely choke the network. Tools such as asping and sendmail can be used to initiate Broadcast Storms. Broadcast Storms can be effectively prevented by blocking illegal broadcast messages in the network.

Smurf DoS

Smurf attacks are named after the program that is used to instigate these attacks. These attacks are sometimes also referred to as ICMP Magnification attacks.

In these attacks, an intruder uses a spoofed IP address and sends a large number of ICMP (ping) echo requests to the network's broadcast IP address. The other network computers send their ICMP echo reply messages to the spoofed source IP in response to the broadcast IP echo request. This results in an enormous amount of traffic leading to network congestion.

 NOTE

In the case of a multi-access broadcast storm, Smurf attacks can assume large proportions; if there are hundreds of computers in a network then each and every computer will reply to each echo request.

Ping of Death

Ping of Death refers to a DoS attack where an intruder floods the network with many IP packets of a size greater than 65,535 bytes. These packets are sent to targeted computers. These computers cannot handle the onslaught of such huge packets and often reboot or freeze. A large number of such packets in the network can also lead to network congestion.

If the intruder is using Windows 95 to initiate the Ping of Death attack, he or she can send large-sized packets to the target host using the following command:

```
ping -l 65527 -s 1 {destination_IP}
```

In this command:

- ◆ `-l 65527` is used to set the buffer size to 65527.
- ◆ `-s 1` is used to specify the time stamp for hop counts.

A Teardrop attack is a category of Ping of Death attacks, where overlapping fragments of ping packets are sent to the target host(s). Upon receiving the complete ping command, each target computer tries to reassemble the packet. However, the size of the data packets is so large that it can't fit into the computer's buffer. As a result, these large-sized packets cause overflow that might lead to system damage in the form of system crash, frequent reboots, or hangs.

A Land attack is yet another category of Ping of Death attacks. In a Land attack the intruder spoofs a TCP connection request from the target host. This spoofed packet is then forwarded to the target machine, so that it appears as if the target machine is trying to establish a connection with itself. This causes the machine to stop responding and hang.

You can counter Ping of Death attacks by blocking pings to your computer. However, blocking all regular pings is not a very practical solution. So, instead of blocking all pings, you need to block only the fragmented pings. When you block fragmented pings, all pings that are bigger than the MTU size of your link are blocked. Regular pings of 64 bytes will be allowed through most systems.

Mail Bomb

A *Mail Bomb* attack is targeted at your mail server(s). In this attack, identical copies of an e-mail are sent to the target host. In addition, sometimes the mail that is sent is capable of replicating itself at the server end. The mail server might not be capable of handling such a large amount of traffic due to low bandwidth, low disk space, or other processing constraints. This puts the mail server in a looping process and may lead to a server crash.

Spam Mailing

Just like a Mail Bomb attack, *Spam Mailing* is also aimed at the mail server. Spam Mailing uses fake reply addresses in e-mail messages. Therefore, when you reply to these messages, the reply bounces back to non-existent e-mail addresses. If there are a number of reply addresses in the Spam mail or the Spam mail is self-replicating, mail server congestion can occur, thereby affecting mail services.

Countering DoS Attacks

DoS attacks are fast becoming the weapon of choice for hackers. However, you can take the following measures to counter these attacks:

◆ Disable unused or unneeded network services.

◆ Maintain regular backups.

◆ Create, maintain, and monitor daily logs.

◆ Create appropriate password policies.

◆ Implement an Intrusion Detection System.

◆ Implement route filters to filter fragmented ICMP packets.

◆ Keep a strict vigil on the physical security of your network resources.

◆ Configure filters for IP-spoofed packets.

◆ Install patches and fixes for TCP SYN attacks.

◆ Partition the file system to separate application-specific files from regular data.

◆ Deploy tools such as Tripwire that detect changes in configuration information or other files.

Summary

In this chapter, you explored the various security threats that your VPN might face. First, you learned what a security threat actually is, its kinds, and the motivation factors behind it. Next, you learned that the security threats that a VPN faces can be broadly organized into four categories. These include attacks on the VPN implementation (individual elements), attacks against VPN protocols, attacks against the algorithms used in VPN protocols, and Denial-of-Service attacks.

Check Your Understanding

Multiple Choice Questions

1. Which of the following statements about security threats are NOT true?

   a. External threats are less damaging than internal threats.

   b. Internal threats are more damaging than external threats.

   c. External threats are easier to trace.

   d. A combination of internal and external threats is easier to trace.

2. Which of the following is not a category of VPN attacks?

   a. Hijacking

   b. Cryptanalysis attacks

   c. DoS attacks

   d. Tunnel attacks

3. The Diffie-Hellman algorithm is prone to which of the following attacks?

   a. Brute Force attacks

   b. Spoofing attacks

   c. Timing attacks

   d. Man-in-the-Middle attacks

4. The latest category of hardware-intensive cryptanalysis attacks is _____.

   a. Timing attacks

   b. Attacks using the underlying hardware

   c. IPSec attacks

   d. Differential cryptanalysis attacks

5. Which of the following are PPTP vulnerabilities that allow an intruder to attack PPTP-based VPN implementations?

   a. Key management

   b. Administrative wildcards

   c. GRE-based encapsulation

   d. Transmitting passwords in cleartext

Answers

Multiple Choice Answers

1. **a, c,** and **d.** Although external threats are highly damaging, internal threats are capable of wrecking greater havoc on your networks as they are more difficult to trace. A combination of internal and external threats is the most difficult to trace.

2. **a** and **d.** The categories of VPN attacks include attacks against VPN elements, attacks against VPN protocols, attacks against VPN cryptosystems (cryptanalysis attacks), and Denial-of-Service attacks. There is no category called tunneling attacks and no category called hijacking attacks.

3. **d.** The Diffie-Hellman algorithm is prone to Man-in-the-Middle attacks. In these attacks, a third non-trusted party intercepts the key exchange and forwards its own keys to both authorized communicating ends. As a result, the original communicating ends do not receive the legitimate key and, instead, end up using forged keys.

4. **b.** The latest category of hardware-intensive cryptanalysis attacks is attacks against or using the underlying hardware. In these attacks, crypto-parameters such as timing, power consumption, and radiation patterns, if any, related to the cryptosystems are measured accurately. On the basis of this information, encryption keys are generated. As these attacks are more dependent on hardware, they are highly independent of the algorithms used.

5. **c** and **d.** PPTP vulnerabilities that allow an intruder to attack PPTP-based VPN implementations include GRE-based encapsulation and the sending of passwords in cleartext. In addition, PPTP is also open to dictionary attacks.

Chapter 11

VPN Security Technologies

VPNs are a strong security technology. The effective use of authentication, encryption, and digital certificates only serve to strengthen the technology further. However, as you learned in the previous chapter, "VPN Security Issues," hacking and attacking techniques have developed in proportion to the security technologies. As a result, even advanced security technologies like VPNs are not completely safe and are vulnerable to security threats. In the present scenario of ever-increasing demands on security, it is important that additional security measures be implemented.

In this chapter, you will learn about additional security measures that can help you to strengthen data transmissions based on VPN technology. You will learn about additional remote authentication techniques, such as Authentication Authorization Accounting (AAA), RADIUS, and TACACS. You will also explore security technologies such as firewalls, NAT, SOCKS, SSL, and TLS, which when used with VPNs can help you achieve a safer environment for data transactions across the Internet and public networks.

Remote Authentication Techniques

With a significant increase in the mobile workforce of organizations all over the world, remote authentication techniques have come to play an important role in ensuring that only trusted and authorized users can access an intranet's resources. This trend has further been fuelled by the global presence of corporations and organizations in which users located in a remote subnet or LAN can access the resources located in the organization's main network. As a result, strong authentication mechanisms need to be in place to prevent the theft of sensitive data stored on the intranet. Some of these authentication techniques have been adopted to complement VPN technology with a goal of increasing the security level of data stored within these private intranets. These authentication techniques include the following:

- Authentication Authorization Accounting (AAA)
- Remote Access Dial-In User Service (RADIUS)
- Terminal Access Controller Access Control System (TACACS)

Authentication Authorization Accounting (AAA)

As the name suggests, AAA is an architectural framework that is used to configure three basic security functions—authentication, authorization, and accounting. Today, the AAA security model is used in practically all remote access scenarios because it allows network administrators to identify and answer the following three important questions:

- Who is accessing the network?
- What is the user allowed to do and what actions are restricted to him or her when he or she accesses the network successfully?
- What is the user doing and when?

Authentication

As you already learned in Chapter 3, "Security Components of a VPN," authentication is the first step toward security. Authentication involves the proper identification of a user before he or she can access any of the resources within the network.

Authentication provides various mechanisms for determining the true identity of the users who access resources located within the intranet. Supplying user ID and the corresponding password is the traditional authentication method. Other methods include challenge and response dialog, messaging support, and, sometimes, encryption, depending on the security protocol used.

Most popular authentication methods that are used today are based on challenge and response. Some of the methods that implement the challenge-response mechanism include PAP, CHAP, EAP, Shiva PAP (SPAP), and IPSec.

NOTE

Refer to Chapter 5, "Tunneling Protocols at Layer 2," for more information on PAP, CHAP, and EAP. Chapter 6, "An Introduction to IPSec," explores the concept and functionality of IPSec in detail. You might also refer to Chapter 3, "Security Components of a VPN," for detailed information on authentication and access control.

Authorization

Authorization refers to the mechanism of controlling the activities that a user is allowed to perform within the network and the resources that the user is allowed to access. As a result, authorization provides the mechanism for remote access control by means of one-time authorization, authorization for each service, per-user account list, or workgroup policy.

Generally, a set of access rights, privileges, and attributes are compiled and stored in a centralized database for the purpose of authorization. These rights and attributes determine the activities that a user is allowed to perform. When a user needs to be authorized after successful authentication, these rights and attributes are verified against the database entry for the given user and the result is forwarded to the involved server (the remote access server, for example).

Usually, authentication precedes authorization. However, this is not a strict sequence. If a network resource, such as server, receives an authorization request without undergoing proper authentication, the authorization agent on the network device must determine whether the user can access the network device and is allowed to perform the services specified in the authorization request.

Accounting

Accounting is the mechanism of recording each activity that a user performs after he or she successfully logs onto the network. Therefore, accounting involves collecting, billing, auditing, logging, and reporting user identities, commands that were executed during the session, the number of packets transacted, and so on. When a user activity is recorded, the time it was performed, the duration for which the entire user-session lasted, and the duration for which each individual activity lasted is also recorded. This detailed user-related information helps the network administrators track errant users and take appropriate actions to maintain network security.

Although accounting is considered to be the next logical step after authentication and authorization, it can be implemented out of the specified sequence. In other words, accounting can be implemented even though authentication and authorization activities have not been performed.

The AAA model can be implemented at the centralized network device, such as at the remote access server and RADIUS server, as shown in Figure 11-1. AAA can also be implemented at the individual network resources, depending on the number of network devices and the complexity of network management. In this case, if the AAA model is implemented at the remote access server, any user accessing the network is authenticated as well as authorized by the remote access server. Accounting is also the responsibility of the remote access server in this scenario. On the other hand, if the AAA model is implemented on individual resources, each resource is responsible for authenticating, authorizing, and keeping account of user activities. The later implementation of AAA is not popular because it can make network management difficult, as it is easier to store, update, and manage all the information related to remote users on a dedicated and centralized device.

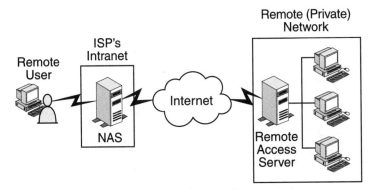

FIGURE 11-1 *A typical AAA-based network configuration.*

Besides easy manageability and enhanced security, AAA offers the following advantages:

◆ **Scalability and flexibility.** The network configuration can be rearranged, changed, or upgraded according to the organization's future needs and requirements without having to change the existing setup.

◆ **Cost-effectiveness.** The solution is highly cost-effective because it does not require huge investments or major changes in the existing network setup.

◆ **Standardization of authentication mechanisms.** With the implementation of standard authentication mechanisms, such as RADIUS, TACACS+, and Kerberos, the entire authentication procedure can be standardized across the entire intranet despite distance-constraints. Here, TACACS+ is the enhanced version of TACACS. Besides the standard authentication services that TACACS provides, TACACS+ offers challenge and response along with data encryption capability.

◆ **Easy recovery.** You can implement secondary authentication servers that can take over in case of primary server failure. This results in the easy recovery of information stored on the remote access servers.

> ## NOTE
>
> Refer to RFCs 2903 and 2904 for more information on AAA. You can find
> RFC 2903 at http://www.armware.dk/RFC/rfc/rfc2903.html and RFC 2904 at
> http://www.armware.dk/RFC/rfc/rfc2904.html.

For some time now, IETF has led the movement to standardize the remote access mechanism. Because centralized storage of user information is a more secure and manageable option, RADIUS and TACACS have emerged as standard solutions in the field of remote authentication.

Remote Access Dial-In User Service (RADIUS)

Developed by Livingston Enterprises (now a subsidiary of Lucent) and supported by IETF, RADIUS has emerged as the de facto standard for remote authentication. It is widely supported by remote access servers, VPN products, and firewalls.

In a network setup that uses RADIUS, user-related information is stored on a central database. All remote access servers share this database. When a remote access server receives a login request from a remote user, RADIUS enables the communication between the database and the remote access server. In fact, RADIUS specifies the format and the flow of packets between the database and the access server. The database supplies the requested information. The remote access server uses this information to authenticate the incoming request and authorize the user to access the requested service or resource.

RADIUS consists of two components, *RADIUS client* and *RADIUS server*, as shown in Figure 11-2. The RADIUS server receives an AAA request from the RADIUS client, which can either be an NAS at the ISP site, a local server, or a firewall protecting the network. The RADIUS server, upon receiving the request, validates the request only if it stores the relevant information. If the requested information is stored on the central database or another RADIUS or TACACS server, the request is forwarded to the device that stores the required information.

Figure 11-3 depicts the flow of traffic in RADIUS-based implementations.

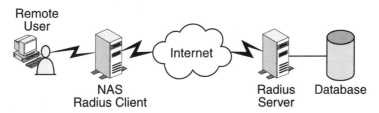

FIGURE 11-2 *The two components of RADIUS.*

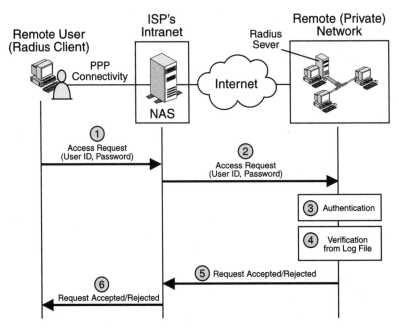

FIGURE 11-3 *RADIUS traffic flow.*

 NOTE

Refer to RFC 2058, 2138, and 2865 for detailed information on RADIUS. You
can find RFC 2058 at http://www.ietf.org/rfc/rfc2058.txt, RFC 2138 at
http://www.ietf.org/rfc/rfc2138.txt, and RFC 2865 at http://www.ietf.org/rfc/rfc2865.txt.

Terminal Access Controller Access Control System (TACACS)

Developed by Cisco Systems, TACACS is very much similar to RADIUS. Like RADIUS, it
also has been accepted as an industry standard protocol specification.

TACACS functionality bears a strong resemblance to RADIUS. As shown in Figure 11-4,
when a remote client issues an authentication request to its nearest NAS, the request is forwarded to TACACS. TACACS then forwards the supplied user ID and password to the central database, which can be either a TACACS database or an external security database. Finally,
the information is retrieved and forwarded to TACACS, which in turn accepts or denies the
connection request on the basis of the information it received from the database.

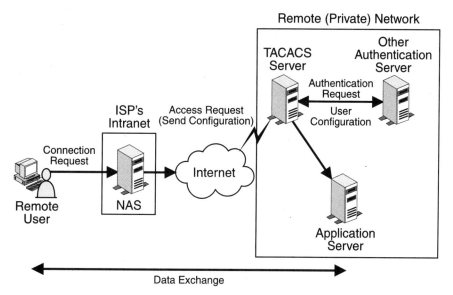

FIGURE 11-4 *TACACS-based remote authentication.*

Currently, there are two versions of TACACS on the market and both versions have been developed by Cisco. These are

◆ **XTACACS (eXtended TACACS).** This is an extension of TACACS, which supports advanced authentication features.

◆ **TACACS+.** This version of the original TACACS uses a dedicated access server in the form of TACACS+ server. This server provides independent authentication, authorization, and accounting services.

 NOTE

Despite the emergence of more enhanced versions, TACACS is still popular. Refer to RFC 1492 for detailed information on TACACS. You can find this RFC at www.armware.dk/RFC/rfc/rfc1492.html.

NASs play an important role in both RADIUS-based and TACACS-based remote authentications. As a RADIUS or TACACS client, NASs encrypt the information (User ID and password) supplied by the remote user before forwarding it to the authentication server at the host-network end. NASs are also capable of routing an authentication request to another authentication server if the target authentication server is unreachable.

On receiving an authentication request from a NAS, the authentication server validates the request and retrieves the user ID and password from the encrypted packet. When a NAS receives the authentication server's identification in the form of an authentication key or a digital signature and acknowledgement packet it notifies the remote user about the success of the login procedure. If the login request fails, the user is again notified of such by the NAS.

 NOTE

The acknowledgement packet that a NAS receives from the authentication server may also contain additional information, such as the protocol that the user will need to work with the destination network or the list of network resources and servers that the user is allowed to access.

Besides remote authentication, other security technologies can help strengthen the security of VPNs. These technologies include firewalls, NATs, SOCKS, SSL, and TLS.

Other VPN Security Strategies

Security technologies and strategies that are implemented to secure LANs and WANs can also be implemented with VPNs to enhance the security of data both during transactions and when it is stored within a network.

Firewalls

A *firewall* is an effective method of securing the data in a network from external threats. Firewalls not only prevent an unauthorized user from accessing your network or specific resources within it, but also act as an effective security blanket, preventing damage inflicted by external attacks from affecting the entire network.

A firewall is comprised of a router or a set of routers implemented at the periphery of a private network, where the network is connected to a public network, as shown in Figure 11-5. Because of their location in a network, every access request—authorized or unauthorized—

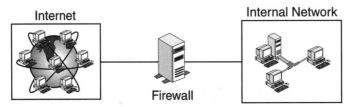

FIGURE 11-5 *A generic representation of a firewall.*

must pass through these security points. Depending on the security filters that you set or the security policies that you apply, firewalls allow or deny a request. As a result, hosts and other resources within the network are shielded from the "outside" world and malicious attacks.

Firewalls, generally, use Access Control Lists (ACLs) to filter incoming packets. These ACLs allow "harmless" traffic from authorized users to be forwarded to the nodes within the network, while blocking data packets from unknown and restricted resources from entering the network. Network administrators can set these ACLs to define precisely what IP traffic should be allowed within the network and what traffic to disallow from it.

Types of Firewalls

Conceptually, there are three types of firewalls that function at various layers of the OSI model. The three types of firewalls are

- Packet filter firewalls.
- Stateful packet inspection firewalls.
- Application proxy firewalls.

Packet filter firewalls use the source, destination, and port addresses carried by the packets to permit or deny their entry into the network they guard. However, packet filter firewalls completely ignore the data content of the packet. As a result, they are fast and independent of all applications. They are also considerably inexpensive when compared to other firewalls. But, because they scan a packet on the basis of the IP addresses and port numbers, they are the least secure category of firewalls. For example, a hacker can fake the source IP address of a trusted user and gain entry into the network.

 NOTE

A router might belong to the category of packet filter firewalls because routers base their decisions to allow or disallow a packet on IP addresses and ports carried within the packet.

In addition to source and destination IP addresses, *stateful packet inspection firewalls* use elaborate conditions to decide whether a packet should be allowed within the network. They also use dynamic state tables to track the state of connections that they have allowed.

Stateful packet inspection firewalls are highly intelligent firewalls that can match an incoming packet with the original request that was sent from a node within the network. Therefore, if a hacker sends a packet (or packets) as a response to a non-existent request from within the network, the packet is stopped from entering the network. This strategy further reduces the security risk to the network. However, stateful packet inspection firewalls are expensive and lack the capability to initiate a user-authentication procedure on their own.

Unlike the previous two types of firewalls, *application proxy firewalls* are mostly software-based, but some solutions are also available as a combination of hardware and software. They use the application proxy software to scan the packets. If a packet is from a restricted Web site, is not from an authorized and trusted source, or contains "unsafe" content, the packet is barred.

The functionality of application proxy firewalls is a little different from the other two types of firewalls. Application proxy firewalls protect the resources within the network by mimicking the specified internal node. As a result, the internal resources of the network they protect are never compromised by the external users. In addition, they can also provide user authentication service. Because of these reasons, Application proxy firewalls are considered to be the best of the three types of firewalls. However, they are also the slowest of the three and are protocol-specific. Another disadvantage associated with these firewalls is that they are the most expensive to implement. In addition, the applications that the application proxy firewalls deal with must be aware of the proxy server.

Firewalls in a VPN Scenario

You can implement a firewall with a VPN solution in the following two ways:

◆ Firewall behind the VPN server
◆ VPN server behind the firewall

If you implement the *firewall behind the VPN server* security strategy, the VPN server should be connected directly to the public network and the firewall must be located between the VPN server and the private intranet (or network), as shown in Figure 11-6. In this case, the firewall must be configured to allow only the VPN traffic received from or directed to the VPN server. To achieve this, you'll need to configure packet filtering on the firewall.

In the scenario depicted in Figure 11-6, when the VPN server receives incoming packets, it decrypts these tunneled packets and forwards them to the firewall. The firewall then scans the

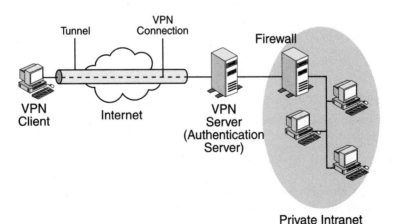

FIGURE 11-6 *The "firewall behind the VPN server" approach.*

data according to the packet filters that have been configured and, if the data is not "harmful," forwards it to the internal destination node. In the case of outgoing packets (assuming that the VPN client is behind the firewall, inside the network) the firewalls do not need to scan the packets because the VPN server is configured to receive data only from authenticated VPN clients. Consequently, you can also implement access control effectively by restricting users from accessing mission-critical network resources. An added benefit of the "firewall behind the VPN sever" approach is that you can prevent the sharing of intranet resources with non-VPN users as all the traffic must go through the VPN server, which doesn't accept requests from non-VPN clients.

The *VPN server behind the firewall* strategy is the most commonly implemented approach in VPN scenarios. In this approach, the firewall is directly connected to the public network while the VPN server is located between the firewall and the private network, as shown in Figure 11-7.

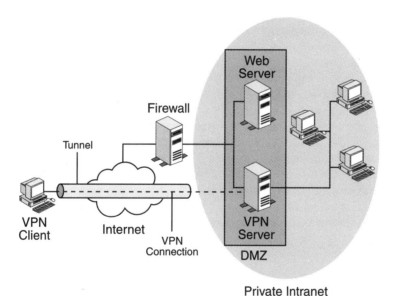

FIGURE 11-7 *The "VPN server behind the firewall" approach.*

Figure 11-7 also shows that the VPN server is a part of the DeMilitarized Zone (DMZ). As you might recall, the DMZ is the zone or segment of a protected network that is accessible to external users. Generally, bastion hosts, such as Web servers and FTP servers belong to this zone. This is an additional measure of network security that allows external users to access certain specified network resources while effectively shielding other resources.

In the "VPN server behind the firewall" approach, input as well as output filters must be configured on the firewall. Unlike the previous approach, these firewalls need to deal with tunneled packets. Therefore, they can only filter traffic on the basis of the plaintext header of the tunneled data packets. In this approach, however, the VPN server is well protected.

Firewalls, regardless of which of the three types you want to implement, are considerably expensive because they all require you to invest money. However, Network Address Translation (NAT) offers you a less expensive method of securing your network resources.

Network Address Translation (NAT)

Historically, NAT was developed by Cisco Systems as a short-term solution to the problem of ever-dwindling IP addresses. However, NAT has emerged as an effective strategy to keep external users and hackers from penetrating the network. Another benefit associated with NAT is that NAT allows networks using private IP addresses to communicate with the outside world across a public network.

 NOTE

In order to communicate across public networks, especially the Internet, a unique IP address is required. However, the number of hosts (or computers) connected to the Internet is extremely large—several hundred million by the latest estimate. On the other hand, per the current IP addressing scheme, IPv4, the pool of IP addresses holds an exhaustible number of possibilities. To make the situation worse, the available number of IP addresses within this pool is fast approaching its limit due to the exponential growth of the Internet in the past few years. A new IP addressing scheme has already been worked out, which is known as IPv6. However, the implementation of IPv6 and the complete transformation of the existing addressing scheme to the newer scheme will take time because IPv6 requires certain modifications to the TCP/IP infrastructure. Required in this prevailing scenario is a measure that will allow prudent use of the available IP addresses and allow organizations that use private IP addressing schemes to connect to the Internet and communicate with the rest of the world without the need to invest heavily in the purchase of unique IP address from InterNIC.

NAT, as depicted in Figure 11-8, is a peripheral mechanism like firewalls. It is implemented at the exit point of an intranet (or a private network) and acts as an agent between the intranet and the outside world by representing the entire network with a globally unique IP address. When an internal user needs to connect to an external entity it forwards the connection request to the NAT device, which is typically a router. This NAT device masks the original (private) address used by the internal node, assigns a globally unique IP address from its pool of IP addresses, and then forwards the packet with the new IP address to the external host. A similar procedure is applied to incoming requests (that might have more than one global IP addresses). As a result, external and non-trusted entities never know the real IP address of the internal nodes shielded by the NAT device.

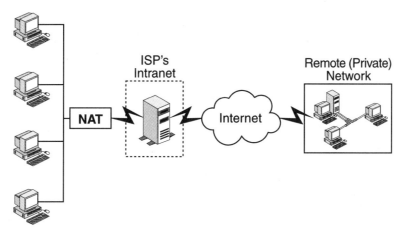

FIGURE 11-8 *The generic implementation of the NAT mechanism.*

Types of NATs

NAT-based solutions can be implemented in two ways.

◆ Static NATs
◆ Dynamic NATs

In the *Static NAT* approach, an unregistered IP address is always mapped to a fixed IP address. This concept is depicted in Figure 11-9. Static NATs are generally used when an external entity accesses an internal network resource.

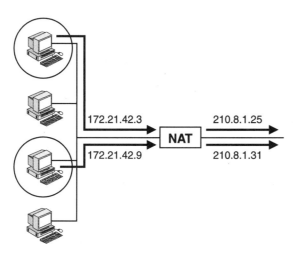

FIGURE 11-9 *Static NAT technology.*

Dynamic NATs on the other hand, map an unregistered IP address to the first-available IP address in the pool of globally unique IP addresses. This mechanism is depicted in Figure 11-10. Dynamic NATs are generally used when an internal host accesses an external entity.

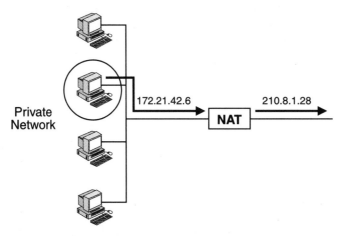

FIGURE 11-10 *Dynamic NAT technology.*

Dynamic NATs are of the following two types:

◆ **Overloaded dynamic NATs.** Per this scheme, you can map multiple unregistered IP addresses to a single registered IP address on different ports. Figure 11-11 illustrates an Overloaded dynamic NAT.

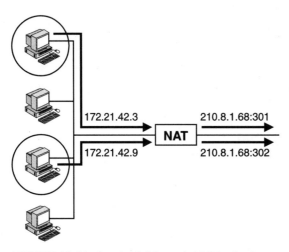

FIGURE 11-11 *Overloaded dynamic NAT technology.*

◆ **Overlapped dynamic NATs.** According to this two-way communication NAT scheme, a globally unique IP address is mapped to the outgoing request that uses an unregistered IP address. When the external entity responds to the request, the NAT device must translate the registered IP address back to the original unregistered IP address. Figure 11-12 shows the Overlapped dynamic NAT scheme.

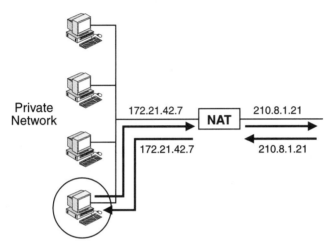

FIGURE 11-12 *Overlapped dynamic NAT technology.*

NATs in a VPN Scenario

For the successful implementation of NATs with VPNs, the NAT must be capable of mapping multiple data streams to and from a single IP address. NAT should also be transparent to the end user. However, NAT works differently with the main VPN protocols PPTP, L2TP, and IPSec because NAT not only swaps IP source and destination addresses, but might also swap TCP source and destination ports, change the IP and TCP header checksums, change the TCP sequence and acknowledgment numbers, and change IP addresses contained in the original data. This is why NAT might be suitable with VPNs based on one protocol, but might not work as seamlessly with the VPNs based on another.

For the success of NAT technology, the Layer 3 (IP) addresses must be changed. This explains why NATs work seamlessly with PPTP-based VPNs as PPTP neither encapsulates nor encrypts the IP datagrams. As a result, NATs can operate freely with PPTP-tunneled packets.

Choosing NAT as an additional security mechanism will bode well if your VPN is based on PPTP. However, you might face problems or the breakdown of the entire tunneling system if your VPN uses L2TP or L2TP over IPSec. Unlike PPTP, L2TP and IPSec encapsulate and/or encrypt the Layer 3 IP address of a packet with another Layer 3 network address. As a result, the UDP port number is encrypted and its value is protected with a cryptographic Frame

Check Sequence (FCS). This makes L2TP or L2TP over IPSec traffic non-translatable by NATs because NAT wouldn't be able to work on the packet after the packet goes through the IPSec or L2TP VPN tunneling process. Therefore, the packet would have the same network address. Moreover, in the case of end-to-end IPSec authentication, a packet whose address is changed will always fail the integrity check provided by the AH. Consequently, NATs can break an L2TP-based tunnel or a L2TP over IPSec-based tunnel as the VPN server will always drop the packets.

If you are planning to implement NAT, you will have to carefully designate which traffic should be allowed through the NAT device; if the traffic is to be tunneled over IPSec it should not pass through the NAT.

NOTE

Refer to Chapter 5, "Tunneling Protocols at Layer 2," to learn more about PPTP, IPSec, and L2TP. You might also refer to RFC 1631 for detailed information on NATs, which is available at http://www.armware.dk/RFC/rfc/rfc1631.html.

NAT allows nodes within a network to connect to the Internet and other public networks without having to expose their real IP addresses. This objective can also be achieved with the help of SOCKS, which is an acronym for SOCKet Server.

SOCKet Server (SOCKS)

Developed by Permeo Technologies, Inc. (a subsidiary of NEC USA, Inc.) and approved by IETF, *SOCKS* is a generic networking proxy protocol that enables hosts on one side of a SOCKS server to access hosts on the other side of the SOCKS server without having to expose their real IP addresses. In addition, the SOCKS server is responsible for authenticating and authorizing requests, establishing a proxy connection, and transmitting data between the two ends. Consequently, SOCKS is often used as a primitive network firewall that redirects connection requests from hosts on opposite sides of a SOCKS server.

SOCKS-based implementations use two components. These are the SOCKS server and the SOCKS client. When a SOCKS client needs to connect to an external entity, it forwards the connection request to the SOCKS server. The SOCKS server then connects to the destination node. After a connection is set up between the SOCKS server and the destination node, the SOCKS client forwards the data to the SOCKS server, which then forwards the data to the destination device. Similarly, the destination device cannot directly connect to the SOCKS client. It forwards the data or request to the SOCKS server, which forwards it to the SOCKS client. Figure 11-13 depicts the SOCKS implementation.

Remote (Private) Network

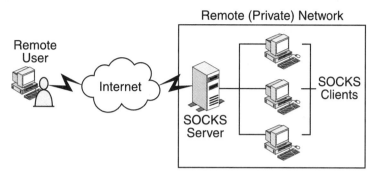

FIGURE 11-13 *An implementation of SOCKS.*

 NOTE

The SOCKS server is implemented at the Application layer of the OSI model. The SOCKS client, though, is implemented between the Application and Transport layers.

SOCKS is available in two versions, SOCKSv4 and SOCKSv5. SOCKSv5 is the latest and most commonly implemented version. However, SOCKSv5 does not support backward compatibility with SOCKSv4. SOCKSv4-based implementations can make connection requests, set up proxy circuits, and transmit data between the destination node and the SOCKS server. SOCKSv5, on the other hand, offers authentication capability in addition to those capabilities supported by version 4.

SOCKS in a VPN Scenario

Present-day VPNs implement SOCKSv5. VPNs built using SOCKS v5 protect internal computers by acting as an agent between the source and destination nodes. SOCKS can also be implemented with firewalls. In this case, the firewall receives the data packets and passes them through port 1080 to the SOCKS server. On receiving data packets from the firewall, the SOCKS server filters them to the destination node. This prevents administrators from opening multiple ports in their firewall for various applications. The VPN SOCKS server also hides the internal setup and the address structure of the network. This makes it more difficult for hackers and unauthorized users to access confidential data.

Due to the fact that SOCKSv5 functions at the fifth layer of the OSI model, the Session layer, it is an excellent complementary security technology that can operate seamlessly with other VPN protocols, such as PPTP, L2TP, and IPSec, which operate on Layers 2 and 3 of the OSI model. In addition, as an upper-layer protocol SOCKSv5 has better control of applications that run on the Application layer. For the same reason, SOCKSv5 works seamlessly with other security technologies and platforms and is especially useful in heterogeneous computing environments. SOCKS also supports authentication, encryption, and key-management methods commonly used in VPNs, further enhancing security in the VPN environment.

 NOTE

Refer to RFC 1928 for detailed information on SOCKS. This RFC is available at http://www.armware.dk/RFC/rfc/rfc1928.html.

In addition to SOCKS, Secure Socket Layer (SSL) and Transport Layer Security (TLS) help secure transactions across VPN tunnels.

Secure Socket Layer (SSL) and Transport Layer Security (TLS)

Developed by Netscape Communications Corporation and RSA Data Security Inc, *SSL* is another de facto security standard for securing transactions across public networks. *SSL* provides a private channel between communicating applications, thus ensuring data privacy and integrity during a transaction. In addition, SSL also provides authentication of the communicating ends. SSL has gained great popularity over the last few years and has been adopted by major Web browsers and Web servers.

The SSL protocol runs over TCP/IP, which can support any TCP/IP-based application without the need of major changes. However, SSL is widely implemented with HyperText Transfer Protocol (HTTP). This is why it has been implemented with most Web servers and browsers. SSL is progressively being implemented with Telnet and Network News Transfer Protocol (NNTP). In addition, SSL is also used for securing access to firewalls.

As shown in Figure 11-14, SSL is composed of two layers, the *upper layer* and the *lower layer*. The protocol that functions at the upper layer is SSL Handshake Protocol and is used for initial authentication. This protocol also plays a key role in the exchange of cryptographic keys between the two ends. The protocol that functions at the lower layer is SSL Record Protocol and it is responsible for data transfer between the two ends. SSL lower layer uses a variety of authentication mechanisms and algorithms to ensure the safety of the data being transacted.

When a client sends a request to the Web server in an SSL-protected transaction, this request must be prefixed with http:. The SSL client (the browser in this case) then initiates a connection through TCP port 443 with the SSL server at the Web server end. If the SSL server accepts the connection request, the client initiates the SSL handshake phase. In this phase, the SSL server is authenticated and the encryption keys are negotiated and established.

TLS was developed using SSL as its base and is considered the successor to SSL. Like SSL, TLS allows the client and the server ends to communicate safely across unsafe public networks.

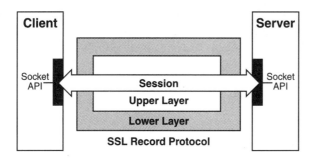

Upper Layer: SSL Handshake Protocol
Lower Layer: SSL Record Protocol

FIGURE 11-14 *The two layers of SSL.*

In addition to the security capabilities provided by SSL, TLS also prevents eavesdropping, sniffing, and spoofing.

TLS is also composed of two layers: the TLS Record Protocol and the TLS Handshake Protocol. The TLS Record Protocol offers connection security by employing encryption mechanisms, such as DES. The TLS Handshake Protocol, on the other hand, provides two-way authentication by allowing the TLS server and the client to authenticate each other. In addition, the two ends can negotiate encryption algorithms and keys that will later secure the data being exchanged between the two ends.

In the VPN scenario, SSL and TLS can be implemented at the VPN server as well as at the client-end, which helps advance the security objective by adding another layer of security.

Summary

In this chapter, you learned about the additional security measures that help you strengthen data transmissions based on VPN technology. You learned about additional remote authentication techniques, such as Authentication Authorization Accounting (AAA), Remote Access Dial-In User Service (RADIUS), and Terminal Access Controller Access Control System (TACACS). AAA allows network administrators to keep tabs on the users who are accessing network resources, control their access by allowing or restricting access to specified devices and services, and log the user activities by recording the day, time, and duration of each activity. RADIUS and TACACS are remote access servers that authenticate remote connection requests. These servers can either authenticate the remote users by themselves or can forward the user information for validation from the central database.

You also explored security technologies such as firewalls, NAT, SOCKS, SSL, and TLS, which when used with VPNs can help you achieve safer environments for data transactions across the Internet and public networks. You learned that firewalls are an effective method of securing network resources as they act as the "security blanket" for the internal network resources. NATs, on the other hand, allow users using unregistered IP addresses and private networks to securely connect to the Internet. However, they support PPTP-based VPNs better than L2TP- or IPSec-based VPNs. You also learned about Socket Servers (SOCKS) that shield internal resources of a network by acting as the "go-between" between the destination node and the internal host. Secure Socket Layer (SSL) and Transport Layer Security (TLS) are used to secure HTTP-based transactions over the Internet. These security mechanisms are basically supported by Web servers and browsers.

Check Your Understanding

Multiple Choice Questions

1. RADIUS stands for _____.
   a. Remote Account Dial-In User Service
   b. Remote Access Dial-In User System
   c. Remote Access Dial-In User Service
   d. Remote Account Dial-In User System

2. TACACS is a proprietary protocol by _____.
   a. Cisco Systems
   b. Netscape Communications Corporation
   c. Microsoft Corporation
   d. InterNIC

3. Keeping a tab on the duration of user activities is a part of _____.
   a. Authentication
   b. Authorization
   c. Accounting
   d. Authentication and Accounting

4. Which of the following security solutions helps preserve IP addresses?
   a. SOCKS
   b. SSL
   c. TLS
   d. NAT

5. Which of the following firewalls keep an account of connection status in addition to checking the IP addresses carried by the datagram?

   a. Application proxy firewalls

   b. Static stateful firewalls

   c. Packet filter firewalls

   d. Stateful packet inspection firewalls

6. What is the difference between a firewall and a SOCKSv4 server?

   a. A firewall masks internal nodes from the outside world; SOCKS do not.

   b. SOCKS authenticates remote users; firewalls do not.

   c. Firewalls authenticate remote users; SOCKS do not.

   d. There is no difference between the two.

7. Which of the following requires compulsory two-way authentication for an HTTP-based transaction?

   a. SSL

   b. SOCKS

   c. TLS

   d. NAT

Short Questions

1. ABLC, Inc. is expanding rapidly. So is their intranet. They use VPNs to exchange data between their various remote offices and the corporate head office. In order to escape the heavy investment required to buy unique IP addresses, Mark, their network administrator implemented NATs. Suddenly, even the connection with remote branch offices is not possible. What might be the reason?

Answers

Multiple Choice Answers

1. **c**. RADIUS stands for Remote Access Dial-In User Service. RADIUS is a remote access server that authenticates remote connection requests. RADIUS servers can either authenticate the remote users themselves or can forward the user information for validation from the central database.

2. **a**. TACACS is a proprietary Cisco protocol and remote authentication solution. It works along the same lines as RADIUS and is available as XTACACS and TACACS+.

3. **c**. Keeping a tab on the duration of user activities is a part of Accounting. Authentication serves to validate the end user, while Authorization determines which services and activities are allowed to a user.

4. **d**. Network Address Translation (NAT) technology helps preserve fast-dwindling IP addresses by intelligently mapping unregistered (and therefore illegal) IP addresses to a small number of globally unique IP addresses.

5. **d**. Stateful packet inspection firewalls are highly intelligent firewalls that use elaborate conditions to decide whether a packet should be allowed within the network. They use dynamic state tables to track the state of connections that have been allowed by them.

6. **c**. Firewalls are capable of remote user authentication. SOCKSv4 does not provide authentication capability.

7. **c**. TLS requires that the server and the client both be authenticated before a data transaction can begin. SSL, on the other hand, requires authentication of the server; authentication of the client end is optional.

Short Answers

1. Assuming that Mark is using an IPSec-based VPN client (not PPTP), the transactions will be carried out in transport mode. The reasoning behind this assumption is that the connection extends from the client to the server, which implies that the administrator is using IPSec in transport mode. You might recall from Chapter 6, "An Introduction to IPSec," that in IPSec transport mode the IP header is not encrypted. In addition, authentication data is calculated based on the values in the IP header (among other things). When the packets arrive at the NAT router, the IP headers are modified by the NAT. Because of this, upon arriving at the VPN server the authentication data in the packet is deemed invalid. So, the VPN server drops the packet and the VPN client never gets connected.

PART V

Managing VPNs

Chapter 12

Managing and Troubleshooting VPNs

As you learned in the earlier chapters, implementing a VPN for an organization is a win-win situation because a secure connectivity solution can be implemented while reducing the cost of WAN connectivity. In addition, you are also familiar with the cost-effectiveness of a VPN-based solution. For example, the cost of VPNs has been calculated to be 80 percent cheaper than a typical leased line connection normally used to secure transactions. So, everybody is happy—your management as well as your end-user.

Implementing a VPN is not enough. Besides the biggest problem of VPN-based connectivity simply not working, there are a few other problems that you might face. What if an employee, who is mostly on the move, needs urgent data from your intranet and cannot connect to it? What if the employee can connect but cannot access data? All activities might come to a grinding halt. No one can afford to be in such a situation given the level of competition in which we operate.

In this world of instant connectivity, it becomes imperative for organizations (and you as the administrator or IS manager) to effectively and efficiently manage and troubleshoot their VPNs. In this chapter, you'll learn about the basics of management of your virtual private network solution and how to troubleshoot any problems that might arise.

Managing VPNs

At this time, the power of VPNs has really revolutionized the remote connectivity world. The deployment of VPNs has now become an integral part of an organization's security policy. However, one area of VPN implementation that seems to have been overlooked is VPN management.

Although organizations might deploy VPNs with enthusiasm, they seldom seem to have the support or management capabilities to sustain their VPN solution for very long. The need for management of your VPN setup can be understood better from the following example.

Suppose, after much planning, research, and development you finally prepare a recommendation report (including costs) that advocates a particular VPN solution for your company. However, due to changes in the technological and operating environments within the organization, you find that within a year of deploying the solution, the cost of the solution you have advocated has sky-rocketed. Not only has there been a miscalculation on the financial front, but due to an increase in the number of users you find that your database is insufficient to accommodate the growing number of users. To aggravate matters further, you find that the new authentication server that you have implemented to accommodate more users does not support a comprehensive authentication mechanism.

Although this is a hypothetical situation, you might find yourself in a similar position if your VPN management is lacking.

Some other questions you might face while planning follow:

◆ Will your VPN solution support changes in tunneling protocols and encryption algorithms in addition to supporting software upgrades?

◆ Do you have enough financial support for hardware upgrades, which are more expensive, relatively speaking, than software upgrades?

◆ Do you have the necessary infrastructure and resources to support such expensive upgrades?

◆ How will you upgrade your bandwidth if there is a decline in the performance of your network due to an increase in the number of VPN sessions? More importantly, who will provide funds to support such an upgrade?

◆ What client software are you using? Is it a freeware? If yes, then will it continue to remain so? What if the vendor decides to license the same? Do you have the required finances to purchase those licenses?

As can be seen from the preceding points, managing VPNs is not restricted to just deciding on someone to be responsible for looking after the operation of the VPN hardware and software. In fact, VPN management includes many responsibilities, such as managing users, databases, tunnels, keys, and also providing support.

The following sections discuss in detail common issues related to VPN management.

Managing Users and Databases

Having separate user accounts for a single user on separate servers is not adequate in terms of keeping the records updated on every server, synchronizing those records, and managing duplications, if any. To overcome these problems most administrators prefer to have a master account database at the Primary Domain Controller (PDC) in Windows. In non-Windows environments, RADIUS servers, TACACS servers, Lightweight Directory Access Protocol (LDAP), and other directory services, such as Novell Directory Service (NDS), are also used widely.

By following the practice of maintaining a separate master database, a central device is available that can be used as a centralized user database. This user database is comprised of the detailed records of all the users that need to be authenticated while accessing your intranet using the VPN. Therefore, most of these centralized devices also provide user authentication capabilities. When the user database is stored on a RADIUS or TACACS server, the user accounts can also be used for both VPN-based and dial-in remote access.

Although having a centralized user database does solve some management issues, it does not provide adequate support to an increase in the number of database users. To handle this, you need to have a scalable user database and you need to have a clear idea about the estimated growth of the number of VPN users. One good way to do this is to contact your organization's recruitment team for an estimate of the number of users they are authorized to hire. With this as a starting point, you can then plan the year-by-year growth in the number of users.

A change in the number of VPN users can also come with a merger or acquisition. In a case like this, the need for scalability is all the more necessary because you may not be able to predict the number of uses to be added. As a result, you need to be prepared to as much as double the size of your existing user database. Of course, you also need to ensure that such an increase does not in any way degrade the overall performance of your VPN or your intranet.

Managing Tunnels

As you already know, at the core of VPNs is the process of tunneling. As discussed in Chapter 4, "Basics of Tunneling Technology," the safety, cost effectiveness, and security that VPNs offer during a transmission are the direct result of tunneling. Because of this, tunnel management is one of the main VPN management issues. However, despite such gravity, tunnel management continues to be ignored by many IS managers or administrators.

Tunnel management involves the following:

◆ Choosing a tunneling protocol

◆ Managing bandwidth usage

Choosing a Tunneling Protocol

As discussed in Chapter 4, "Basics of Tunneling Technology," tunneling technology makes use of three types of protocols, namely:

◆ Carrier protocols

◆ Encapsulating protocols

◆ Passenger protocols

When implementing a VPN, you need to ensure that you are using the right protocol. To do this, you'll need to conduct extensive research to understand the requirements of the organization as well as the end-user, who will actually use the technology.

Analyses and opinions of most VPN administrators demonstrate that today, the most preferred protocol in a VPN deployment is IPSec. As discussed in Chapter 6, "An Introduction to IPSec," IPSec offers a VPN confidentiality, authenticity, integrity, and anti-replay functionality.

 NOTE

Refer to Chapter 4, "Basics of Tunneling Technology," for detailed information on tunneling. Refer to Chapter 6, "An Introduction to IPSec" for detailed information on the features and advantages offered by IPSec.

Managing the Usage of Bandwidth

As the number of VPN users increase, the amount of available bandwidth decreases proportionally. Therefore, it is very important that when you are planning to increase the number of users, you keep in mind the effect this increase will have on available bandwidth. You also need to study the effect of tunnels on the bandwidth available for your network.

Even if you've passed the VPN implementation stage you might later face the inevitable bandwidth pinch (or the increased demand for bandwidth), in which case, you'll need to increase your bandwidth. Despite the additional work required to implement them, you can upgrade the existing cables with cables that support a higher capacity and better transfer rates. In this situation, you might also need to upgrade the termination devices. As a part of this process, you'll need to answer a few questions. These questions include:

◆ Do you have adequate finances for supporting such an upgrade? You might need to implement additional hardware, such as routers or switches, to balance the load on existing equipments. As a result, your expenditure might increase further.

◆ Is there uneven distribution of bandwidth among various applications? There is no guarantee that when the user launches an application, the extra bandwidth will be available to him or her. Although an increase in the cable capacity might provide better bandwidth performance to applications such as the Internet, other critical applications, such as SAP, may still not get the bandwidth required. As a result, there is unequal distribution of the bandwidth.

To a large extent, bandwidth management in VPNs is taken care of by the QoS specification as defined in the SLA between your organization and the service provider. Therefore, as has been stressed earlier, you need to have a well-defined SLA.

It is a good management practice to constantly monitor and evaluate the performance, effectiveness, and integrity of the solution provided by the service provider. Doing so could prevent your end-users from experiencing unnecessary hassles as they feel the bandwidth pinch. However, this can only be achieved if you are vigilant.

 NOTE

As discussed, in Chapter 2, "VPN Requirements, Building Blocks, and Architectures," QoS is the ability of a network to respond to critical situations by assigning network and resources to mission critical and delay sensitive applications. QoS ensures that all business critical applications, such as financial transactions and order processing, are allocated sufficient bandwidth.

Managing Keys

Keys are an integral and very important part of your VPN solution. Management of keys involves generating, distributing, storing, securing, and backing up the keys. When managing keys, the most basic questions that you will need to answer are listed below:

◆ Who will be responsible for generating keys?

◆ Do you have the required expertise and employees for carrying out each of the functions of key management?

◆ What will be the mode of key distribution? Will that method provide security to the keys? What will be the cost incurred for distributing these keys?

◆ Who will be responsible for key backup?

◆ What will be the methods of key recovery in case of an accident or disgruntled employee?

◆ Is there another employee who can take over the responsibilities of any of the key management tasks in case an employee with any of these responsibilities leaves the organization?

NOTE

Refer to Chapter 3, "Security Components of a VPN," for detailed information about keys and key-based encryption techniques.

As mentioned earlier, the two most important issues related to key management are

- ◆ **Key generation and distribution.** Key generation and distribution are the most important tasks in key management. In the case of key generation, the user should generate the key pair. If the CA generates the key pair, it would also have the private key of the generated key pair. This private key would then have to be transferred to the user, which could lead to certain security threats. For example, if the private key is compromised during its transition, another user could use the key to carry out transactions without the knowledge of the original user. In such a situation, the original user would not have any knowledge of the transactions carried out and would subsequently deny being a part of the transaction in question. As a result, if the key pair is generated at the user-end, the private key doesn't need to be transferred because the owner generates the key; the owner cannot deny being a part of the transaction.

- ◆ **Key backup.** Another essential task of key management is key backup. Generally, a CA performs key backup to ensure that if a user loses his or her private key, the data that was encrypted using the corresponding public key can still be decrypted. A private key is usually backed up when the certificate is generated. In cases where the private key is used for signing documents, the CA need not back it up. Currently, there are no well-defined rules for backing up keys. These policies essentially depend upon the use of the keys.

TIP

If two key pairs are used, one for data encryption and the other for digitally signing documents, then the key that is used for the digital signature need not be backed up at all because, even if the key is lost, there would be no encrypted data that this key would need to be decrypt.

Managing VPN Hardware and Software

When managing your VPN you need to keep in mind both your hardware and software requirements. Managing your VPN software is not just restricted to simply upgrading your software. In fact, managing software takes into consideration many more issues, such as the ones that follow:

◆ How will the remote users receive all updates and upgrades?

◆ Who will be responsible for upgrading all the software, including the client, server, and VPN software?

◆ Who will be responsible for applying the patches?

◆ How will the servers be secured?

◆ In case the security of the server is breached, what will be the backup plan? Also in such a situation, what will be the costs involved with and the amount and value of the data compromised?

◆ How will the VPN be affected by a server security breach?

◆ Which security software will be used?

◆ What resources and expenditures will be required to apply patches and upgrades to the server on which the VPN software is installed?

◆ Is the software being used a freeware? What if a software license is introduced? Do you have the required finances to purchase the licenses?

Hardware-based VPNs are quickly gaining popularity over software-based VPNs. This paradigm shift is largely due to their edge on important issues relating to security and performance. Hardware management in a VPN can be divided into two categories: security and connectivity.

Security includes device authentication, authorization, and implementing the overall security policies. Connectivity includes configuration, device management, and provisioning. To guarantee both, you need to ensure that there exists no single point of failure (SPOF) in the solution that has been deployed.

Managing Support

Last but not least in the discussion of VPN management is providing and managing support to the implemented VPN solution. Managing support is not restricted to just seeking and providing technical support from the vendor. Trained personnel is an important aspect of supporting your VPN solution.

When managing support for VPNs you need to answer the following questions:

◆ Do you have enough Help Desk personnel to provide support?

◆ Can all the members of the Help Desk team handle any query? What about one entailing an error occurring in tunneling or its protocols?

◆ Do you have all the documents that can be referred to by the users?

◆ Is there any kind of training requirement for support personnel so that they can provide the necessary services and support? Also, do the users need to be trained about how to make the best use of available VPN infrastructure?

◆ Who will maintain and monitor the log files? How often will these log files be analyzed?

◆ Is the server backing up the log files secure?

Concluding the topic of VPN management is the golden rule of documentation. I highly recommended that you maintain detailed documentation for every problem that you face, big or small. This documentation will serve as a wonderful reference later, when you encounter a certain problem more than once. The second time a problem occurs, you won't have to waste time looking for the appropriate solution—you'll already have it.

Now that you have been sensitized to the management of VPNs and issues related to it, you can now consider how you'll go about troubleshooting problems when they arise.

Troubleshooting VPNs

When talking about troubleshooting VPNs, the focus is on IP connectivity, remote access and demand-dial connections, routing, and, of course, IPSec. In this section, you'll look at some common VPN problems in both Windows and Linux environments and their possible solutions.

Troubleshooting Windows-based VPNs

The most common VPN problems in Windows environment can be placed into the following broad categories:

◆ Client cannot establish a connection with the VPN server.

◆ Client cannot connect to hosts beyond the VPN server.

◆ Client cannot browse the LAN after logging on.

◆ Client is unable to connect to the Internet.

Client Cannot Establish a Connection with the VPN Server

If a client cannot establish a connection with the VPN server, the cause could be attributed to one of the following:

◆ A physical connectivity problem

◆ A protocol has been configured incorrectly

◆ An authentication error

To define the problem area and, subsequently solve the problem, you need to perform a standard set of checks to verify the connection and configuration parameters. The basic points you need to examine to troubleshoot such a problem include the following:

◆ Verify that the VPN server is reachable. To do this, you can ping the IP address of the server. If the ping is not successful, packet filtering might be the problem area.

NOTE

It's the public IP that needs to be pinged, not the private IP address. Also it should be tried from outside the network; otherwise might always succeed.

♦ Simple as it may sound, the next step should be to check that Routing and Remote Access is enabled on the VPN server.

♦ If the VPN server is a part of a Windows 2000 Active Directory domain, verify that the VPN server is a member of the RAS and IAS servers group and that the group type is set to security.

♦ If the host name is being used instead of the IP address, verify that the host name is resolved to the correct IP address.

♦ Verify that the PPTP and L2TP (if using IPSec) ports are configured for inbound remote access. If behind a firewall, PPTP ports need to be allowed access too.

♦ Check the authentication and encryption methods used on the server and on the client. The server and the client must use at least one common authentication and encryption method.

♦ Ensure that the VPN server supports the LAN protocols used by the client. These protocols should be enabled for remote access on the server.

♦ Make sure the VPN server supports the tunneling protocol used by the client.

♦ Make sure the remote access permission for the user account is set to Allow access.

♦ Ensure that the number of PPTP and L2TP ports is configured correctly for the number of concurrent connections you need. The default number of ports for PPTP and L2TP is five each. However, if you want a PPTP only server, set the number of L2TP ports to zero; if you want an L2TP server, set the number of PPTP ports to zero.

♦ Verify that the client is passing an authentic user name, password, and domain name to connect to the server.

♦ Ensure that the IP address assignment is correct. The client's IP address should be a part of the server's IP address pool. If the server is configured to use a static pool of IP addresses, ensure that there are enough addresses available.

♦ For connections over IPX, if the server is configured with a range of IPX network numbers, ensure that the numbers within the range are not used anywhere else in the IPX network.

♦ If the client is configured to request its own IPX node number, verify that the VPN server is configured to allow IPX clients to request their own IPX node numbers.

♦ If the VPN server uses RADIUS to provide authentication, ensure that the VPN server and the RADIUS server can communicate.

◆ If you are not using MS-CHAP v1, make sure that a user password does not exceed 14 characters. If a password does, you either need to use a different authentication protocol, such as MS-CHAP v2, or modify the password so that it doesn't exceed 14 characters.

Client Cannot Connect to Hosts Beyond the VPN Server

After the initial connectivity issues have been settled, VPN clients may still encounter problems remotely accessing the resources in the private network. The clients might be able to connect to the VPN server, but might not be able to access the resources that are part of the VPN server's internal network. Possible causes for and solutions to such problems follow.

◆ If the VPN server is configured to use a static address pool, the other resources on the network might not be configured to access the IP addresses in the static address range. Check that the IP addresses in this range are reachable by the hosts on the internal network. If not, you'll need to add the range of addresses to the routers in the network to enable communication. You can also enable the routing protocol for the network on the VPN server. If the routes to the remote access VPN client subnets are not configured, the VPN clients will not receive data from hosts on the internal network. Routes for the subnets are configured either by specifying static routing entries or by using a routing protocol, such as Open Shortest Path First (OSPF) or Routing Information Protocol (RIP).

◆ Check that the LAN protocols on the VPN server are configured to allow access to the entire network. Configure the VPN server to allow clients to access the entire network. You can also configure the VPN client to act as a router. Also ensure that IP forwarding and packet forwarding are enabled as well.

◆ Ensure that TCP/IP packet filters are not implemented. Packet filters might prevent flow of data over TCP/IP.

Client Cannot Browse the LAN after Logging On

You may encounter a situation in which clients are able to log on but are unable to browse the LAN. In such a situation, you must:

◆ Ensure that you have set the workgroup to the target domain in all the clients.

◆ Manually map or predefine the *Uniform Naming Convention* (UNC) connections to the required resources. However, before this you need establish the PPTP session. Predefining or manually mapping the UNC connections is useful when you have more than 20 visible nodes and your dial-up connection is slow.

◆ Understand the affect of the following four TCP/IP settings on your network:

◆ **WINS server.** Translates a NetBIOS name into a TCP/IP address. In a Windows NT environment, your clients cannot browse Network Neighborhood if a WINS server has not been assigned to them. However, they can access the print and file shares by manually specifying the UNC.

- ◆ **DNS server.** Resolves user-friendly names to IP addresses and vice versa. In the absence of the DNS server, you can connect to a computer only through its numeric IP address.

- ◆ **Default gateway.** Specifies the destination of the data when the destination is outside the local subnet.

- ◆ **DHCP server.** Assigns TCP/IP addresses to computers when they boot. In addition, it assigns TCP/IP addresses to RAS clients when they remotely connect to a network.

 NOTE

If your client is still not able to browse the Network Neighborhood after you have addressed the preceding issues, then you need to check the configuration of your VPN server.

Client is Unable to Connect to the Internet

This is a common problem when your client is running Windows 95. There are two possible reasons for this kind of a problem:

- ◆ **VPN server-defined gateway overwrites the ISP gateway.** In this situation, Windows 95 causes the VPN server-defined gateway to overwrite the ISP's gateway. As a result, when the client tries connecting to the Internet, the path to the Internet cannot be found. A possible solution to this problem is to manually add a static route to the ISP's default gateway. Note the metric for this static route as 2. As a result, the VPN gateway will be tried first and only after that will the ISP gateway will be tried. Another option would be to not check the Use default gateway or similar option in the Dial-Up Networking (DUN) dialog box. Then add the static route for your organization's gateway over the VPN.

- ◆ **VPN server denies remote clients to access the Internet.** This problem might occur if the default gateway of your network does not point to the gateway at the ISP end. In this situation, the VPN server will not allow the remote clients to access the Internet during a remote connection. A possible solution to this problem is to close the VPN connection before the user tries to access the Internet. As a result, the default gateway will point to the ISP's gateway and the remote clients can then access the Internet.

The few VPN troubleshooting utilities covered in the next section will ease the task of VPN management.

Troubleshooting Utilities

In this section, you'll look at some of the utilities that you can use to diagnose VPN-related problems.

Event Logging

In the Event Logging tab in the VPN server properties dialog box, you can select the Log the maximum amount of information option. This option allows you to view information regarding events that occur during the attempted connection. You can then use this log to identify problems.

Tracing

You can use tracing to record the function calls during an attempted connection. You should be experienced enough with routing and remote access to understand the traced information. You enable tracing by selecting Enable Point-to-Point Protocol (PPP) Logging from the Event Logging tab in the VPN server properties dialog box.

Network Monitor

You can use Network Monitor to capture and view the information exchanged during an attempted VPN connection. To understand the information captured by the Network Monitor, you need to be well versed with PPTP, PPP, and IPSec, among other remote connectivity mechanisms and protocols.

Troubleshooting Linux-based VPNs

In this section, you'll look at the common problems that you could face in Linux-based VPNs. You'll then look into possible solutions to these problems.

Common VPN Problems in Linux include the following:

- Client cannot establish a connection with the VPN server.
- Client is successfully authenticated but cannot establish a network connection with the server.
- Multiple PPTP clients cannot access the same server simultaneously.
- Intermediary firewall is creating problems.
- Problems occur when accessing Windows-based components and networks.
- IPSec session expires after some time.

Client Cannot Establish Connection with the VPN Server

The inability of the client to establish a connection with the VPN server is one of the most common problems in a VPN setup. The first and most basic step toward a solution is to ensure that the number used by the client to dial into the server is the IP address of the VPN server, or the IP address of the firewall if the server is "behind" the firewall. However, you might need to check the availability of the server or the firewall with the help of ping command first.

Another reason the client may not being able to connect to the server is that client cannot locate the server at all. In this case, you need to ensure that the VPN client points to the VPN router (behind which your VPN server is situated) by default. To do so, run the "route print" command and verify that it contains a 0.0.0.0 entry. A better option for this purpose would be to use the netstat -nr command because it is platform-independent.

Client is Authenticated Successfully but Cannot Establish Network Connection with the Server

This problem commonly occurs with IPSec-based VPN clients because of the intermediary firewall's inability to filter the ESP traffic properly. Check the log entries in the /var/log/messages directory to ensure that the VPN traffic is being logged and then enable VPN debugging to determine if the patch is at fault.

Multiple PPTP Clients Cannot Access the Same VPN Server Simultaneously

This problem with simultaneous access usually occurs in the case of a patch running older version of PPTP. In this case, consider setting up a separate router for your PPTP clients. If you are using Call-ID masquerading and you are masquerading a PPTP server, do not enable PPTP Call-ID masquerade because the server's outbound traffic will be rejected by the firewall.

Intermediary Firewall is Creating Problems

The following are problems that may be caused by intermediary firewalls:

◆ **The client is able to dial the ISP but cannot reach the VPN server.** In this case, the firewall located at the server-end must be configured to allow the IP address allocated dynamically by the ISP.

◆ **The IPSec client is able to dial the ISP but cannot reach the VPN server.** In this case, the firewall located at the server-end is not configured to send and receive IPSec data.

◆ **The PPTP client is able to dial the ISP but cannot reach VPN server.** In this case, the firewall located at the server-end is not configured to send and receive GRE packets.

◆ **An intermediary router is blocking the VPN traffic.** In this case, all the routers between the firewall and the VPN client are not configured to allow IPSec packets through port 50 or PPTP packets through port 47.

◆ **Not all protocol traffic can be routed across the firewall.** In this case, the firewall is configured to allow only a few services and the "All protocol" option has not been checked.

◆ **VPN masquerading doesn't work after the system is rebooted.** In this case, the `modprobe ip_masq_pptp.o` or `modprobe ip_masq_ipsec.o` commands are missing from your `/etc/rc.d/rc.local` startup script.

Problems Occur When Accessing Windows-based Components and Networks

Windows-based clients might generate the following problems for your Linux-based VPN:

◆ **The client and server cannot establish a secure session.** If this happens, you might not receive a specific error messages, but the client will keep trying to establish the connection in vain. This problem generally occurs if the client is Windows-based and either the client or the server lacks the 128-bit `NDISWAN.SYS` or Windows 95/Windows 98 PPTP software.

◆ **The client can access the VPN server but cannot access other resources located within this network.** If this is the case, you need to remember that you require two separate passwords—the VPN password and the network password—while working with Windows-based networks. While the VPN password allows you to access the VPN server located in the remote Windows-based network, only the Network password allows you to access the resources located in this network.

TIP

An easy method of eliminating the hassle of working with two sets of usernames and passwords is to use the same password for both your network password and your VPN password.

IPSec Session Expires After Some Time

When the ISAKMP packets being received contain "zero cookie" values, the IPSec session may expire. This phenomenon generally occurs with earlier versions of the IPSec Masq patch, which causes the remote IPSec host to assume a link failure between the two communicating ends. As a result, the connection between the ends is terminated abruptly.

If you are using version 2.0.x, there is a patch available to help you overcome this problem. You can download this patch from the Internet, run it on your machine, and reconfigure the kernel per the instructions provided with the patch.

Troubleshooting Utilities

You can use the following utilities to troubleshoot problems in Linux-based VPNs:

◆ VPN debugging
◆ Packet sniffers

VPN Debugging

You can run the VPN Debugging utility by adding the following statements to the /etc/sys-
log.conf file:

```
# debugging
*.=debug /var/log/debug
```

You'll then need to recompile the kernel, after which all the VPN-related activity will be logged
in the /var/log/messages and /var/log/debug files.

 NOTE

Logging is a disk-intensive activity. Therefore, it is recommended that it be enabled
only when it's required.

Packet Sniffers

As you learned in the previous section, "Troubleshooting Linux-based VPNs," a large number
of problems occur at the firewalls implemented as part of the VPN setup.

You can run a packet sniffer by executing one of the many sniffer commands, such as tcpdump
-v, on the VPN firewall. When implemented successfully, a packet sniffer will allow you to
monitor IPSec and PPTP traffic from the client end, UDP, ESP/TCP, and GRE traffic from
the firewall and ISP end, and traffic at the server end.

Summary

Just implementing a VPN solution is not the answer to all your remote connectivity problems.
After you have successfully implemented a VPN, you need to effectively and efficiently manage it. Managing a VPN includes managing users, databases, tunnels, keys, and also providing
support after a VPN solution has been deployed. In this chapter, you learned about all of these
aspects of VPN management.

You also learned about some common VPN problems that might occur in Windows-based
and Linux-based VPNs and how to troubleshoot them. And, you learned about the utilities
that you can use to troubleshoot these problems.

With the fast-changing pace of any technology, especially network technology, you (and your organization) need to view VPNs as a very dynamic medium. Tunneling technology and encryption algorithms, which lie at the base of VPNs, have changed dramatically in last three to four years and there is no guarantee that the evolution of VPNs is over.

Though you can't predict the future, you can monitor trends and act upon them in such a manner that you can support the current needs of your organization now and prepare for the future. Well-grounded research and analysis will stand you in a good stead. And don't forget to learn from your mistakes. These are the keys to the longevity of your VPN solution.

Check Your Understanding

Multiple Choice Questions

1. While attempting to connect to a VPN server, you notice that you cannot ping the server IP address from the client. What could be the possible problem?

    a. The client IP address is not a part of the static IP address pool assigned by the server.

    b. The server does not support TCP/IP.

    c. TCP/IP packet filtering is implemented on the server.

    d. The server is not configured as a router.

2. A VPN client is configured to request its own IPX node number. What settings should you configure on the VPN server?

    a. Do not allow IPX clients to request their own IPX node number.

    b. Allow IPX clients to request their own IPX node number.

    c. Specify a fixed range of IPX network numbers to be used.

    d. Disable IPX routing on the server.

3. You have a VPN server configured as a PPTP only server. How many L2TP ports can you configure on this server?

    a. 16,384

    b. 5

    c. 0

    d. As many concurrent connections as you need.

4. You notice that a VPN client can connect to the VPN server, but cannot access resources on the server's internal network. What could be the problem? (Select all that apply.)

    a. The static IP addresses configured on the server are not routed on the internal network.

    b. The LAN protocols on the VPN server are configured to access only the server computer.

    c. TCP/IP packet filtering is implemented on the server.

    d. Enough IP addresses are not configured in the VPN server's static IP address pool.

Answers

Multiple Choice Answers

1. **c.** If you cannot ping a VPN server, it implies that TCP/IP packet filtering is implemented, preventing data flow.

2. **b.** If the client is configured to request its own IPX node number, the VPN server should be configured to allow IPX clients to request for their own IPX node numbers.

3. **c.** If you want a PPTP only server, set the number of L2TP ports to zero.

4. **a, b, c.** All three are possible causes that prevent a client from accessing hosts beyond the VPN server.

5. **a, b, d.** These three utilities can be used to diagnose remote connectivity problems.

PART VI

Appendices

Appendix A

VPN Implementation Best Practices

Based on their past experiences, experts recommend a few practices that might prove to be very useful—not only during the deployment of the VPN setup, but also for the consistent operation of the VPN.

When implementing the VPN solution, consider the following:

◆ Before you even decide to implement a VPN solution, you must assess throughput, traffic patterns, user requirements, service level guarantees, support resources and infrastructure, the total cost of implementation, and so on, against the cost of existing (or proposed) leased line solutions. After the calculations and assessment, you might find that VPNs are not the right solution for your organization after all. You might also find that implementing an outsourced solution is a better option.

◆ If you decide to outsource your VPN solution, do not choose the first-suggested service provider. Gather quotes from multiple service providers and conduct good research before committing to the services of one specific service provider. Also, it is recommended that you pay attention to the SLA offered by the service provider. The SLA should be well-defined and clear. The points in SLA that you need to pay attention to include latency, availability, busy-free connect speed, packet loss probability, the number of concurrent operations supported, and outage notifications.

◆ When deciding between a leased line and dial-up connection that stretches from your intranet to the ISP's POP, you should base your decision on the comparison of average throughput with the maximum number of concurrent users it can support.

◆ If your VPN uses a diverse range of VPN client operating systems, ensure that the range is not too wide. Huge diversity of VPN clients will only complicate the management of your VPN. Standardizing the configuration of VPN clients as much as possible will help a great deal when you need to troubleshoot client-related VPN problems.

◆ It is highly recommended that remote access clients have a host-based intrusion detection system installed. This system will alert the user of any unauthorized activity, especially from the Internet connection.

◆ If possible, it is recommended that you configure a personal firewall on the client machines of users who are always on the move.

◆ The VPN gateway should be placed behind the firewall because the firewall can inspect decrypted packets, thus exerting better control of the data that enters your network.

◆ Implement dynamic allocation of addresses to VPN clients, if possible. This will reduce the management overhead and will ease the configuration and deployment of VPN clients across your intranet. However, you'll need to keep the downside associated with this practice in mind—you will not be able to easily map a given client to the corresponding address in order to control the accountability of your VPN clients.

◆ If you have multiple subnets or have decided to use a static IP address pool, it is recommended that you configure the address pool at the VPN router or gateway. In this scenario, clients will be allocated an IP address by the gateway. Because the VPN addresses and DHCP addresses are separate, the task of mapping the IP address of the client with the client name can be done easily. As a result, you'll have better control of the information related to the accountability of each client.

◆ If you have a single subnet only, allocation of static IP addresses is recommended.

◆ If your VPN is based in the U.S. and is based on a Microsoft Windows 2000 platform, it is recommended that you select the strongest level of encryption. However, if you are deploying the VPN connection outside of North America, you'll need to use basic level encryption because the strongest level of encryption is supported only by the Windows 2000 version available in North America.

◆ The best recommended way to implement IP addresses in VPN clients is with a RADIUS server. You can specify a pool of static IP addresses at the RADIUS server-end and the server will allocate an address from this pool to a VPN client authenticated by it. Because a RADIUS server also controls accountability, each session is logged comprehensively and accountability information can be accessed easily.

◆ It is a good practice to maintain detailed logs of each and every activity that occurs on your VPN. These logs ease the task of troubleshooting and management considerably. It is also recommended that these logs be transferred to a separate machine periodically. This serves as an effective precautionary measure, as an intruder cannot hide their tracks by altering these logs. Besides VPN servers, you must also configure VPN routers and gateways to log every access request, as well as every VPN session in detail.

◆ The VPN gateway (or what I have referred to as the host network gateway) should be different from the peripheral gateway.

◆ A VPN firewall should be protected by the peripheral router.

◆ In addition to implementing redundant paths and devices, redundant routing protocols, such as BGP and Virtual Router Redundancy Protocol (VRRP), should be deployed.

◆ NAT within the VPN setup can cause IPSec-encrypted data packets to be dropped due to integrity value check failure. (Refer to Chapter 11, "VPN Security Technologies," for more information.) As a result, NAT must be placed in such a manner that NAT-based operations take place outside the realm of your VPN. In simpler terms, with regard to incoming data packets, NAT-based operations must take place before the data is encapsulated and tunneled. Similarly, in the case of outgoing data packets, data should be de-tunneled and decrypted before the NAT can operate on them.

◆ Advanced user authentication services, such as AAA, RADIUS, TACACS, and so on, should be implemented without fail. Of these, your best option is the implementation of RADIUS because it offers scalability, flexibility, and advanced authentication features.

◆ If you use policy-based access, make sure that the policy is concise and easily understandable. As many experts agree, any policy that goes beyond 15 pages is a waste of valuable time and will not succeed.

◆ Never forget the power of training. Well-trained users who are alert to any possible invasion attempt are an asset and can help you control the security of the organization's intranet considerably.

◆ If you are using IPSec VPNs, you can either use pre-shared keys or digital certificates for authentication purposes. Use the pre-shared key method if your network is small and you do not foresee much growth in terms of scalability. However, if scalability is a concern, you should go for digital certificates. Although the use of digital signatures might increase the total cost of implementation (because you'll need to buy certificates from a Certificate Authority (CA) and implement a CA server), they are secure and highly scalable.

VPN Tunneling Protocols—Best Practices

PPTP, L2TP, and IPSec are the three most commonly implemented VPN tunneling protocols.

The recommendations and best practices related to the use of PPTP in your VPNs include the following:

◆ If you're implementing a Windows-based, low budget, relatively secure, and simple VPN solution, choose PPTP as the VPN protocol.

◆ PPTP supports multiple protocols. Therefore, if your VPN setup involves an assortment of protocols, or if multi-protocol support is must in your VPN, PPTP should be considered.

◆ Use PPTP if you are planning to implement a NAT because PPTP functionality does not "clash" with NAT functionality.

◆ If you are using PPTP and want additional security, it is recommended that you implement IPSec. This will allow your traffic to be IPSec-encrypted while still being tunneled in PPTP packets.

◆ If you want a VPN solution that is easy-to-implement and manage, you should opt for a PPTP-based VPN.

◆ If you are not planning to implement PKI for security purposes in your VPN solution, PPTP is an ideal choice.

◆ PPTP supports legacy devices. If you have a large number of legacy devices (especially VPN clients) in your intranet, PPTP will prove to be a good choice.

The recommendations and best practices related to the use of L2TP in your VPNs include the following:

◆ If you're implementing a VPN solution and you are planning to deploy a comprehensive PKI-based security structure, L2TP is recommended.

◆ If you would like to implement a faster and "leaner" VPN solution, L2TP is recommended.

◆ If you are implementing a VPN solution where interoperability between platforms is a major issue, you should consider L2TP.

◆ Do not use L2TP if you are planning to implement a NAT because the functionality of data tunneled using L2TP "clashes" with NAT.

◆ L2TP supports multiple protocols. Therefore, if your VPN setup involves an assortment of protocols, L2TP works fine.

◆ L2TP also supports legacy devices. Therefore if you have a large number of legacy devices (especially VPN clients) in your intranet, L2TP again will prove to be a good choice.

One major point that you'll need to keep in mind when implementing an L2TP-based solution is that L2TP on its own doesn't support data confidentiality in the form of encryption. Therefore, it is always preferable to use L2TP in association with IPSec.

The recommendations and best practices related to the use of IPSec in your VPNs include the following:

◆ If you're implementing a VPN solution where security is the biggest consideration and you are planning to deploy a comprehensive PKI-based security structure, IPSec is an ideal protocol candidate.

◆ Do not use IPSec if you are planning to implement a NAT. IPSec clashes with NAT functionality; every packet, even if correct, will be dropped by the VPN end because it will fail the integrity check.

◆ Current recommendations of IPSec do not support any other protocol beside IP. Therefore if your VPN is a multi-protocol and multi-vendor environment, the use of IPSec is not recommended at all.

◆ IPSec does not function well in a legacy-based environment. Therefore, do not use IPSec if you are planning to use legacy devices in your VPN.

◆ IPSec does not support standard user authentication mechanisms. Therefore, the use of a RADIUS-based authentication strategy is a must in the case of IPSec. Similarly, IPSec does not support standard dynamic address assignments. Therefore, you cannot use standard DHCP assignments with IPSec.

VPN protocols are vulnerable to certain security attacks. Therefore, it is important that you keep these vulnerabilities in mind when developing your VPN solution. Table A-1 lists the vulnerabilities of these protocols.

For your reference, Table A-2 summarizes the communication protocols and the security features supported by the three popular VPN protocols—PPTP, L2TP, and IPSec.

Table A-1. VPN Protocol Vulnerabilities to Security Attacks

Attack Type	PPTP	L2TP	IPSec
Spoofing	Vulnerable	Vulnerable	Resistant
Dictionary attack	Vulnerable	Vulnerable	Resistant
Brute Force attack	Vulnerable	Vulnerable	Resistant
Man-in-the-Middle attack	Vulnerable	Vulnerable	Resistant
Denial-of-Service attack	Vulnerable	Vulnerable	Resistant
GRE attack	Vulnerable	Resistant	Resistant
Implementation attack	NA	NA	Vulnerable
Key Management attack	NA	NA	Vulnerable
Password attack	Vulnerable	Resistant	Resistant

Table A-2. VPN Protocols—at a Glance

Attack Type	PPTP	L2TP	IPSec
Functions at OSI Layer	Layer 2	Layer 2	Layer 3
Tunneled Protocols	IP, IPX, NetBEUI	IP, IPX, NetBEUI	IP
Supported Infrastructure	IP, FR, ATM	IP, FR, ATM, X.25	IP
Transport Protocol	TCP	UDP	NA
Tunnels Supported	1	Multiple	Multiple
User Authentication	Password-based & smart cards	Password-based & smart cards	No standard mechanism
User Authentication Algorithm	PAP, CHAP, EAP and SPAP	PAP, CHAP, EAP and SPAP	NA
Packet Authentication	NA	NA	Yes
Packet Authentication Algorithm	NA	NA	HMAC (SHA-1, MD5)
Key Management	NA	NA	IKE
Address Assignment	Static and standard DHCP	Static and standard DHCP	Proprietary DHCP

Best Practices for Users

As a user, you ought to keep the following facts in mind when implementing passwords on your machines:

◆ You should always secure your workstation when not in use. The best way to secure your workstation is to lock it. Optionally, you can also log out of your account. This prevents any one from walking up to your work station and accessing confidential data.

◆ You should never open attachments that are from strangers. These attachments might contain malignant software or Trojan horses.

◆ You should never reply to "Spam" messages. Responding to Spam messages might lead to the conclusion that your mailbox is active and, therefore, it becomes an easy target for hackers.

◆ You should never share your passwords with anyone. An unauthorized user can ask for your passwords by impersonating an authorized user. Because of this possibility, you should never discuss your password with anyone.

◆ You should regularly change your passwords. In addition, your password should be an amalgamation of letters, numbers, and special characters.

In addition to these simple but imperative practices, you need to ensure that the security policy of your network is comprehensive and provides an end-to-end security solution.

Connecting to the Internet— Best Practices

You might find the best practices listed below of use:

◆ The physical security of all the components within your setup is extremely important. It is advisable to keep these devices from the physical reach of your users. Use separate rooms, if available, to ensure the physical security of your devices.

◆ You should create users with minimal rights that allow a person to perform their work without any hassles. The best strategy is to create a group of such users and assign members to this group. This approach is fast and easy and will effectively limit user rights. As a result, users will not be able to misuse or abuse their rights.

◆ Preferably, you should restrict all guest accounts to prevent unauthorized users from accessing your setup as even those with minimal rights can pose a risk.

- ◆ A two-tier DNS infrastructure will help you protect the identity of servers and other resources located within your intranet. The first tier of this DNS infrastructure is located "in front" of the firewall and can be queried by external entities. The second tier of the solution is located "behind" the firewall and cannot be directly accessed by external entities.

- ◆ It is extremely important that you have an effective intrusion detection system (IDS) in addition to mandatory firewall(s). However, integration of this IDS system with your firewall(s) depends on the requirements of your organization and (to an extent) on your allocated budget.

- ◆ Test your firewalls from inside as well as outside on a weekly basis. This practice will help you to detect internal as well as external intrusion attempts early.

- ◆ You should run port scans and Internet scans fairly regularly to detect if an authorized user machine has been infected by viruses. If so, disable the user account until the virus menace has been eradicated.

- ◆ Run frequent virus scans on VPN servers and clients. Also, update anti-virus updates without fail.

- ◆ If an employee leaves the company, disable his/her accounts without delay.

- ◆ Review the logs of various VPN servers and RADIUS authentication servers at least once a week.

- ◆ It is advisable to keep track of new hacking tools. You can use these tools to detect gaps in your security solution. Although time-consuming, this exercise can prove to be extremely helpful in detecting vulnerabilities within your security solution.

- ◆ It is advisable to run brute force and dictionary attacks regularly—at least on your administrative accounts—to test the passwords in use. You can also run these attacks on random user accounts to test the strength of passwords that are being used by your users.

- ◆ Force your users to change their passwords regularly. In addition, limit the number of login attempts so that if an attempt fails repetitively, the account is locked out.

- ◆ Run regular checks on ACLs, routers, and firewalls to test their strength.

- ◆ Run only minimal services (those that will allow users to only perform the most essential activities) on your VPN servers.

- ◆ Audit the directory service regularly (at least once a month) to ensure that user rights and permissions have not been altered.

Recommendations for Choosing a CA for Your Security System

A CA is a trusted third party that distributes keys used for the encryption or decryption of data. Another important responsibility of a CA is the distribution of digital certificates to requesters. These digital certificates play a significant role in the authentication of all parties involved in a transaction. Generally, you can avail the CA services of a trusted vendor for secure key exchanges. However, you can also establish the infrastructure to operate your own CA services. In either case, the recommendations for choosing a CA service for your setup follow:

◆ The CA should not only issue keys, but also update, back up, recover, reissue, revoke, disable, and enable keys.

◆ The CA should provide support for X.509 v3 certificate standards as well as X.500 directory standards.

◆ The CA should provide support for redundant certificate directory services that can be used in the case of failure of the primary directory infrastructure.

◆ The CA should provide detailed policies for the proper working and administration of CA services. In addition, the CA should provide expert support when required.

◆ The CA should provide centralized and scalable support for key management. In addition, the CA must provide separate key pairs for encryption and digital signatures.

◆ The CA should comply with the FIPS PUB 140-1 standard, which governs the requirements for products that protect sensitive information.

◆ Preferably, the CA should offer a Local Registration Agent (LRA) model, which allows the CA to administer the setup while the control of the certificate recipient is under the realm of the subscriber organization. This model, as a result, allows the organization to eliminate certificate administration overhead, but still control the security of its intranet.

◆ You should ensure that the CA supports cross-certification and that it complies with the X.509-based PKI (PKIX) standard. Cross certification, incidentally, is the capability of a CA to validate certificates issued by another CA.

◆ The keys and certificates issued by the CA must be time-stamped. In addition, the CA should provide a CA archival service, which allows the digital certificates to be verified over long period of times.

◆ Ensure that an independent third party, who can also analyze the risk factor in the services of the given CA, certifies the CA security measures.

◆ It is recommended that the CA that you choose support role-based operation. This increases the security of the operation and reduces the possibility of internal compromise.

◆ The CA should maintain secure audit records. This practice helps effectively reduce the risk of compromise.

◆ The CA must have a Certification Practice Statement (CPS). A CPS ensures that you are dealing with a credible and legitimate CA.

Recommendations for Choosing a VPN Service Provider

As you learned earlier, a VPN service provider is a very significant aspect of your VPN setup, especially if you have outsourced the VPN solution partially or completely. Therefore, considerable thought must go into the choice of a service provider. The recommendations for selecting a service provider are as follows:

◆ Select a service provider that offers comprehensive data encryption services. Generally, data is encrypted from the service provider's intranet or POP to the destination network gateway. However, data travels in clear from the remote user-end to the ISP POP. Some service providers offer encryption services only while the data is traveling on their backbones. Some service providers do not provide the encryption facility at all. This is the worst scenario because the security offered in such a case is minimal. The best solution is to go for those service providers that offer robust end-to-end encryption because the security level offered with end-to-end encryption is the highest.

◆ Your service provider should offer a strong encryption mechanism, preferably the Triple DES (3DES) encryption algorithm.

◆ Your service provider should support both Layer 2 and Layer 3 tunneling protocols.

◆ Your service provider should offer system level security to its subscribers. In addition, it must prevent direct and indirect security breaches with the help of efficient external security devices.

◆ Your service provider should offer simple and uncomplicated configuration of network elements so that the end user can use them easily.

◆ The solution provided by your service provider should be such that no upgrades or major changes are required within the organization's intranet.

◆ The solution provided by your service provider should not force major addressing changes within your intranet.

◆ The VPN protocol used by the service provider is another important criterion. As you already know, PPTP offers low level of security, while L2TP offers mid-level data security. IPSec offers the highest level of security. Therefore, choose a VPN service provider that offers IPSec-compliant VPN service.

◆ Authentication services provided by the service provider are also important. User- and packet-based authentication are extremely important. Therefore, again an IPSec-based authentication service is the apt choice. If security is the most important issue in the setup, your service provider should also support certificate-based authentication. In this scenario, your service provider should also be a CA or must work closely with a CA.

◆ The encryption services offered must be hardware-based rather than software-based because encryption performed on a specialized hardware device is much faster and high-performing when compared to software-based encryptions performed on a router or firewall. In the case of hardware-based encryption, the devices used by the service provider must offer 10–100 Mbps throughput, simultaneous support of 500–1000 requests, and the capability to handle at least 1000 concurrent tunnels.

◆ An SLA is a must for every service provider you consider. A strong SLA takes care of situations in which the contracted service levels are not adequately met and the administration and monitoring of offered services is required.

◆ In the case of dial-up connections, you should look at the call success rates and the modem connection-speed guarantee. However, if you plan to use dedicated connections to the service provider's POP, you should look at the guaranteed availability level and the maximum latency that might arise.

◆ Service provider infrastructure is another important consideration. Besides having business-class switching and an IP backbone, the service provider's infrastructure must also be capable of supporting various networking technologies (ATM, Frame Relay, SONET, X.25, and so on).

◆ A service provider's commitment to future growth and their accommodation of newer technologies is a very good indicator of the efficiency of the service provider.

◆ The service provider must offer 24-hour management and monitoring capabilities. In addition, they must use proven and mature administration and monitoring tools for the purpose.

◆ The available assistance and proven expertise of the staff at the service provider end is also a very big consideration. After all, these are the people who will be responsible for the proper working of your VPN and you'll have to deal with them.

◆ You must closely examine the service provider's track record to understand their level of maturity and experience in dealing with the technology. If necessary, get in touch with their costumers to get the real picture.

◆ Your service provider should provide complete and accurate documentation that can help IS managers and administrators at the subscriber end with initial configuration, basic troubleshooting, and management purposes.

Appendix B

Q. What is a VPN?

A. A VPN is an extension of a private intranet across a public network (the Internet) that ensures secure and cost-effective connectivity between the two communicating ends. The private intranet is extended with the help of private logical "tunnels." These tunnels enable the two ends to exchange data in a manner resembling point-to-point communication.

Q. What is a public network?

A. As the name suggests, a public network is a network available to general public. There are three major categories of public networks. These include:

- **POTS (Plain Old Telephone Service).** Used in homes and offices.
- **PSTN (Public Switched Telephone Network).** Interconnected voice-oriented public telephone networks. They might be used for commercial purposes or belong to the government.
- **The Internet.** A global connection of computer networks and individual computers.

Q. Why should I implement a VPN?

A. VPNs offer a large number of benefits to your organization. These advantages include:

- Reduced cost of implementation
- Reduced management and staffing costs
- Enhanced connectivity
- Transaction security
- Effective use of bandwidth
- Enhanced scalability

Q. What are the possible disadvantages that I might come across if I implement a VPN setup?

A. VPN disadvantages include:

- High dependence on the Internet
- Lack of support for legacy protocols

Q. What are the most important features of a VPN?

A. The most important features of a VPN solution include:

- Security
- Interoperability of devices from multiple vendors
- Centralized VPN management
- Easy implementation
- Easy usability

- ◆ Scalability
- ◆ Performance
- ◆ Bandwidth management
- ◆ Service provider's infrastructure
- ◆ High availability

Q. What are the requirements of a VPN?

A. The basic requirements of a VPN are

- ◆ Security
- ◆ Availability
- ◆ Quality of Service (QoS)
- ◆ Reliability
- ◆ Compatibility
- ◆ Manageability

Q. What are the building blocks of a VPN?

A. The building blocks of a VPN include the following:

- ◆ VPN hardware, which includes VPN servers, clients, and other hardware devices, such as VPN routers, gateways, and concentrators.
- ◆ VPN software, which includes server and client software and VPN management tools.
- ◆ Security infrastructure of the organization, which typically includes RADIUS, TACACS, NAT, and AAA-based solutions.
- ◆ Service provider's supporting infrastructure, which includes the service provider's network access switching backbone and the Internet backbone.
- ◆ Public networks, which include the Internet, PSTNs, and POTs.
- ◆ Tunnels, which might be PPTP-based, L2TP-based, or L2F-based.

Q. What are the common VPN architectures?

A. Common VPN architectures include:

- ◆ Implementer-based VPN architecture (Outsourced VPNs, In-house VPNs, and Hybrid VPNs)
- ◆ Security-based VPN architecture (Router-to-router VPNs, Firewall-to-firewall VPNs, Client-initiated VPNs, and Directed VPNs)
- ◆ Layer-based VPN architecture (Link-layer and Network-layer VPNs)
- ◆ Class-based VPN architecture (Class 0 through 4)

Q. What is the most common type of VPN architecture?

A. The most basic classifications of present-day VPNs include the following three categories:

- ◆ **Remote Access VPNs** that provide remote, mobile, and telecommuting employees anytime access to corporate network resources.
- ◆ **Intranet VPNs** that are used to interconnect an organization's remote branch offices to the corporate intranet.
- ◆ **Extranet VPNs** that are not entirely segregated from the "outer world." In fact, extranet VPNs allow controlled access to necessary network resources by external business entities, such as partners, customers, and suppliers that have a major role to play in the corporate business.

Q. What are the generic categories of network setup attacks?

A. The generic categories of attacks to a network setup include the following:

- ◆ Interruption of network services
- ◆ Interception of data
- ◆ Modification of data
- ◆ Fabrication of data

Q. What does user authentication mean?

A. User authentication is the process of verifying that users are who they claim to be.

Q. What is access control?

A. The process of allowing access to certain network resources while denying access to others is referred to as access control.

Q. What is encryption?

A. Encryption of data, also known as cryptography, is one of the most important components of VPN security and plays major role in securing data during transit. Encryption is the mechanism of converting data into unreadable format, known as *cipher text*, so that unauthorized access to the data during transmission can be prevented.

Q. What are the two types of encryptions?

A. Symmetric cryptography and asymmetric cryptography are the two types of encryption. Symmetric cryptosystems are based on a single key, which is a bit string of fixed length. Therefore, this encryption mechanism is also referred to as *single-key encryption*. The key is private and is used for both encryption as well as decryption. Asymmetric cryptosystems use a pair of mathematically related keys. One of the keys is private and is known only to the owner of the pair. The second key is public and is freely distributable. The public key is used for encryption purposes whereas the private key is used for decrypting the encrypted messages. This asymmetry in encryption and decryption is the reason behind its name.

Q. What is PKI?

A. PKI is a framework of policies for managing keys and establishing a secure method for data exchange. These data transactions can take place within an organization, country, industry, or zone. To accomplish key management and highly secure data transactions, the PKI-based framework is comprised of policies and procedures that are supported by hardware and software resources.

Q. What is tunneling and what are its advantages?

A. Tunneling is the technique of encapsulating (or placing) an entire data packet within the packet of another protocol format. The resulting packet is then transferred to the destination node or network across the intermediate infrastructure. The major advantages of tunneling include:

◆ Simplicity and ease of implementation

◆ Security

◆ Cost-effectiveness

◆ Ability to route non-IP packets across the Internet

◆ Sparing the ever-dwindling pool of globally unique IP addresses

Q. What are the components of tunneling?

A. The target network, initiator node, HA, and FA are the tunneling components.

Q. What are the two types of VPN tunnels?

A. Based on the manner in which it is created, a tunnel can be of two types:

◆ **Voluntary tunnels.** Because they are created at the request of a user (client) computer, the initiator node acts as the tunnel endpoint. Therefore, a separate tunnel is created for each communicating pair. After the communication between the two ends is complete, the tunnel is terminated.

◆ **Compulsory tunnels.** The initiator must use the tunnel created by the intermediate device, which is why this is called compulsory tunneling. NASs and dial-up servers are examples of intermediate devices.

Q. What tunneling protocols function at Layer 2 of the OSI model?

A. PPTP, L2F, and L2TP function at the second layer (Data Link layer) of the OSI model.

Q. What tunneling protocol functions at Layer 3 of the OSI model?

A. IPSec functions at the third layer of the OSI model.

Q. When should I use PPTP?

A. You should use PPTP when data security is not the most important issue. Interoperability, ease of implementation, and a low-cost solution are the major considerations warranting PPTP use for a proposed VPN.

Q. When should I use L2TP?

A. You should use L2TP when security, interoperability, and multi-vendor support are the major issues you need to address.

Q. When should I use IPSec?

A. You should use IPSec when security is your biggest consideration.

Q. What is an IPSec security association?

A. SAs are a fundamental concept of the IPSec protocol suite. As quoted by the developers of IPSec, an SA is a logical unidirectional connection between two entities that use the services of IPSec. IPSec SAs define authentication protocols, keys, algorithms, the mode and keys for the authentication algorithms used by the AH or ESP protocols of the IPSec suite, encryption and decryption algorithms and keys, key-related information, such as the change interval and time-to-live interval of the keys, information related to the SA itself, which includes the SA source address and the time-to-live interval of the SA, and the usage and size of any cryptographic synchronization used for IPSec-based tunneling.

Q. What are the AH protocol and ESP Protocol in IPSec terminology?

A. The Authentication Header (AH) protocol adds an additional header to the IP datagram. As the name suggests, this header serves to authenticate the origin (or the source) of the IP datagram at the receiver end. In addition, this header also helps identify any undetected modifications to the content of the datagram by an unauthorized user during transit. However, AH does not provide confidentiality. The main aim of ESP is to provide confidentiality in addition to the processing of sender authentication and the verification of the data integrity during transit. ESP encrypts the content of the datagram using advanced encryption algorithms, as specified by the SA.

Q. What are the modes offered by IPSec for the safe transmission of data?

A. IPSec offers two modes of transmission, the transport mode and the tunnel mode. Transport mode protects upper-layer protocols and applications. In Transport mode, the IPSec header is inserted between the IP header and the header of the upper-layer protocol. Unlike Transport mode, Tunnel mode protects the entire IP datagram. The entire IP datagram is encapsulated in another IP datagram and an IPSec header is inserted between the original and the new IP header.

Q. What is IKE?

A. IKE (Internet Key Exchange) is a third-party protocol used by IPSec that helps the communicating parties negotiate security parameters and authentication keys before a secure IPSec session can begin. The security parameters negotiated are the ones defined in the SA. Besides negotiating and establishing security parameters and cryptographic keys, IKE also modifies these parameters and keys (when required during a session). IKE is also responsible for deleting the SAs and keys after an IPSec-based communication session is completed.

Q. **What are the main issues that I should keep in mind when designing a VPN solution for my organization?**

A. The main issues that you'll need to consider when developing the design of your VPN include the following:

◆ Security
◆ Addressing and routing
◆ DNS-related issues
◆ Issues related to routers/gateways, firewalls, and NAT
◆ Server and client issues
◆ Performance
◆ Scalability and interoperability

Q. **What are the generic steps that I need to follow when building my VPN solution?**

A. The complete implementation of a VPN-based solution can be broken down into following steps:

1. Laying the groundwork
2. Choosing products and a service provider
3. Testing the results
4. Getting down to design and real implementation
5. Managing and monitoring

Q. **What are the common attacks that my VPN solution may have to face?**

A. A VPN-based implementation can be attacked in many ways. The following is a list of possible attacks on VPNs.

◆ **Security threats to VPN elements**, such as the dial-in remote user, the dial-in ISP segments, the public network or Internet, and the host network gateway.

◆ **Attacks against VPN protocols**, such as PPTP and IPSec. PPTP is vulnerable on two fronts: GRE and passwords exchanged during authentication process. IPSec, on the other hand, is vulnerable to attacks against IPSec implementations, attacks against key management and administrative and wildcard attacks.

◆ **Cryptanalysis attacks**, such as ciphertext-only attacks, known plaintext attacks, chosen plaintext attacks, Man-in-the-Middle attacks, brute force attacks, and timing attacks.

◆ **DoS attacks** that make some services or target computers or the entire target network inaccessible to authorized users. These include attacks such as SYN floods, smurf attacks, broadcast storms, mail bombs, pings of death, and Spam mail.

Q. How can I successfully counter DoS attacks?

A. Although very harmful, you can take the following steps to counter various DoS attacks:

◆ Disable unused or unneeded services on the network.

◆ Maintain regular backups.

◆ Create, maintain, and monitor daily logs.

◆ Create appropriate password policies.

◆ Implement an IDS.

◆ Implement route filters to filter fragmented ICMP packets.

◆ Keep a strict vigil on the physical security of your network resources.

◆ Configure filters for IP-spoofed packets.

◆ Install patches and fixes for TCP SYN attacks.

◆ Partition the file system to separate application-specific files from regular data.

◆ Deploy tools such as Tripwire that detect changes in the configuration information or other files.

Q. What are the remote authentication techniques that have been adopted as complementary solutions to VPNs?

A. The most commonly used remote authentication techniques adopted to complement VPN technology to increase the security level of data stored within these private intranets include the following:

◆ Authentication Authorization Accounting (AAA)

◆ Remote Access Dial-In User Service (RADIUS)

◆ Terminal Access Controller Access Control System (TACACS)

Q. What is AAA?

A. AAA is an architectural framework used to configure three basic security functions—authentication, authorization, and accounting. Today, the AAA security model is used in practically all remote access scenarios because it allows network administrators to identify and answer the following three important questions:

◆ Who is accessing the network?

◆ What is the user allowed to do and what actions are restricted to him or her when he or she successfully accesses the network?

◆ What is the user doing and when?

Q. What is RADIUS?

A. RADIUS is the de facto standard for remote authentication in which user-related information is stored on a central database. All remote access servers share this database. RADIUS enables the communication between this database and the RASs when a RAS receives a login request from a remote user. In fact, RADIUS specifies the format and the flow of packets between the database and the access server. The database supplies the requested information that the RAS uses to authenticate the incoming request and authorizes the user to access the requested service or resource.

Q. What is a firewall?

A. A firewall is an effective method of securing data in a network from external threats. Firewalls not only prevent an unauthorized user from accessing your network or specific resources within it, they also act as effective security blankets that prevent any damage due to external attacks from affecting the entire network. Conceptually, there are three types of firewalls that function at various layers of the OSI model. The three types of firewalls are

- Packet filter firewalls.
- Stateful packet inspection firewalls.
- Application proxy firewalls.

Q. What is a NAT?

A. Historically, NAT was developed by Cisco Systems as a short-term solution to the problem of ever-dwindling IP addresses. However, NAT has emerged as an effective strategy of keeping external users and hackers from penetrating a network. Another benefit associated with NAT is that it allows networks using private IP addresses to communicate with the outside world across a public network. NAT-based solutions can be implemented in two ways:

- Static NATs
- Dynamic NATs

Q. Why would I need to be careful while implementing a NAT-based VPN solution?

A. For the success of NAT technology, the Layer 3 (IP) addresses must be changed. NATs work seamlessly with PPTP-based VPNs because PPTP neither encapsulates nor encrypts the IP datagrams. As a result, NATs can freely operate on PPTP-tunneled packets. Unlike PPTP, L2TP and IPSec encapsulate and/or encrypt the Layer 3 IP address of a packet with another Layer 3 network address. As a result, the UDP port number is encrypted and its value is protected with a cryptographic FCS. This makes L2TP or L2TP over IPSec traffic non-translatable by NATs because NAT isn't able to work on the packet after the packet goes through the IPSec or L2TP VPN tunneling process. Therefore, the packet would have the same network address. Moreover, in the case of end-to-end IPSec authentication, a packet whose address is changed will always fail the integrity check provided by the AH. Consequently, NATs can break an L2TP-based tunnel or an L2TP over IPSec-based tunnel because the VPN server will always drop the packets.

Q. What is SOCKS?

A. SOCKS is a generic networking proxy protocol that enables hosts on one side of a SOCKS server to access hosts on the other side of the SOCKS server without having to expose their real IP addresses. In addition, the SOCKS server is responsible for authenticating and authorizing requests, establishing a proxy connection, and transmitting data between the two ends. Consequently, SOCKS is often used as a primitive network firewall redirecting connection requests from hosts on opposite sides of a SOCKS server.

Q. What are SSL and TLS?

A. SSL (Secure Socket Layer) is a de facto security standard for securing transactions across public networks. It provides a private channel between communicating applications, thus ensuring data privacy and integrity during the transaction. In addition, SSL provides authentication of the communicating ends. SSL has gained a large popularity base over the last few years and has been adopted by major Web browsers and Web servers. TLS (Transport Layer Security) was developed using SSL as its base and is considered the successor to SSL. Like SSL, TLS also allows the client and the server ends to communicate safely across unsafe public networks. Besides the security capabilities provided by SSL, TLS also prevents eavesdropping, sniffing, and spoofing.

Q. What are the main issues of VPN management?

A. The main issues related to VPN management are as follows:

- Managing users and databases
- Managing tunnels
- Managing keys
- Managing VPN hardware and software
- Managing support

Q. What are the common problems with VPNs?

A. The common problems that might arise in a VPN setup include the following:

- Inability to establish a connection with the VPN server
- Inability to connect to hosts beyond the VPN server
- Inability to browse the LAN after logging on the network
- Inability to connect to the Internet

Q. What are the common utilities used to troubleshoot VPN problems?

A. The common utilities that can help you troubleshoot a VPN-related problem include:

- Event logging
- Tracing
- Network Monitor

Appendix C

Trade experts predict a steady growth of VPNs in the market. Some credit in the growth of VPN technology goes to industry giants Cisco Systems and Microsoft Corporation. With more and more organizations waking up to the advantages of VPNs, new vendors and solutions are introduced every now and then. With this increase in competition, newer and more advanced VPN products and services are introduced and the cost of a typical VPN implementation continues to fall. The ultimate winner of this competition and its outcome is the buyer—you. In addition, many vendors are gearing up to offer integrated voice and data services across the Internet.

So, what exactly lies in the future of VPNs? According to trade analysis, two VPN technologies are being predicted as the "future" of VPNs. These are the Border Gateway Protocol/Multi-Protocol Label Switching (BGP/MPLS) technology and broadband VPNs.

BGP/MPLS VPNs

Originally known as *RFC 2547bis*, these VPNs are popularly known as BGP/MPLS because they use the Border Gateway Protocol (BGP) to distribute VPN routing information across the service provider's backbone. The infrastructure that is used to forward this BGP-based routing traffic from one site to another is based on MPLS (as you learned in Chapter 2, "VPN Requirements, Building Blocks, and Architectures"). Figure C-1 depicts a typical BGP/MPLS VPN.

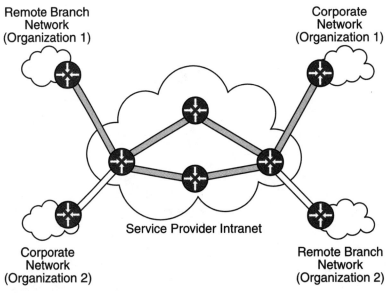

FIGURE C-1 *The BGP/MPLS VPN setup.*

As shown in Figure C-1, the subscriber organization's intranet is connected to the service provider's intranet through a "port" associated with a VPN routing table. This VPN routing table in BGP/MPLS terminology is referred to as a VPN Routing and Forwarding (VRF) table.

At the customer end, a Layer 2 switch, an IP router, or a host is connected to one or more routers at the service provider end. These routers at the subscriber end exchange VPN routing information with the routers located at the service provider end. These routers at the service provider end are dedicated to VPNs and use routing protocols, such EBGP, RIPv2, and OSPF for exchanging available VPN route information in the form of a VRF. Each individual VRF is associated with a direct customer connection. Therefore, a port of a service provider's peripheral router is associated with a specific customer rather than a site.

Any router at the service provider end that is not directly connected to a subscriber router acts as an MPLS router and is responsible for forwarding data across the MPLS backbone.

In this manner, BGP/MPLS VPNs offer connection-oriented services that are analogous to the Virtual Circuits (VCs) found in ATM and Frame Relay networks. These connection-oriented virtual circuits are commonly referred to as Label Switched Paths (LSPs). After an LSP is established, packets can be prioritized per the application priority as best effort, real-time, or absolute. As a result, BGP/MPLS natively supports important VPN requirements, such as QoS and traffic management.

The main advantages of BGP/MPLS VPNs include the following:

◆ Being independent of Layer 2, BGP/MPLS does not have to face the same problems and limitations associated as other Layer 2 VPNs.

◆ BGP/MPLS VPNs are easy to implement and configure because only routers located at the periphery of the subscriber's intranet and the service provider's intranet need to be configured.

◆ BGP/MPLS VPNs offer scalability and flexibility for customer VPN services.

◆ BGP/MPLS VPNs support various network topologies, such as hub and spoke, mesh, and hybrid.

◆ BGP/MPLS VPNs can support separate routes between the same set of routers, thus providing remote access, access to supported extranets, as well as access to the Internet. As a result, service providers can use the same IP-based infrastructure to deliver both VPN and Internet traffic.

◆ Even without encryption, the security provided by BGP/MPLS VPNs is equivalent to ATM- or Frame Relay-based network backbones.

◆ In a BGP/MPLS setup, routing information is not exchanged between BGP/MPLS VPN routers and other routers at the customer site. Therefore, the subscriber doesn't have to deal with inter-site routing traffic, which falls under the realm of the service provider.

Broadband VPNs

Bandwidth management has been a sore point of any VPN setup. It is an expensive exercise when compared to ATM-based transmission infrastructures and it does not allow the customer much choice in line speeds per their requirements. Broadband VPNs, or BVPNs, are gearing up to solve this problem by providing broadband transmission services between the various remote branches and the main corporate network of an organization's intranet.

Broadband VPNs leverage ISDN connectivity to transfer data securely. Broadband VPNs are a solution that is based on the Switched Virtual Circuits (SVCs) that are commonly used in B-ISDN and ATM.

Figure C-2 depicts a BVPN network setup.

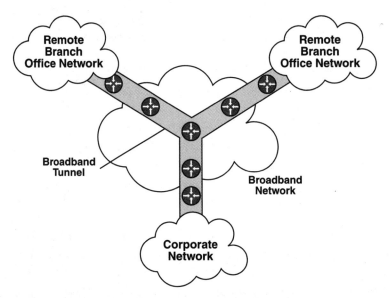

FIGURE C-2 *A generic representation of a BVPN.*

The BVPN infrastructure is strongly based on ATM technology, which provides increased bandwidth and services. As a result, audio as well as normal data can be exchanged between two sites of a VPN. Other benefits of BVPN technology include the following:

◆ Increased flexibility

◆ Cost-effectiveness

◆ Access to broadband services and capabilities.

Although BVPNs have much to offer, this technology is still is in the experimental stage; a few issues need to be resolved before it can be rolled out to the general public. Compatibility between various broadband-signaling systems is a one such consideration. A proper and workable addressing scheme for routing calls is another consideration. However, experts predict that this technology will progress rapidly and will be available to all in the near future.

Appendix D

Your network security policy plays a significant role in defining your organization's stand on security and the steps it has taken to implement network security. No product or solution comes with a security policy. It is something that you have to create and implement based on the needs of your organization.

As the IS manager or administrator, you need to ensure that the security policy of your network is comprehensive and provides an end-to-end security solution. What follows is an explanation of the way a security policy forms the heart and soul of any network security design.

Security Policies—The Basics

A *network security policy* defines an organization's vision of the way it will use its computer and network infrastructure to provide better service and enhanced productivity. It also outlines the procedures to take to respond to security threats.

The security policy of an organization should provide answers to the following questions:

◆ Who has access to the organization's network? If needed, how are clients, partners, and vendors to be provided access to the organization's network?

◆ Who can connect to external networks, such as those of clients and partners?

◆ Who can access the Internet from the organization's network?

◆ How do the organization's employees access the Internet?

◆ When should a user's account be deleted?

◆ How secure must computers be before they are placed in a network with unprotected Internet access?

◆ Can users download random executables from the Internet?

◆ How is the data traveling over the organization's network protected?

◆ How is confidential employee information protected? Are there any laws regarding the handling of this type of information?

◆ What kinds of passwords should employees use and how often should they change their passwords?

◆ What safety measures must be taken against viruses on personal computers?

◆ How are the computers of remote and mobile users secured? How do they get secure access to the organization's network?

A network security policy streamlines an organization's response to the various risks and possible threats associated with corporate assets, including data and network resources. Because it outlines your organization's security needs, you should have the company's network security policy in hand before you start planning your organization's network security.

In practice, a network security policy delicately balances the weight of possible threats and the value of personal productivity and efficiency. Without a proper network security policy, a functional and operational security framework cannot be established. However, you need to realistically assess your organization's security needs and requirements before you design and implement the policy, else you might neglect important aspects of security or end up focusing on trivial issues.

A functioning security policy is not only a set of rules governing user access to corporate assets, it's also a general agreement to accept and abide by those rules. The ideal security policy provides a framework that safeguards corporate resources and enforces security regulations, but still allows secure and transparent user access. The following section discusses risk analysis in detail.

Risk Analysis

Risk analysis, also popularly referred to as risk assessment, is the first step in deciding upon a suitable security policy. Risk analysis helps you assess the vulnerabilities and loopholes in a network setup and, subsequently, identify the potential threats that your organization faces. As a result, risk analysis, if done properly, allows you to prioritize an organization's requirements, decide upon the strategies to be implemented, and define the budget allocated to implement the required security measures.

In the process of risk analysis, you first must identify the following:

◆ Assets that must be protected

◆ People who can attack assets

◆ Tools (and their sources) that can be used to attack the assets

◆ Immediate cost of an asset attack

◆ Time needed to recover the attacked asset

The following are some basic guidelines for designing a well-defined security policy:

◆ Consider your residual risk factor. Residual risk is the risk that remains even after proper security measures have been considered. Is your estimated residual risk factor acceptable?

◆ Contingency measures must be included in case the primary security measures fail.

◆ The policy must be documented properly and all reasons for strategy decisions (why one strategy was picked over another) should be provided.

After you have identified the risks that your network setup faces and documented the results of your risk analysis, you need to get down to actually designing the policy. To begin, you'll need to identify the various components of the security policy.

Components of a Network Security Policy

Before formulating a security policy, it's a good idea to study the components of an effective security policy. The content of your network security policy will depend on various factors, including the network size, topology, internetwork devices, and usage. The following section discusses some common components of network security policies.

Physical Security

An organization's network can span floors, buildings, and even diverse geographical locations. Implementation of such a network involves many components and devices. A good network security policy addresses the physical security of these components and devices.

Network Security

A network serves as a repository of resources and data that can be shared with authorized users. These resources are valuable to an organization and must be protected. Therefore, your network security policy should address how your organization's network data repositories should be protected. It should also include implementation and configuration information for access control, firewalls, network auditing, remote access, directory services, Internet services, and file-system directory structures.

Access Control

Access control is the mechanism used to ensure that only legitimate and authorized users have access to network resources and services. Your security policy should define a guideline for access-control mechanisms that streamlines legitimate user access within or outside the network. However, your policy should not be overly complex; it needs to be easy to implement.

Software Security

The software component of the security policy should define how commercial and non-commercial software packages are to be installed and implemented on the network. The policy should also address software copyright and OEM support issues, as well as how to purchase, upgrade, or procure licenses for the software. You should also ensure that security guidelines for downloading new software, upgrades, or patches from the Internet are included in the policy.

Audits and Reviews

Your security policy should be reviewed and audited regularly to make sure it maintains its relevance, addresses potential needs to update security measures, and ensures that all components and users are complying with the standards it outlines. Monitoring resources and components for any inconsistencies is a natural outgrowth of this practice. Auditing helps identify new security holes as they develop.

Disaster Contingency Plan

Your security policy should include procedures to follow in case of disaster. A *disaster contingency plan* details how an organization deals with a natural disaster, a significant hardware failure, or attacks from hackers. When a disaster, hardware failure or hacking attack does occur, the security of corporate data is of utmost importance. Apart from regular access policies and user permissions, a plan for data backup and restoration is essential. The backup plan should indicate the frequency and scheme of backup, where to store backup media (onsite or offsite), and how to recover data in case of a system failure.

Preparing the Security Policy

The following considerations should be kept in mind when designing your security policy:

◆ **Accessibility.** An organization's security policy affects all of its employees. Hence, it is important that all employees have access to the policy. A good idea is to include the security policy in the organization's employee handbook and/or the company's intranet site.

◆ **Goals.** Any change in the existing setup of an organization is bound to meet resistance from the employees. The same holds true when you try to introduce a network security policy. It is important that the security policy's goals and objectives are outlined. Employees must know why the security policy is important to the organization.

◆ **Clarity.** To avoid any misinterpretation, the security policy should be clear, easy to understand, and precise. The language of the security policy should be accurate and unambiguous.

◆ **Roles and responsibilities.** Your security policy should clearly define the employees' roles and responsibilities with regard to maintaining network security. The policy should also specify those people who are responsible for enforcing the security policy, creating backups, and conducting audits.

◆ **Consequences.** Employees should know the impact of security policy noncompliance. Hence, the security policy should include the consequences that an employee would face if he or she does not comply with a particular policy issue.

Keeping the results of your risk analysis and the previous considerations in mind, the security policy must contain the following:

◆ A description of vulnerabilities points, such as mission-critical information and sensitive resources.

◆ A description of the organization's security goals.

◆ A description of the way the security goals of the organization are to be achieved.

◆ A description of local, state, and federal laws that have been incorporated in the policy.

After the policy has been developed, you also need to ensure that it is properly documented. Once documentation is in place, you can implement your policy.

Implementing the Security Policy

Good intentions are never enough, which is why you need to actively implement the security policy as well. The following is a list of steps you need to take to implement the security policy you've designed:

◆ Appoint a dedicated expert or administrator to be responsible for the security of the setup.

◆ Ensure that the employee handbook reflects the organization's security policy. Also, update the security policy as and when required.

◆ Brief all new employees about the organization's security policy. And, increase awareness among veteran employees by communicating the organization's security needs, requirements, and expectations frequently. You can organize regular workshops or use visible reminders, such as posters, pamphlets, and memos for the purpose. Also, publicly appreciate employees who exhibit "security consciousness."

◆ Train the staff vigorously about security best practices. Encourage employees to report any suspicious behavior or incident that might threaten the security of the setup.

◆ Enforce security laws and regulations at all levels, including top management.

You can use the following checklist to ensure that your security policy is being implemented correctly:

◆ Have all levels of staff been included in the development and implementation phase of policy creation?

◆ Is the policy written in a manner that can be universally understood?

◆ Does your security training program cover all aspects of the policy?

◆ Are all new employees aware of the security needs, requirements, and procedures of the organization?

◆ Is a dedicated administrator assigned to manage and monitor the security of the network setup? Is the administrator well trained?

Implementing a policy is not enough. You'll also need to review it periodically to accommodate your organization's changing needs and requirements.

Appendix E

Table E-1. VPN Hardware, Software, and Complete Solution Vendors

Vendor	Product Description
3COM	Hardware and software enterprise VPN solution for internetworking and remote access
ADC Kentrox	WAN access solution (Secure Vision Series), SecureVision Software solution
Alcatel	VPN services
Altiga Networks	Specialized VPN hardware and AGIS Express Connect Plus Series
Ascend/Lucent	VPN hubs, gateways, and management tools
Ashley Laurent	Remote solutions (Enterprise and Extranet) and VPCom Software Series
Assured Digital, Inc.	Plug-and-play VPN solutions (hardware as well as software)
AT&T	VPN services/solutions (hardware as well as software)
Aventail Corporation	Extranet solutions
Axent Technologies	VPN software products
Bay Networks	Carrier-class VPN products (internetworking and remote access)
CAIS Software Solutions	Management tools (IPORT Server Series)
CheckPoint	VPN solutions (CheckPoint Series) and VPN-1 product family management tools
Chrysalis ITS	Specialized VPN hardware
Cisco Systems	Routers, switches, hubs, gateways, management tools, internetworking, and remote access solutions
Compatible Systems	VPN switches
Concentric Networks	Complete VPN products and product management tools
CoSine Communications	Managed VPN solution for service providers
Data Fellows, Inc.	Integrated (software-based) enterprise security solutions
Ennovate Networks, Inc.	WAN solutions for service providers
Entrust Technologies	Providers of security software solutions
Epoch Internet	Software-based management and access solutions

Table E-1. Continued

Vendor	Product Description
Exodus Communications (with Cohesive Solutions)	VPN services (software)
Extended Systems	Specialized VPN hardware and solutions
FiberLink	Complete VPN solution
FirstVPN	VPN services
Fortress Technologies	NetFortress-series hardware products
FreeS/WAN	VPN solution for Linux platform
General Electronics (with Spacenet, Inc.)	Satellite-based VPN solutions
GTE Internetworking	VPN services/solutions and VPN Advantage software series
HiFN	Encryption solutions
IBM Corporation	VPN services, routers, and switches
Indus River Networks	Specialized VPN hardware and RAS solutions
Info Express	VTVP/Secure software product series
Intel Corporation	Gateways and Shiva product line for VPNs
Intelispan	VPN services (exSPANd)
Internet Devices	Specialized VPN hardware
Internet Dynamics, Inc.	Dynamic VPN products
iPass, Inc.	VPN services
IRE, Inc.	VPN product and services (SafeNet Series)
Isolation Systems (with Intel and Shiva)	VPN product and services (LanRover Series)
Matrox	Internetworking and remote access solutions
Microsoft Corporation	VPN server/client operating systems
Netopia, Inc.	VPN (software) solutions for Class 0 and 1 VPNs
NetScreen Technologies	Software-based firewalls and management tools
Network Alchemy, Inc.	VPN software-based security solutions (CryptoCluster series)

Table E-1. Continued

Vendor	Product Description
Network Associates	Software-based security solutions
New Oak Communications (with Nortel)	Carrier-class VPN products (hardware/software)
NewBridge Networks	Carrier-class VPN products (hardware/software)
Nokia	Partner in CheckPoint Series
NetGuard (with LanOptics, Inc.)	VPN services
Nortel Networks	Carrier-class VPN products
Novell, Inc.	Management tools and VPN server/client operating systems
OneBox Networks	Specialized VPN hardware
OneBSD	VPN server operating system and IPSec-based solutions
Onix Networks	VPN integration services
Pilot Network Services	VPN services
Raptor (with Axent)	VPN software solutions
RASGuard, Inc.	VPN products (cIPRO Series)
Redcreek Communication	VPN products (Ravlin Series)
RSA	PKI, User Authentication, Intrusion detection
Scientific-Atlanta, Inc.	Satellite-based VPN solutions
Secure Computing Corporation	Authentication, firewalls, Web tools
SDDI (with VPN Solutions)	VPN integration services
Shiva Corporation	Internetworking and remote access solutions
Signal-9 Solutions	Desktop firewalls (ConSeal series)
SLM Software	VPN-based e-commerce solutions
SplitRock Services	VPN products (dial access)
SPYRUS	Cryptographic products and enterprise services
Sun Microsystems, Inc	Operating system and management tools
TimeStep	Specialized VPN hardware

Table E-1. Continued

Vendor	Product Description
Technologic	Interceptor Firewall
Toshiba America	ISDN routers and broadband access devices
Trusted Information Systems, Inc.	VPN software solutions
UUNET Technologies (with MCI WorldCom)	VPN integration services
Verio, Inc.	VPN integration services
VirtiCon Communications	VPN design and integration services
VirtuaLINC	Video services
V-ONE Corporation	VPN software solutions
VPNet Technologies	VPN services and solutions
VPNSolutions	VPN services and solutions
Xedia (with Lucent Technologies)	VPN gateways and services
XyPlex	VPN solutions (EdgeGuardian Series)

Table E-2. VPN Service Providers

Service Provider	Description
3COM	Enterprise/WAN access solutions
Apex Global Internet Services	ISP
Ashley Laurent	Broadband solutions and security
AT&T	ISP and comprehensive solutions
Avaya	Enterprise/WAN access solutions
CAIS Internet	ISP
Cisco Systems	Enterprise/WAN access solutions
CoVad Communications	ISP (DSL-based connectivity)
Epoch Internet	Access solutions

Table E-2. Continued

Service Provider	Description
Evidian	Secure access and e-commerce solutions
FiberLink	Access solutions
FirstVPN	Access solutions
FlowPoint	Access solutions
Genuity	Enterprise/WAN access solutions (combines VPN service by Cisco and Nortel)
GTE Internetworking	Access solutions
IBM Corporation	Access solutions
Icon CMT	Access solutions
Impertio Networks	Access solutions
InetU	VPN outsourcing solutions
Interliant	ASP and enterprise/WAN access solutions
iPass, Inc.	WAN access solutions
Matrox	Enterprise/WAN access solutions
Myrient	Managed access solutions
Nokia	Access solutions
Nortel	Enterprise/WAN access solutions, managed services
OpenROUTE Networks, Inc.	Enterprise/WAN access solutions
Nextra	Enterprise/WAN access solutions, managed services
Qwest	Broadband-based enterprise/WAN access solutions
Scientific-Atlanta, Inc.	Satellite-based access solutions
Secure Computing	Highly secure enterprise/WAN access solutions
Shiva Corporation	Enterprise/WAN access solutions
SnapGear	Access solutions
SpaceNet, Inc. (with General Electronics)	VSAT satellite-based access solutions
Sprint	Managed access solutions

Table E-2. Continued

Service Provider	Description
TCG CerfNet (with AT&T)	Access solutions
Varadox	Enterprise/WAN access solutions
Verio	Enterprise/WAN access solutions
WatchGuard Live Security	Outsourced security solution provider
WorldCom	Enterprise/WAN access solutions

Table E-3. Information Security Solution Providers

Service Provider	Description
CertiCom Corporation	Encryption technologies
CryptoNym	Encryption technologies, risk management
CyberGuard Corporation	Security products for NT
Data Fellows	Enterprise security solutions
E-Lock Technologies	PKI solutions
Entegrity Solutions	E-commerce security solutions
Entrust Technologies	Complete security solutions
ICSA, Inc.	Comprehensive network security solutions
IFsec Security	Security products and services
SSH Communications (with IPSEC.com)	IPSec development
Riptech	Security consultation services
RSA (with Security Dynamics)	Authentication and intrusion detection solutions
SLM Software, Inc.	End-to-end e-commerce security solutions
SPYRUS	Cryptographic products and enterprise services
Technologic	Firewalls and intrusion detection solutions
Trusted System Services	Windows NT security solutions
Ukiah Software	Firewall solutions

Table E-3. Continued

Service Provider	Description
Verisign, Inc.	PKI solutions
WatchGuard Live Security	Outsourced security solution provider
Who Vision	Software-based security solutions

Index

Numbers

168-bit 3DES encryption, 282
3COM, PPTP development role, 104
3DES (Triple Data Encryption Standard), 65

A

AAA. *See* Authentication Authorization
    Accounting (AAA) model
ABR (Available Bit Rate), 39
Absolute QoS, described, 24–25
access control
    network security policy, 390
    PPTP, 114
    user identifications, 62
access points, destination network design
    considerations, 166
accounting, Authentication Authorization
    Accounting (AAA), 319–320
Address field, PPP frame, 102
addressing
    Extranet VPNs, 185
    Intranet VPNs, 184
    Remote Access VPNs issues, 182
ADSL (Asymmetric Digital Subscriber
    Line), 38
Aggressive mode, Internet Key Exchange
    (IKE), 155–156
AH. *See* Authentication Header
algorithms
    168-bit 3DES encryption, 282
    Data Encryption Standard (DES), 65
    Diffie-Hellman (DH), 66–67
    NULL, 306

    Rivest Shamir Adleman (RSA), 68–69
    Ron's Code 4 (RC4), 65
    symmetric cryptosystems, 65
    Triple Data Encryption Standard (3DES),
        65
application proxy firewalls, 326
architectures
    Bridge CA, 79–80
    Class 0 VPNs, 51
    Class 1 VPNs, 51–52
    Class 2 VPNs, 52
    Class 3 VPNs, 53
    Class 4 VPNs, 53–54
    class-based, 51–54
    client-initiated VPNs, 46–47
    Cross-certificate, 79
    dependent VPNs, 40–41
    directed VPNs, 47–48
    Extended Trust List, 78
    firewall-to-firewall VPNs, 44–46
    Hierarchical, 75–76
    Hybrid VPNs, 42, 77–80
    implementer-based VPNs, 40–42
    independent VPNs, 41–42
    in-house VPNs, 41–42
    layer-based, 49–51
    link-layer VPNs, 49–50
    Mesh, 76–77
    network-layer VPNs, 50–51
    outsourced VPNs, 40–41
    Public Key Infrastructure (PKI), 72–80
    router-to-router VPNs, 43–44
    security-based, 42–48
    Single CA, 73–74
    Trust List, 74–75

GAME DEVELOPMENT.
IT'S SERIOUS BUSINESS.

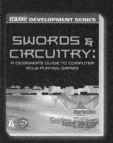  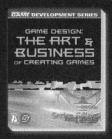  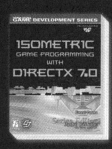